Rutter

Michael Rutter

The Life of a Racer

by

MICHAEL RUTTER
& JOHN MCAVOY

THE CHOIR PRESS

First published in the United Kingdom in 2020 by

The Choir Press

ISBN 978-1-78963-116-6

Picture Credits:

Simon Lee/SLDigital: Front Cover, Back cover, Helmet collection
Double Red
Pacemaker Press
Michael Rutter
Hedley Whewell/Snapchap
Honda UK
Alan Flack
Bauer Archive
Stephen McClements
John Hackett
Glynne Lewis

Contents

For my late Nan.

You left me some money, which I used to start my racing career – against your wishes.

Perhaps this book can make it up to you a little bit.

Thank you to everyone who has supported me along the way. There are simply too many of you to name and by attempting to do so, I'd inevitably miss some of you.

I have been lucky to know so many incredible people and to have been a part of so many great teams.

My sincere thanks to each and every one of you.

Foreword

BY JOHN MCGUINNESS

know Michael looks a lot older than me, but we were actually only born two days apart. As hard as that is to believe when you look at him, it means that our racing careers have spanned the same era. We've shared the same track and enjoyed the same highs as much as we've felt the lows.

Although we'd raced together beforehand, the first time Michael grabbed my attention was at the TT in 1994. I was still a spectator at the Isle of Man back then. I was stood up at Kerrowmoar, a really bumpy bit of the track. I saw a rider coming towards me wearing a newcomers' bib but riding a mint-looking Honda RC45. The bike was bouncing off the lockstops; it looked really unstable and as the rider's feet were being chucked off the pegs'. I was chuckling to myself, thinking, 'Jesus, is this what the TT is really all about?' I was with Becky, and each time the out-of-shape RC45 came into view we were like, 'Ah, here comes that Michael Rutter fella, the ex-superteen guy.' He was wearing a Tony Rutter replica helmet, but obviously Tony was miles more famous and better looking than Michael could ever hope to be.

Michael wasn't easing himself into his TT career: the RC45 wasn't the best-handling bike in the world and Michael hadn't spent any time on 125s or 250s beforehand. It was a brave move and fair play to him for doing it like he did.

Michael always seemed to stay one step ahead of me with everything when it came to racing. I don't know if maybe it was because his dad was a famous racer and he had some doors opened for him that just didn't open for me. In them early days in the 90s he always seemed to be on good bikes. We were both snotty-nosed kids doing superteens in 1991 but he was on the Merrydown-sponsored RGV and I was on my private KR-1S doing it 'lad and dad' style out of a van.

To be fair to him, he lived in the Midlands, which was a popular place for bikers and it might have been easier to knock doors for sponsors there. That said, I get the feeling he didn't listen too much at school; he certainly isn't the brightest bulb in the box. Like me he probably spent more time looking out the window thinking about motorbikes. Didn't matter though; he always seemed to have cool cars and cool stuff. When me and Becky were racing out the back of my old Iveco truck with bits dropping off it, Michael had a proper race truck and better kit than me. I'm not kicking him in the bollocks for that, he must have worked for it. He certainly wasn't gifted any of it because of his looks. I think he picked up that scar on his lip when he fell over at Scarborough. He says he rolled down the bank and hit a load of tree stumps, but I reckon he fell out of the ugly tree, hit every branch on the way down and somehow landed in a big pile of fifty-pound notes. The jammy bastard.

We weren't always racing against each other: sometimes we shared the same bike and raced as part of a team in World Endurance. All Michael did was moan from start to finish about everything. We were just trying to get on with the job and he was just moan, moan, moan, in his Brummy accent. 'Ahhh bloody 'ell, the boike's ccccrappp.' Non-stop moaning.

Michael was and still is a good rider though, joking aside, and for all the slagging we give each other, I looked up to him and viewed him as a top jockey. The first time we shared a podium was in 1998 at Macau. I was gifted third place but Michael and Simmo were long gone for first and second place. We were just three young lads. We had our own hair and everything back then and I was really proud to stand next to the old goat. That was a good do; Macau always has been a chance for Michael to shine. I've never beaten him there.

Over the years he's had Alpinestars, Dainese, Spyke, Spidi, this leathers and that leathers, he's had the lot. He's been through every manufacturer of motorcycles and equipment and he's been through every type of woman as well.

In my opinion, we've only properly fallen out once, and it was over an electric bike race back in the early days of the Zero TT. I'd been about nine seconds up in practice and thought I had it won. Michael played me all the way through practice, telling me that he was maxed out. He wasn't, and he caught me with my pants down. Going up the mountain in the race, I was nine seconds up and he just opened the taps up on the MotoCzysz and flew. He beat me by a couple of seconds over the line and I was fuming. I properly spat my dummy out and he just smirked at me. I had a diva strop and fired into him and everybody else, called him twat for doing what he did. Then I thought about what he'd done, how clever a move it was and took it on the chin. I went and apologised to him. Later that year we were on the plane to race at Suzuka. We'd had a couple of cheeky ones at the airport and then a few more drinks on the plane and Michael just launched into me. We were up the back of the plane near the toilets, and everyone else on the flight was asleep. He called me an ungrateful wanker and said he'd swap all his electric TT wins for one of my Senior TT wins. I stood back and thought, 'Fair enough, mate.' I took the bollocking on the chin and we were better mates for it. We've shared the job for a long time and I think that's the only cross word we've had to say to each other. We sorted our differences out in the back of a jumbo jet at 40,000 feet. Good craic, that was.

After all this time, it's quite hard to believe we're still riding together. Michael is still fast and super smooth on the bike. He's never really been one for training or watching what he eats; he likes a beer or a glass of wine. Sometimes he can be massively infuriating and you want to give him a jab in the eye, but he's just got a dry sense of humour and that's how he his.

I've stood on the podium with him many, many times. Even after all these years, the last time we both shared a race, we shared the podium (at the Classic TT). Michael can jump from a 250, to a 350, and then straight to a big 1300cc Yamaha and go well. He can ride any bike and be competitive. I know it's important to have the right setup, and his dedication to perfection is unquestionable.

Despite me always feeling like I'm one step behind him, I still have the utmost respect for him. In the last year or two, me getting a bigger house and having a bit of a nest egg helped me feel like I was closing the gap on him a bit, but then he got himself a new girlfriend and it feels like he's completely accelerated away from everyone again. He's had the lot. He might have had a poke at me on Twitter for getting the chance to ride a factory racebike, but I'm not the one that had a Honda RC213V MotoGP bike bought for me by my bird.

He's a dad, he's a racer, and deep down he's kind. He will go to the bar and buy a drink, and long may that continue. Look at him now, running the Bathams team and bringing on other riders. He's doing something that I probably couldn't do. I'm not clever enough to do that, so good luck to him.

The pair of us are 47 years old, we've done thousands and thousands of laps all over the world on all kinds of different bikes, and yet here we still are. We're probably closer now than we ever have been; you can't roll the dice as many times as we have and not have something in common. Whatever that thing is, I'm glad we share it; Michael is a good man.

I know for sure the one thing we don't share is my good looks: we've been using a picture of him to keep the kids away from the fire for years.

Enjoy his book. He's worked hard for every page.

Introduction

My first-ever race was on a Yamaha TZR125 against a bloke called Carl, who had the same bike as me. I really didn't want to do it, but he was a proper show-off and was dead keen to race me. On top of that, all my mates were on at me to beat him.

I'd got a reputation because Dad was the local hot shot, so for my generation, and despite my best efforts not to be, by association I became the person for this guy to beat, in order for him to be top dog in the area and feel good about himself. He wouldn't take no for an answer, so it became a big thing that went on for ages.

Eventually I gave in and agreed to race him. When I say 'race', I only mean in the sense that the outcome mattered, and there would be a result at the end of it. It wasn't a race like all the ones I'd been to watch Dad at, on racetracks lined with tens of thousands of people, TV crews and global superstars as competitors. This was much more low-key . . .

A few people from the Rock Tavern in Brierley Hill had turned out to see who would win, because there had been a lot of bets on the result. We raced round a five- or six-mile lap in the countryside, not far from Mum and Dad's house, on an open road in the middle of the day, absolutely flat out. I knew what I had to do that day, and by the end of the day I knew what I wanted to do for the rest of my life.

The rest is history, and most of it is in this book. Some of it isn't here because I simply can't remember it all, and some of it isn't here because I've made some really good friends along the way, and I'd like to keep it that way! If I'm completely honest, it took me a long time to come round to the idea of writing a book, mainly because I really didn't see anything special about my career, or about having a Dad who is a multiple world champion and TT race winner. But as I've gone through the process of trying to relive it all, I have realised just how lucky I've been. Back when I first started racing I never dreamed that I could meet such amazing people, have such incredible experiences and visit such outstanding places.

I started racing bikes in 1989, and I turned pro in 1993, which feels like a lifetime ago – probably because it is. But before that, I spent my childhood following my dad everywhere; I was his shadow and wouldn't let him out of my sight. If you look at pictures of Dad at any of his races, I'm usually nearby, somewhere in the background, because there was nowhere else that I'd have rather been.

Mine and Dad's roles reversed pretty soon once I started racing. He became the spectator, steering me through my very early years of being a bike racer. He passed on some of his experience and wisdom on things like bike setup and how to learn circuits. Dad also taught me a lot without realising it, especially on how to survive in the cut-throat business of motorcycle racing, and that it only takes one accident for it to all come to an end.

I've competed in so many races in so many categories against so many competitors all over the world during the last thirty years, but my first was reluctantly against a fella from the local pub on a learner bike. How did it go? Let's just say that my life as a racer started with a win, and I'll leave it at that ...

1
Montjuic Park

My earliest memories as a child weren't of being at school, or holidays with my parents, or playing with friends on the street – you know, the usual stuff. The earliest memories I have of my life are to do with bike racing, being at racetracks, being around bike racers and being around race bikes. It is all I've ever known. Dad had been racing in the Grand Prix World Championship already for three years when I was born, so this isn't a book about how a passing interest in motorbikes turned into a hobby that eventually turned into a career; this is a book about my life as a racer, and my life with a racer.

There are three things that Dad is probably best known for: obviously his four world championships and success at the TT are the main two things, but also his accident in 1985, when I was just thirteen. The accident was at a street circuit called Montjuic Park, near Barcelona, during the F1 race, basically the same as a World Superbike (WSB) race today. I think he won the F2 race earlier that day, and then, as he used to do, he also took part in the F1 race. He would use the same bike but swap the engine in between the races to convert it from F2 spec to F1 spec. By 1985, he was virtually untouchable, having just won his four consecutive world championships, and was the man to beat.

1

What I was told about that day was that Andy McGladdery's Suzuki blew up and dropped a load of oil on the track. Joey Dunlop missed it, and Dad – who was in the pack behind in 2nd or 3rd – hit the oil and went down. A lot of riders crashed on the oil, but Dad was really unlucky because he got run over a few times by following riders. I suppose one thing that was lucky was that he landed right next to a doctor. He was actually officially dead at the scene, in as much as his heart had stopped beating. The doctor resuscitated him at the track-side, but his heart stopped again in the ambulance, and again they resuscitated him. The doctors put him on a life support machine for weeks because his body was so damaged.

My nan was living with us at the time, and she was really supersti-tious, as was Mum, who was always visiting fortune-tellers. Apparently, not long before Dad set off for Spain for that race, a blackbird flew into Mum and Dad's bedroom and landed on Dad's side of the bed. I remember Nan saying to Dad that it was bad luck for him, and Dad telling her not to be so bloody stupid. It did make me wonder if there's anything in the superstition stuff, because that blackbird flew through a tiny window and surely must have really tried to get in, which always seemed odd. It does make you wonder.

As well as the blackbird, Mum went to see a fortune-teller shortly before the accident, and they told her that she would be going abroad soon, except it wouldn't be a holiday. I didn't go to Spain after the accident, but Mum did because it was touch-and-go for Dad. He had broken his neck, ribs, arm, hip and leg. The impact shook his eyeballs so hard that all the nerves behind them got broken, so his eyes just fell and pointed in different directions. I was told that they had to take his eyes out to repair the nerves and put them back in; it was extreme stuff. Needless to say, his Arai helmet got ripped to pieces; in fact, it was donated to Arai afterwards, who used to take it to bike shows as a way of shocking visitors by saying 'look at the state of this, yet the person wearing it survived'.

When Mum went to Spain, I stayed at Dave Burr's house. He was sponsoring my dad and managing the team at the time, plus I was friends with his son Scott. By chance, Dave and I have ended up being neighbours today. I remember the TV news reported how 'Tony Rutter has had a massive crash, and he may never race again'. They said he was on life support, so I remember thinking that I wasn't going to see him again because he wasn't going to survive. Back then, of course, there was no internet, so getting updates wasn't easy, and I would listen to the radio and watch the local TV stations for news on Dad.

Eventually they flew him back after a few weeks, then drove him to Sandwell hospital in the Midlands, near where we lived. When I visited him for the first time, his top half was completely encased in plaster, from his head right down to the end of his arms, the lot. You could see his face and that was about it. It was incredible, but I think it was to make his neck as stable as possible for the journey back from Spain.

The next time I saw him, he had this cage on his head, connected to bolts that had been drilled into his skull. Dad told me that when they fitted the framework, the surgeons had to keep him awake while they were drilling and tapping his skull, in order to tell if they'd gone too far. The only way they could be sure was to keep him awake and constantly ask him questions. Every day the doctors would come around with a spanner and move the bolts in his skull, so that the wounds wouldn't heal and fuse the bolts into his skull.

It was the first time that I ever saw Dad cry; he must have been so low. To see him just start crying was a big shock for me; he never cried at anything. Dad is mentally so strong, even to this day. He'll make himself do what's needed; even if his arms and legs are falling off, he'll just carry on – so it was hard to see him cry.

When Dad came home, he was a nightmare because he wanted to get back on a bike straight away. He was so frustrated, because he'd been told it would be ten weeks with the cage on his head, before he could even begin to think about any rehab or physiotherapy to get fit again.

One day I came back from school, and I remember walking across the landing and seeing Dad in the corner of my eye. He shouted at me to come into his room. He was being really aggressive because he was in so much pain and everything he loved had just stopped. He was in a bad place.

Dad said he needed me to adjust his cage, but I was terrified of having anything to do with it because I remember seeing blood seeping out of it whenever the doctors or nurses adjusted it. I said, 'Dad, I'm not doing it', which made him even more angry. In the end he bollocked me so much that I had to do it, so I got a couple of 10mm spanners that I could use to undo the pinch bolts that held the bars together. Dad was desperate to move his head, so there I was with the spanners, and then he started begging me to take the cage completely off for him, saying that he just wanted to move his head again.

I told him that it could kill him if I took it off, but he said that he'd do it himself if I wouldn't help him. So I slackened the bolts off, and all of a sudden his head just flopped to one side – not even like a slow slump; it just fell as a dead weight. Dad started scream-ing at me, 'Bloody hell, pick my bloody head up!' So there I am with his head resting limply in my hands, and I can't get the bolt back in because his head weighs so much that I couldn't hold it with one hand and put the bolts back in with my other hand. All the while he's in agony. In the end I got him to hold his head in place with his one good hand while I put the bolts back on the cage and tightened it all back up.

Fair play to him, two days later he was doing it himself, slackening it off just enough to give his neck something to do, and about one week later, when I came home from school, Dad was sitting there in the chair, looking like Jesus: he had taken the whole cage off by himself, except the four studs sticking out of his head and the ring on top of them which now looked like a halo. He had dismantled everything else, but he couldn't get that bit off. We would put it all back on for hospital check-ups to stop him getting told off.

4

We became very friendly with Dad's neurosurgeon; he had to do so much work on Dad over such a long period of time that it was sort of inevitable that he, Dad and Dave became quite close friends. He was called Bernard Williams, and he came to the Isle of Man and on holidays with us once Dad was back on his feet. He died on a motorbike five or six years later, which was a blow to us all, and like a real punch in the stomach after all he did not just for Dad but for all the other patients he'd helped.

Bernard used to say that with his injuries Dad absolutely should have died; he'd never seen anything like it before. He explained how occasionally he would be working on a person in the operating theatre and they would just die for no obvious reason. Some people just give up, he'd surmised, but sometimes some people defy all the odds and want to live, no matter what. Bernard was certain that my dad owed a lot of his recovery and survival to his wanting to race again, as simple as that. That's all he wanted to do. He didn't care about anything else or anyone else; all he wanted to do was get back on that bike. And to be fair to him, he eventually did it.

He came back in 1987, but he was never like he was before his accident. He couldn't see properly – he had tunnel vision – and his body didn't really work, but his personality was different too – he was actually much nicer. He also had a massive hernia – huge as far as I could tell, and it seemed as if most of his insides were sticking out – and the only way he could get into his leathers was to wrap himself in duct tape, about twenty times around, to pull it in.

Before long he fell off somewhere and had to go to the doctors at the track, who asked what was with all the duct tape. Cool as a cucumber, Dad just replied that it was all there just to hold his guts in. He eventually had the hernia sorted, but it was much later, after the race season had finished.

Dad loved racing so much that I believe he'd still be racing to this day if he could get on a bike. I think the fact that I started racing a couple of years after he came back made it a little easier for him to stop. He was a physical wreck by then and probably shouldn't have even made a comeback in the first place.

After Dad's accident in 1985, I really appreciated how lucky he was to survive it, and I also learned a massive lesson in the way sponsors and the paddock treated him afterwards. It has absolutely influenced the way I have gone about my racing career and deals. It's ironic that the biggest lesson he taught me wasn't a lesson he actually purposely taught me.

I get a hard time for being motivated by money to earn a living, and I'll mention it plenty of times in this book, but I have always struggled to get past my dad's experience of being shafted, and left with nothing when most of his sponsors and the teams wanted nothing to do with him after his accident. You're only as good as your last race. If you have a manager, you need a special manager. I never had one, and probably would have struggled with one because I know that I would have been advised to take some rides for free and play a longer game, which is what Dad tried to do. I decided early on that I wouldn't go about my racing career in the way he did. I have always looked to make as much money while I could.

From: Midland Centre for Neurosurgery and Neurology

Re: Anthony Rutter (age 44)

26/03/86

This racing motorcyclist fell off his machine at high speed in Spain, on 14/7/85. The accident details were not known to me.

He was treated in Spain and then transferred to Sandwell D.G.H. where I came into contact with him and took over several aspects of his management.

He sustained a head injury with a fractured skull, a fracture of the atlas vertebra. A fracture of the right ankle. A fracture of the right femoral head and acetabulum of the hip joint, and there was an old fracture of the left wrist. He was concussed for several days, and his retrograde amnesia was about a week and post-traumatic was over three weeks.

When I first saw him in Sandwell, he had a normal mental state. He had a possible 6th nerve palsy on the right and a certain, quite severe 6th nerve paralysis on the left, which means that he had double vision in most directions of gaze. He had extensor plantar, indicating persisting brain damage. The limbs were normal apart from the fractures. The skull radiograph did not show a basal skull fracture, but this diagnosis is almost certain to count for the 6th nerve palsy. There was forward dislocation of the arch of the atlas on the peg of the odontoid exaggerated in forward flexion. The arch of the atlas had sustained multiple fractures.

I carried out an operation on the neck on 20/9/85 to fuse the atlantoaxial facet joints. This was followed by a period in the halo hoop where the head is immobilised.

When I last saw Tony, he was still suffering from the effects of the hip fracture, he still had a severe limp with limitation of hip movement on this account. The left 6th nerve palsy had not recovered, and this means that his double vision is almost certainly to be permanent. His left wrist fracture is still troublesome to him, and adds to all his other difficulties. He has an abdominal hernia on the right side associated with the severe bruising and loss of tissue at the time of the accident. This may also require further surgery in the future.

Tony's injuries may improve in the future, but he would always be substantially impaired in respect of his previous abilities at motorcycle racing. He is absolutely unfit to race at the present, or indeed to drive either a car or a motorcycle or to practise any aspects of his profession. If he has his hip replaced and his double vision problem can be corrected, he might be able to carry out some advisory or other work, but I am still very doubtful about his fitness for racing.

Yours sincerely,

Mr Bernard Williams

2
Dad

At twenty-five, Dad came late to racing – but it quickly became a way of life for him. The locals who used to hang around with him when he was young would tell me how fast he was on the roads; he had a reputation for being naturally good at riding bikes fast. Before he started racing bikes he was a toolmaker, and, just like pretty much every other bike racer ever, he had to do it all himself in the beginning. He didn't have any help from my grandad, who hated bikes and wanted nothing to do with them.

In contrast, I was lucky and had some help from Dad when I started racing. He got it just right with the amount of help he gave me – too much help from parents can ruin everything, not just with racing but at home too. I think Dad did just enough for me, although once it got to a point where he did go a bit too far.

At one of my early TTs, when I was with Honda, so 1997 or 1998, Dad started having a go at me, saying, 'Bloody hell, Michael, you're not very good at the end of Cronk-y-Voddy', which is a really fast, very tricky section of the course. He followed this up with 'Yeah, all my friends have been standing there, and reckon you're bloody useless there'. I asked him if he thought he was perfect everywhere at the TT, and he said he wasn't, and that he was just trying to help. I said, 'Tell your bloody mates to come down here, put a set of leathers on and show me how it's done then.' He said again that he was just trying to help, and for the first time in my life I raised my voice to Dad and said, 'Well don't. I don't want your help any more', and that was the end of that. Dad stuck to spectating and kept his opinions to himself after that. Ultimately, you've got to find your own way through, and I think that was the moment that mine and Dad's roles were completely reversed: I was the racer and he was the spectator.

I think I must have gone to 90% of Dad's races, and I just loved it. I would get picked up from school on a Friday and I wouldn't be back until late on Sunday, absolutely knackered. My childhood was brilliant; I think I've been the luckiest with my upbringing, because I was around Mum and Dad so much. In contrast to my enthusiastic attendance, Mum only came to a few races. I think she was sick of it by the time I was old enough to fend for myself at the circuits.

It was nothing like it is now; it wasn't nearly as glamorous. Then, you lived in a caravan with no hot water – in fact you were lucky to have water at all – and a camping stove to cook the meals on. It's no real surprise that Mum preferred to stay at home. It's a different world now of course: air conditioning, endless electricity, and satellite TV in the paddock. Back then, at Cadwell Park I used to be terrified about going to sleep in the caravan and it rolling off down the hill in the middle of the night with all of us in it.

I always did, and still do, look up to Dad, but I'm under no illusions: to be a bike racer, you've got to be a selfish bastard, and I think my dad was one of the most selfish of them all. He would do things with me, but only if he enjoyed doing them too, or if I could be of use to him. He was also away from home a lot when he was racing abroad, and when he was at home he was working in the workshop, or off doing other things, which was hard on Mum, I think. I wouldn't say I'm really close to my mum or dad, which I think is sad in a way, but I know they cared for me. We just weren't really a close family.

I understand it now because I've been through it; racing takes over your life and rules every part of it. Racing is such a selfish thing; it's an addiction. It's not just the times when you go to a race meeting and come back; it's the whole week in between too. I used to dream about it and think about it in my sleep, and I'm certain that Dad would have been the same, completely obsessed with it all day, all night, every day, every night. When I first started racing, I didn't have a night when I didn't have a crash in my sleep. Nowadays I only have two or three in a year but it still scares me whenever it happens, and I wake up absolutely convinced that I've just had a crash. It just shows that it's always on my mind, even when I'm asleep.

Most people who I've spoken to over the years about Dad all say that he was a hard and aggressive rider on track, which I always found strange because I don't class myself as hard or aggressive on track. That said, one similarity between me and my dad is that he didn't like the attention from the media and fans that comes when you're doing the business, and this is something I've struggled with too.

I remember at the North West 200 I'd often be looking for him after a race, and he would have run off to get away from all the media stuff and was nowhere to be found. I remember Dave Burr telling me a story about Dad at the TT. The commentators asked Dad to do an interview after the race, and Dad got Dave to do it for him. He thought Dave could do it better than him, and he really believed that the listeners didn't really want to hear from him. He really didn't see anything that he did as being that special or interesting.

If I'm honest, I feel a bit the same way about this book. I really don't understand why anyone would be interested in anything I've got to say about my racing or my life. I don't see anything I've done as being in any way special or interesting to anyone apart from me. But enough people have said over the last few years that I really should put it all down (or at least as much of it as I can remember). It's made me realise that what's normal to me, might not be to anyone else.

Looking back there was nothing normal about my childhood, but it was brilliant. When I was at the racetracks with Dad, I used to be pretty much left to my own devices. We would get to the circuit, and straight away I'd go off with a few people I knew, and you wouldn't see me again the whole time. I would be gone, just wandering, sometimes on my own, sometimes with other kids, just exploring all over the circuits. Sometimes I had a 50cc scooter, which was an absolute ball.

In the late seventies and early eighties Oulton Park was a bit of a dumping ground, and there used to be thousands of old car tyres everywhere. I remember people would make bonfires with the tyres, and the smoke was so thick that I would come back to the paddock black with soot. I never really understood why people set fire to the tyres, but it's the main thing I remember about Oulton Park as a child.

I used to race my scooter around the marshals' campsite at Donington Park with probably about four others. It got pretty full-on, and eventually me and someone else on a scooter collided, and I got sent into the middle of the lap we were using, and into where all the marshals pitched their tents. I rode right over the middle of three or four tents at about 20mph – it's so lucky that there wasn't anyone in them or it would have been messy. As it was, it was just the tents that got ruined. Obviously, being young lads, we just went elsewhere to carry on the racing and left the mess behind.

It was at Scarborough that I got the scar on my lip. Everyone thinks it is from fighting, but it isn't. I was playing around as a kid and Barry Sheene had won the race. There were hundreds of people all coming down the hill straight at me to try to get to see him on the podium. It was a stampede, and I got knocked over, fell on to a jagged tree stump and ripped my lip open. I can't actually remember any of it, but that's what Mum and Dad told me. What I *do* remember is having to drink through a straw for ages while it healed.

A few years later, Dad was racing at Scarborough. The year was perhaps 1983 or 1984 – not long before his big accident at Montjuic Park – and I was twelve at that time. Having decided to watch Dad's race at the hairpin, I started to make my way to the spot. The race before my dad's was still going – the sidecar race. As I was walking down the side of the track the sidecars were braking for the hairpin, and suddenly there was a massive bang, and this bloke came flying through the air and landed right in front of me.

One minute I was wandering along, looking forward to watching Dad race, the next minute there was this body right there, and the bloke was groaning inside his crash helmet. His leg had been all but ripped off and I was just stood staring at it and not knowing what to do. Then suddenly there were loads of people all there, and I was ushered away. To this day, I don't know who it was or whether he survived, but I can still see vividly his leg ripped off but still sort of attached to his body. It was the first time I'd seen something really grizzly like that, but it was all part of racing and paddock life back then, so there wasn't much of a fuss.

I've been going to the TT since I was born, but the first memory I have of it is as a toddler, when I woke up one morning, and went down to the bar because Mum and Dad had left me in bed and I didn't know where they were. A fella called Neil Tuxworth found me wandering around the hotel bar and looked after me until Mum and Dad reappeared. Neil really shouldn't need any introduction, but just in case you're a new race fan, Neil is the guy who would go on to run Honda's racing programme in Europe, and I would eventually ride for him. I've never admitted it before, but I always thought this fact was quite cool, given that he is my very first memory of the Isle of Man TT. I think I've only missed a handful of TTs in my whole life: 1986, because Dad wasn't riding after his accident, and a couple more recently, but that's all.

There are other people in the paddock today who have known me since I was a baby – so many other riders, mechanics and people from the teams in the paddock past and present who all had a hand in raising me in one way or another. The paddock has been like a family to me; it's been as much of a home as the house in Kingswinford, which is the West Midlands town we called home when we weren't at races.

This 'paddock family' would spend time with me, talk to me or play with me in the pub after the race. All too often if a familiar face was missing I'd ask Dad where they were, and Dad would just say, 'Oh he got killed, he's dead'. I remember that so many times – not just once or twice but enough times to lose count. I'll never forget that.

When I was really young, my reaction to people dying was pretty blunt; I was more concerned about finding the next person that was going to spend time with me, but as I got older I started understanding that it could happen to Dad, and I started to worry for him. I remember Dad going missing loads of times at the TT and being terrified. By then I'd already been around racing long enough to know that there's a room they take you to if you're about to get bad news. I'd be there in the pits, and I'd see the officials looking for the family and team to take them to that room.

Back then, the first thing that happened when someone had died at the TT was that the helicopter would take off from next to where the police station is, close to the paddock. If the helicopter went up, everyone would know that the officials would soon be in the pit lane, looking for relatives and team members. They would walk along looking for the rider's team by looking for their pit number and then they'd take you to the room. Watching the officials walking along the pit lane looking at the numbers was horrible, and I'd just stand there and pray they didn't stop at Dad's. As I got older, it became the worst thing in the world, being in the pits at the TT and having someone you know who is out on the course.

On one occasion at the TT Dad went past the start/finish while leading the 350cc race and his gear lever fell off; we saw it go bouncing down the road past us. One of the marshals picked it up, brought it to us and said, 'Here you go, that's Tony's brake lever', but one of the mechanics said that it was his gear lever, so it seemed Dad wouldn't be going much further. If it was his brake lever, he would have probably carried on, and managed with just his front brake, especially as he was leading. A few moments later, sure enough it came over the tannoy that Dad had stopped at Braddan

Bridge a couple of miles later. That was definitely one win that got away from him.

Another one was in 1985, just a few months before Dad's career effectively ended. I remember being really sick that year and I was puking all the time, and because I was sharing a room with Dad, he inevitably picked up whatever bug I had and he too started puking. By the time he came to race, he was so dehydrated and weak that he finished in second place behind Joey Dunlop, but, as I would discover years later for myself, there's no shame in finishing second to Joey. I still think it was my fault though. Dad did win the F2 race that year on his Ducati though, which would be his last TT win.

Dad won seven TTs all in all, which, spookily, is the same amount that I've won. He started eighty-three TT races – finishing fifty-one and retiring from thirty-two – over a period of twenty-six years. His record is seven wins and nineteen podiums. The 2020 TT will mark twenty-six years since my first TT, and I'm on seven wins and eighteen podiums, so if I'm lucky enough to get on the podium one more time, I'll have the exact same record as him in the exact same time frame, although I've had much better reliability than him, with seven more finishes from one start fewer.

1985 was a mad year; for some reason, it was just carnage everywhere. Dad's garage used to be at the old Majestic Hotel and I remember walking from the Rutland Hotel on the seafront, which is where we stayed every TT, to the garage at the Majestic. It was a bloody long way, and there were so many accidents that year that I remember seeing people lying on the floor after getting run over or falling off their bike, and being asked to lend my coat to a policeman so he could cover an injured person with it. Looking back, it was absolutely nuts, but at the time, because all I'd ever know was racing and people getting injured or dying, it didn't seem to affect me too much.

In 1983, Dad crashed at Mallory Park and his gear lever went through the back of his leg and made a real mess, breaking his leg and ankle. The TT was the following week, and in those days you had to push-

14

start the bike at the beginning of the race, so the organisers said to Dad that he had to have a medical before he could race. He had to walk up to the top of the control tower in the TT paddock to meet the officials, and that meant walking up about four storeys of stairs.

Just getting to the top of the tower was the test. I went with him, and he also got someone else to help him with the steps. Each step was a massive effort for him but eventually he got to the top where the clerk of the course was waiting. The clerk said, 'Tony, we've heard you've done a bit of damage', and quick as a flash, and as cool as you like, Dad said, 'What do you mean, "damage"?' They said that they had heard that he had hurt his leg really badly and were just checking if he was going to be OK to race.

Dad put on this brilliant act and made out that he was disgusted that someone could put out such a rumour, and whoever said that he had an injured leg had told them a load of rubbish, and there was nothing wrong with him. To prove his point, he stood there and stamped his foot on the floor a few times. They bought it completely and signed him off as fit. As soon as he got out the door, he collapsed in pain, so me and this other fella picked him up and got him down the stairs. At the start of the race, he walked up to the bike with a stick, put the stick down and somehow push-started the bike. To this day, I don't know how he did it, but the bike started, and he just flopped onto it ... and promptly went on to win the race.

Mike Hailwood was Dad's hero, and he used to come to our house now and again and go to Dad's old bike shop in Birmingham. He was just amazing; the stories that Dad used to tell me about him were incredible, like when he and Mike were both on properly sorted Suzuki RG500s in 1979 – they were the bike to have back then. He would recall the times whenever the two of them were riding together, when Mike would use half the track and go twice as quick, and Dad said that his brain couldn't accept what it was seeing.

He used to tell me that Mike was from another planet and could ride anything, as demonstrated by one time when they were Donington

Park, testing. Mike came straight back in at the start of the day after his first run on the bike and said the bike was perfect, and all it needed was 2 inches cutting off each of the foot pegs, and that was all. Meanwhile Dad spent the rest of the day testing all sorts to get to a setup that he was happy with, but despite all Dad's efforts, when the race came, Mike just cleared off.

Once, Dad tried to be clever at the TT and bought a 32-litre fuel tank for his bike, ironically from Mike. Dad thought that the key to victory was to do three laps per tank of fuel, thus only having to stop once in the six-lap race. He was sure that he could beat Mike that way, but he knew he'd made a mistake at the first corner when with 32 litres of fuel on board the bike was way too heavy and all the weight was up high, it quickly became clear that the bike's handling was terrible. As well as having a heavy bike that didn't handle, any time Dad saved by only stopping once instead of twice was lost not only by his slower pace but also the longer pitstop required to refill the 32 litres. Mike had obviously made the tank, tried it and worked all that out before, so he had sold it to Dad! I've still got that tank.

Another mad thing that happened was when I got lost in Tokyo. It must have been about 1980/81, and Dad was out there racing at Suzuka with George Fogarty. It was amazing and I was so lucky to be able to go. I remember there were so many people it was incredible. I'd never been anywhere like it before; until then, Dudley was about the busiest place I had ever been, and there I was, in the middle of Tokyo. I think it was probably one of my very first foreign trips.

The group was Mum and Dad, one of Dad's sponsors called Kenny, George Fogarty and his wife (parents of Carl), Steve Wynne (who ran Sports Motorcycles), the team that Mike Hailwood used to ride for, and me. Kenny had given me a note written in Japanese, which included my name and a phone number, and made me put it in my shoe.

We had been out for the day in Tokyo and had stopped for some lunch, then the next thing I knew was that everyone was gone. They were all there one minute and gone the next, so I got this note out of my shoe and gave it to this bloke, who then must have called Kenny, and they all came back for me. Basically they'd all jumped in to two cars, half in one car and half in the other, so they all thought I was in the other car. Dad told me how when they got back to the hotel everyone was in a right state once they realised I was missing, all alone in the middle of Tokyo, aged eight years old.

Carl wasn't on that trip; he is just that bit older than me, so we never really had as much to do with each other as our dads did, but I think Carl bought a 250cc race bike off Dad when he started racing.

But anyway, getting lost wasn't even the worst bit about the trip for me: When I got back from Japan, the teachers announced during assembly that there was someone who had been to Japan, and they made me go up to the front and tell everyone about it. I don't like to be centre of attention, so doing that was my worst nightmare, much more traumatic than being abandoned in a place like Tokyo all alone.

Dad also raced in the Daytona 200 in 1983 and 1984, and because the race is in Florida we planned to go to Disneyland the day after, which was so exciting for me, more so than the race. Race day was really hot, so when Dad finished and got back to the garage he picked up the first bottle he saw in the pit and took a big swig from it. Someone had left fuel in it after using it to measure some before the race. He drank quite a lot and, understandably, he was really rough the next day, so we didn't bloody go to Disneyland. I was gutted.

It's safe to say that my childhood was not normal, but it was brilliant to be around bikes all the time, and Mum and Dad. I felt so lucky, but the downside was, and still, is that my mates at home would get pissed off with me because I would disappear at the weekends and never be able to go out with them. Eventually, they would just stop asking what I was up to at the weekend, and I'd drop out of favour because I was never there.

It's a little known fact that Dad won as many world championships for Ducati (four) as Carl Fogarty has won. To this day, he's the only person who is equal to Carl in that respect. It's funny, because I really don't recall it being a big deal at the time. For Dad, it was all about road racing back then and so that's where all his attention seemed to be, which is amazing when you think about how big a deal a world championship is today. Dad had virtually nothing to show for his world championships, certainly compared to someone who wins just one in the modern era. If you win a world championship these days, you're set up for life. In the grand scheme of things, there are very few people who make money out of bike racing. If you've made money, you've been very lucky.

Dad had no control over money. If he had a fiver in his pocket, he'd spend it on racing – not on anything or anyone else, just racing. He was hard on track but a soft touch off it. He made money – don't get me wrong, he did OK – but everything he made went back into the bike. He never had any left over.

At the big races that weren't championship races, Dad and the other top riders would get paid per person on the gate. I went with him once when he was racing at Cadwell Park and he was told to go and collect his start money from the house at the bottom of the hill by the start/finish line (which is still there today, but it's derelict and close to falling down). The field in front of the top paddock was full of people as far as you could see, literally tens of thousands of people, but the bloke who used to run Cadwell said, 'Sorry, Tony. It's been a bad day today', and Dad just accepted it. He wasn't strong enough with people like that; he said there were riders getting paid loads more than him, but he wouldn't kick up a big enough fuss. If Dad got paid a couple of hundred quid, which was a lot of money back then, people like Sheene were getting £10K, and you could buy a house for £3K. Dad was getting bugger all, and he was running his own bikes.

I absolutely loved following Dad around throughout my childhood, but I'd never been on track with him until one day, during my novice season as a club racer, he and I were at Mallory Park at a test day. I was on my Suzuki RGV250, and he was on his Ducati. I was giving it all I could on my Suzuki when he came around the outside of me in the middle of Gerard's Bend, which is a really long, fast right-hand corner, with his boot and knee on the floor, fully leant over. It was amazing, the coolest thing I ever saw. I was so proud.

Then he lent me his Ducati and let me have a shot on it, and very soon after he just started to give up racing. Maybe it was easier for him to give up because he had me to get behind and steer, but that day at Mallory, when he nailed my hat on, was maybe his way of signing off, and teaching me my first lesson at the same time, by showing me where he had set the bar.

3
Blade

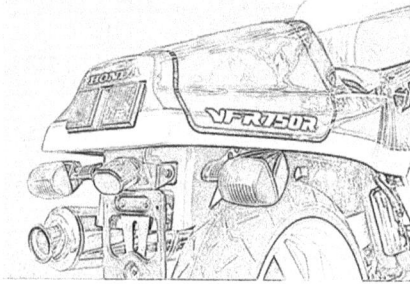

When I wasn't away with Dad at his races, my childhood was fairly normal, in as much as I went to school, I had some mates that I used to knock about with outside of school on pushbikes – then later on motorbikes once we all passed our tests – and I got a job when I left school. There's really nothing extraordinary about my youth, apart from the fact that I had a dad that raced motorbikes all over the world, and took me with him.

During the seventies and eighties the area that we lived in was dominated by a steelworks, and they were one of the biggest employers in the area, maybe even *the* biggest, so for me to have a dad that wasn't in some way connected to the works was out of the ordinary. However, for him to be a bit of a jet-setting local hero celebrity type was something that I never really felt was out of the ordinary, though looking back I suppose it must have been.

School wasn't really for me. I'm quite badly dyslexic – as in I can't even spell it. Back then the schools didn't really know what to do with kids like me, so they just left me to my own devices, which suited me just fine. I wasn't that interested anyway.

When I was a kid, I used to go out on my BMX or Raleigh Chopper and pretend that I was racing. I'd just go around and around in circles on my street in my own little world, imagining that I was in a race somewhere I'd just been to with Dad. I'd even do it in the rain. The neighbours must have thought I was the village idiot, but I just used to love going outdoors all the time.

When I got a Yamaha TY80 trials bike, I used to go riding it up and down a nearby railway track and nearby fields for hours and hours at a time. I was so lucky where I lived because it was quite a rough area and there were always people nicking bikes and riding round on them, so if anyone saw me riding round on mine, obviously underage, it wouldn't raise any eyebrows. I was basically allowed to do anything I wanted. When I got back from school, I would just launch my homework into the corner of the room and go straight back out and not come back until all my mates had gone home. It's the same today in that I'm the first one into the pub and the last one out. Nothing has changed, honest.

On one occasion when Dad was away racing abroad, it was raining and I was bored, so I thought I'd strip the top end of my TY80 engine to see what was going on inside. It all came apart OK, and as I looked at the inside of the little two-stroke engine, it sort of made sense to me how it all worked. I put it back together but it wouldn't run at all, so I panicked and closed it all back up. When Dad came back, I said that I'd got the TY80 out for a ride while he was away, and it wouldn't run, Dad said, 'You've had this apart, haven't you?' I lied through my teeth and said I hadn't, but he obviously knew that I had, and he sorted it without making a big deal of it.

When I was eight or nine years old, I badly wanted a disc brake on my bicycle. I think it was the Raleigh Chopper or something like that, but I really wanted it to look like Dad's race bike. Dad told me that it was a stupid idea and that I'd never get one to fit, but I'm one of those people who won't stop once they get an idea. Eventually I lock-wired a disc from Dad's Yamaha TZ700 race bike onto the front of my bicycle, but I soon realised that it wasn't going to work and that in fact it was a stupid idea, but I did get it on the bike.

I used to love taking things apart but I was never any good at putting them back together. I remember Dad's TZ700 was on the workbench at home, and I had got hold of a load of ball bearings that I had collected from all around where I lived. It was a heavily industrial area and for some reason there were ball bearings everywhere, from the size of your hand to little ones. I used to collect them, and according to Dad I took a handful of them and put them into the crankcases of the TZ when the barrels were off. Oblivious to this, Dad built the engine back up, started it, and it immediately shit itself; there were bearings and bits of engine all over the place. I did some real damage.

In the seventies and early eighties Dad had a bike shop in Lye, near Stourbridge. He had a lot of good years until the steelworks closed, killing the employment in the area and transforming it into a ghost town. Dad's heart wasn't really in it anyway; he just wanted to race, so it was more of an inconvenience for him, a means to an end. He was away so much that most of the time he left it to other people to look after.

I used to love going to the bike shop when I must have been eight or nine years old, and I would sit on the Moto Guzzis and touch the switchgear, and go up and down the gears as though I was riding it; it was fantastic. The Moto Guzzis in particular were really special at the time. There weren't many of them about back then, so when Dad had one in the shop I'd be over there, sitting on it.

Dad used to sell his old race tyres, and one bloke on a six-cylinder Honda CBX1000 was a right show-off. He would often buy Dad's used race tyres and do massive burnouts for show. He'd hold the front brake on at a standstill and get the rear wheel spinning until smoke started coming off it in enough of a quantity to make a massive cloud.

One time, he ended up with one of Dad's really grippy race slick tyres, which had some cuts put into the surface in a half-hearted attempt to make it look like a road tyre. The thing about slick tyres is that they are rubbish when they're cold but mega grippy when they're hot – it's why race bikes use tyre warmers before the race, to pre-heat the slicks so they're grippy from the word go. Anyway, this fella was outside the shop doing a burnout, and the slick must have just got to temperature because when he stopped one burn-out and went to do the next, the tyre just gripped instead of spinning. The bike reared up onto its back wheel into a vertical, out-of-control wheelie across the road and down some steps, straight through the doors of a small sweet shop. There was so much damage it was unreal. I was only eight or nine years old but strangely I didn't have a lot of sympathy for the bloke because he was such a show-off. I did feel sorry for the shop owner though; the shop was a write off – and it was my favourite sweet shop.

I think in the end the shop cost Dad a lot of money, so he closed it in the mid-eighties.

Once upon a time I had a regular job at a bike shop in Kingswinford called Phil's Motorcycles, which I absolutely loved. For the two years of my employment I did a Youth Training Scheme (YTS), where the government funded placements so school-leavers without qualifications could learn a trade while in a job. Phil still works on a load of classic bikes today, but when I worked there I just loved it. Even the days when I had to go to college to learn the theory were so much more interesting than school, and back at Phil's I was working on really flash bikes, like the Honda CBX1000 that the show-off used to have.

I did make some stupid, even unforgivable, mistakes in the work-shop, but Phil taught me that it's OK to make a mistake once, though a second time is stupid. I'd been working on a Honda four-stroke bike for ages and had fully restored it by stripping it right back to the engine cases, which got vapour-blasted so that the engine looked like new. The bike got the full treatment, and it looked a million dollars. The big moment came to start it up, which I duly did in the garage, and while the bike was sitting there ticking over, Phil said that he hadn't seen me put any oil in the engine and asked me if I had. I said to him that of course I'd put oil in it, but I was wondering to myself if I had … and of course, I hadn't. I switched it off quick, and Phil gave me a right bollocking, which I totally deserved. I didn't do it again.

We rebuilt another bike for this lad, another four-stroke Honda SS50, and it was beautiful. Whatever Phil did to a bike, it was perfect. He was really good at finishing all the details, so that everything that left his workshop was immaculate. We finished the bike, and this kid was so proud of it when he collected it, and about an hour later, he came back and it was rattling its brains out, the exhaust downpipe glowing bright red.

Phil looked at me and asked what I had done. I said it was running OK when it left, and it definitely had oil in it. The kid said he was bringing it back when it started rattling, and he asked if I could have a look at it. He was a really nice lad, and I remember thinking it was odd that he'd picked his bike up only an hour ago, and now he was back in the workshop with the bike sounding like shit, and he wasn't jumping up and down shouting at me.

I asked him what he had done to it, and he explained that because he had spent so much money on it, that when he got it home he thought he'd treat it to an oil change. He drained the oil from it but didn't realise that he didn't have any fresh oil at home, so he rode back to us to get some – *with no oil in his engine*. He said he thought it would be OK as we were only up the road, so I put some oil in it and it seemed OK. He never came back, probably due to embarrassment.

After I finished the YTS course, I went and worked at the Motorcycle Mart in Kidderminster, who were one of my Dad's sponsors. I was working in the workshop, carrying out PDIs (pre-delivery inspections) on new bikes, and I was even allowed into the showroom to help with sales. I would just talk shit to the customers, and it seemed to work fine. A bloke called Jeff Turner ran Motorcycle Mart – and he took Phil's place when it came to bollocking me for stuff.

We had a Honda RC30 in to get some crash damage repaired. The RC30 was THE poster bike of the time; it was unbelievably exotic, expensive and rare. Some of the bodywork for it had just come back from a paintshop called Dream Machine, and there was a brand-new seat unit that cost £2,500. I unwrapped this seat unit, and it was a thing of absolute beauty, especially to my young eyes. I'd never seen anything more perfect. The quality of the paint was stunning, and it was as light as a feather. I was mesmerised.

I'd just put the RC30 seat unit down when a YTS placement student was walking up the really steep stairs next to my workbench. She was carrying a 50cc scooter engine barrel – until she suddenly wasn't anymore. It bounced off all the steps all the way down in slow motion, heading straight for the seat unit; I couldn't move fast enough to get to it before it landed right on top of it. It was a direct hit and it put a hole straight through it. I couldn't believe it when I got a bollocking for leaving the seat unit out. I didn't drop the bloody engine barrel.

One day, I'd PDI'd five bikes and was lining them all up outside the shop, ready for collection by their new owners. The last one I had to bring out was a Honda CBR1000F, which is a massive bike anyway, not least when you're a scrawny teenager. The CBR had a centre stand, and my technique was always to put them on their side stand before I put them on the main stand, just so I had a backup.

I started pulling this CBR up on its centre stand, and it had virtually got to the top, where it locks in, but I hadn't pulled it hard enough, so it didn't quite make it. The bike rocked forward off the stand, onto the suspension, then hit the side stand onto the ground, just hard enough to jolt the bike away from me. I was holding onto it for dear life as it teetered just past the vertical away from me, until inevitably physics won, and it pulled me over the top of it as it fell onto its right side and onto another bike in the line, which knocked over three other brand-new bikes like dominos. I did more damage at Motorcycle Mart than anywhere else.

I would go on to have more side stand woes, again with a Honda but this time with a brand-new NS125, which I always wanted but was way out of my league. I'd PDI'd it and was bringing it around to the showroom via the double doors into the shop. The doors were closed and had hooks on them, so I parked the bike outside and went to open the doors, just like I did every day. I remember putting the bike on the side stand, walking to the door, and all I heard was krshhhh. I turned around and the NS125 had flipped over onto its side, right there in front of the shop. The Hondas back then had a rubber on the side stand that I suppose is there to give it some grip, but it had folded over under the stand and prevented it from going all the way out, probably because I hadn't put the side stand out all the way. That resulted in another massive bollocking.

Some of the people that came into Motorcycle Mart were hilarious. Even when I was still at school I'd work there on Saturday mornings because I enjoyed it so much. Sometimes, though, it was painful. To this day, I still remember a bloke that came in and said he wanted a light bulb. I asked him what sort of bike it was for and, deadly serious, he said to me, 'A red one'. I asked him if it was a Honda or Suzuki, and what size engine it had. He didn't know anything at all about his bike, apart from the fact that it was red. So I had to go outside to see what it was – down the stairs, back up the stairs – just for a 10p bulb. He was like a lot of commuters, who aren't really into bikes, unlike your typical bikers, for whom it is a hobby where they're really enthusiastic and knowledgeable about their bikes.

I must have been fourteen or fifteen years old when Dad entered me into a motocross race meeting. I'd never even sat on a motocross bike, but it didn't really matter because I used a trials bike, a Suzuki TY175, basically a more powerful version of what I used to ride around our estate and fields on. It was totally the wrong type bike to try and ride around a fast motocross track with big jumps, let alone enter a moto-cross race. A trials bike is supposed to be ridden really slowly over obstacles like rocks and steep faces.

So there I was, the only one on the grid on a trials bike, which was my dad's idea. I have no idea what he was thinking. I think he wanted to kill me. To complete my humiliation, I was also wearing Dad's racing kit, so I looked a right dickhead. I remember thinking, what am I doing here?

Straight after the race started, I had such a massive crash. I got stuck in a rut that had been carved out in the mud by the proper, more powerful motocross bikes, which, from what I understand now, having only recently taken up off-roading, only a very powerful bike would get out of or drive through. In other words, what you don't need is a gutless trials bike with no suspension. I basically just followed the rut, and because a lot of the time, they pass close to the big wooden posts that marked the edge of the course, I hit most of them too, flat out. I spent most of the day just hitting those posts. At the end of the day loads of people came up to me and said well done, because what the hell was I doing on a trials bike?

That wasn't my first-ever race though. The first race that I ever took part in on anything was at the Motorcycle Show at the NEC in Birmingham when I was ten years old. There was this little course for kids to ride around on electric bikes and set a lap time. The fastest time of the day won a prize, and I won one of those Kodak cameras that folds out. Technically I suppose it was a time trial rather than a race, but there was still a stopwatch involved, so that makes it a race in my book.

When I was seventeen, I had a Yamaha TZR125 with a Micron race exhaust pipe and long gearing for higher top speed, plus the engine's power valve was fixed permanently open. The idea of a power valve on those 125cc learner bikes was that they could restrict the power to the legal limit for learners, but you could easily open the valve to make the bike full-power. With the power valve permanently open, I had to rev the engine to 8,000 rpm before I could even think about pulling away from a standstill, and this, combined with the race exhaust, was deafening. It was virtually impossible to ride at a slow speed, and really, really loud.

I took the old style of bike test, when you had to ride around the block and the examiner used to run around when you were out of sight and change position to make sure you didn't slack off. Anyone could pass that test, except me: I needed three attempts.

The first time, I saw the examiner out of the corner of my eye at a junction, and I had to pull across the road. There was a lorry coming, and I thought I'd make the gap dead easy, but because I was trying not to rev my bike too much and make myself look like a dickhead, I ended up stalling. The lorry had to stop, and I was stood there in the middle of the road on a stalled bike; it was a mess, and I failed.

The next time, it was the new type of test, where I got an earpiece and the examiner followed me on another bike, giving instructions and watching the whole time. I failed that one too. He said that I was perfect but did one thing wrong, and if I could tell him what it was then he would pass me. I couldn't think what it was, so I failed. Apparently, it was a stop sign where I didn't completely stop and put my foot down. I passed at the third attempt.

My mate Neil Bartlett had a TZR125 also, and we used to go everywhere on our bikes. I used to know the lanes between mine and Scott's house way better than Neil, but he still used to try and keep up, and time after time I used to turn around to see where he was, and say, 'Oh no, not again'. I'd go back and look for a hole in the hedge somewhere, and usually see his tail light sticking out of a hedge. He usually had a rucksack on his back, which might have something to do with how he got away without any injuries every time, because more often than not he would slide down the road on his back.

I crashed into the back of Neil at a roundabout in Redditch once when it was really icy. He stopped for some stupid reason, so I hit the brakes, locked the front brake and slid into the back of him. We had a few crashes between us – unlike our other mate Darren Gould, a childhood friend who I used to fly model planes with. That was something that I also really enjoyed, and Darren was really good at it. He was also really handy on a motorbike, or rather a Honda C90 scooter that he used to go around on. It was hilarious: he used to get it hopping around corners on the absolute limit, and hold it there. How he stayed on it I'll never know.

28

It wasn't all bikes back then that me and my mates – Andrew Oakes, Scott Burr and Alan Cox – would get into scrapes with; we had cars too. My first car was a yellow Mini, and just like when I was on my BMX bike, we used to race round the estate in it, just racing around and around, being a nuisance. What we got away with was just wrong: we'd go out racing round the estate in the snow, and just slide off the road across people's gardens and back on the road the other side, and carry on.

When I think back to what we got up to then, it's a miracle that we survived. I look at the price of insurance premiums now for my teenage kids, and I feel responsible; it's all my generation's fault. One day, I hit a kerb while I was driving the Mini and broke the steering rack. At every junction that I got to, I had to get out and turn the wheels by hand, then drive round the junction, then get out again and straighten them up to carry on. That was just how it was back then.

Andrew picked me up in his Austin Metro one time, and as we came round a corner his car just went into a spin. All I could see was the massive oak tree that we were heading for. Somehow we missed it but we did end up in a hedge, upside down. We were both fine, but then we had to try and get out of the car. Andrew was above me in the car, so he had to get out the back window first. He undid his seat belt, which smacked me in the face, then he fell on top of me, and he's a big lad. I'd been perfectly alright up to that point. Eventually, we both got out of the car via the back window, and the wheels were still spinning. It was a mess.

Like Darren, my mate Alan was really into flying model aeroplanes when we were young, and he was much cleverer than me. Even back when we were twelve years old, he was making model cars and aeroplanes, and he even made an engine; in fact, he's still an engineer by trade today. He wasn't really into bikes that much, but if he was then I'd employ him in a heartbeat to work with us at Batham's Racing. Alan built this stunning model aeroplane that he let me fly when his grandad took us to a field to try it out. His grandad was totally deaf and was sat on a chair in the middle of this field where we were. Needless to say, I crashed Alan's plane about 2 feet behind where his Grandad was sitting. I mean, it came down from a long way up, and buried itself into the ground good and proper. If it had hit him, it would surely have killed him, but he never noticed a thing. All around him was carnage, and the old boy was oblivious.

It was around this time that my nickname 'Blade' came about. It's actually a Black-Country expression that often gets used in place of the word 'mate', so all my mates and I would call each other 'blade' instead of 'mate', or even – heaven forbid – our real names. It's totally normal in our region for a group of mates to all be known to each other as 'blade', so for some reason it stuck with me as I went into racing. I didn't adopt it as a nickname like a lot of racers do (and some are genuinely cringe worthy), so I never had it made into a logo for my leathers or helmet, but I also never corrected anyone over it. I'm proud to come from the Black Country region of the West Midlands, so to end up with a nickname that is a regional term is quite cool.

For those who don't know, the Black Country is an area to the west of Birmingham, made up of Dudley, Sandwell, Walsall and Wolver-hampton. There's a bit of uncertainty about how it came to be known as the Black Country; depending on who you talk to, it's either because during the industrial revolution there were a lot of iron foun-dries, steel mills and coal mines, so there was a lot of soot in the air that made everything black, or because there was a large seam of coal just below the surface. Either way, it wasn't a pretty place back then, and legend has it – according to Matt and Tim Batham, whose brewery has been there for 140 years – that it was Queen Victoria who first referred to it as a 'black country' when she passed through the area on the Royal Train, before she closed the blinds so that she wouldn't have to look at it.

I only managed a year and a half at Motorcycle Mart before I started racing full-time. I genuinely cried when I left because I absolutely loved it – but I bet they were glad to see me go. I was so lucky to work in the spares department, I did everything from making brake hoses and serving at the service desk to being in the showroom on Satur-days trying to sell bikes, which I was actually OK at, and I PDI'd new and used bikes. I did a bit of everything, but they wouldn't let me work in the main workshop; they wouldn't let me loose in there.

If I could turn back time and do any of it again, I would 100% abso-lutely go back and work at both Phil's Motorcycles and Motorcycle Mart; it was bloody brilliant. Motorcycle Mart is still going today but at a different site. Some of the staff rightly started getting upset because I had started to go club racing and I'd be away at weekends. Then Ray Stringer from the Medd Kawasaki team said, 'Do you want to go and do this properly or what?' – so, much to the relief of Motor-cycle Mart's customers, I decided to pack my job in and have a go at racing. I have never worked a regular job since.

1989–1992: The Early Years

ROAD RACE AND GRASS TRACK RIDERS ONLY					
DATE	RACE	CIRCUIT	POSITION	TIME	SIGNATURE
12.5.90	VoC	Cadwell	1ST		VH Bales
13-5-90	13co Allconers	MALLORY	7TH		B.J.Charlio'
24.6.90	S/S 400.	Darley Moor	3rd		E.Appleton.
8-7-90	S/S 400	Drury Moor	2M		
22.7.90	S/oot 400	Knockhill	6th		Wso.Campbell
22.7.90	S/oot 400	Knockhill	6th		Wso.Campbell
11.8.90	251 Prod	Cadbrey	2nd		Simony
25.8.90	250 Prod	Snetterton	3rd		B Smyth

I'd not long left school and I had a job and some money from my nan, so I bought my first race bike. It was a Suzuki RGV250, which was the go-to bike at the time for racers starting out. The RGV was a little 250cc two-stroke bike, and it was a thing of absolute beauty. I was seventeen years old (younger than my youngest daughter is now, which is a scary thought) and was really just looking forward to getting out and doing my own thing.

I can't honestly say that I had a burning desire to race and fulfil some sort of destiny. For me, it was as simple as just getting my own bike and going to a racetrack to ride, instead of going to watch Dad. I was just going to go and have a bit of fun, and nothing else. There was no agenda of following in Dad's footsteps or trying to emulate him. I just wanted to go and have a crack at racing myself.

I ran the RGV's engine in on the roads around where I lived – the same roads that I know Dad used to run his race bikes in on. Then I took it to Mallory Park with Dad to a test day that he was riding at. It's the only time I really remember riding on a track at the same time as Dad, and I vividly remember being blown away at how fast he was compared to me. That was the time he swept round the outside of me on the fast, long Gerard's Bend, and I simply couldn't believe what I was seeing. He was leaning his bike so far over, and making it look so effortless; he looked incredible. It was great after all the years of watching him from the sidelines to finally see him at work first-hand. In contrast, I was holding on for dear life and trying to take it all in, but I was having a ball and spent a lot of time just thinking to myself, 'Wow!'

Back then, at the test days, it was normal for sidecars to be out on track at the same time as the solos. It seems incredible now to think how mad that was, but at the time it was normal. Phil Mellor was testing his Durex-sponsored Suzuki that day too, and I remember Ron Haslam was also on track, but I don't think he was on his GP bike; I'm pretty sure I'd recall that. There were all these massive names, on properly trick bikes, all on track at the same time as the sidecars ... and the inevitable happened: There was a massive crash when a sidecar pulled across the track in front of Phil Mellor, who collided with it on the start/finish straight.

I was in the paddock at the time and heard the noise, so I wandered up to see what had happened. The passenger of the sidecar had got thrown out, hit the pit entrance wall, and chopped his arm off. There was this bloke's arm just lying there on the floor in front of me – I couldn't believe it. Then a marshal came along, picked up the arm and took it over to the poor sod who had lost it. For some reason, the marshal was trying to push the arm back onto the bloke's body, as though it was a bit of Lego. I was in the pits just watching, and even I knew that wasn't going to work. I don't know how the bloke was in the end, but I do know that it was the most horrendous day, and the most brilliant day. Not only had I had my first go on a racetrack but I'd also ridden with my Dad for the first time.

Dad was still doing a bit of racing in 1989, so he was just coming with me to a few practice days that he probably would have done anyway.

We went all over, even as far as Knockhill in Scotland. Then later on, in the spring, I went to Snetterton for my first-ever race and got a massive shock. I'd been going to these test days and was getting more and more comfortable being on track, and less overwhelmed by it all, but at that first race I really had my eyes opened. I was last or last but one in all the races I entered that day, and I remember thinking, 'Bloody hell, this is hard'. I don't really remember anything about the race at all, other than feeling really slow.

Being on a track with everyone going the same way was fantastic, despite being thrashed. I didn't mind the beating that I took on track; I just loved being around other lads the same age as me with the same interest. All my life I had been going to racetracks with adults – which was great, but this was different. It was new, fresh and exciting. After the meeting, Dad and I drove all the way home in our white Talbot Express van, and the mood was brilliant. Before Snetterton, I didn't realise how hard it was, but like just about everyone who's ever decided to give racing a go, after my first race, I knew.

For my first couple of seasons, Dad made me race at as many circuits in the UK as possible to experience as many different tracks in as many different conditions. We didn't concentrate on a particular championship; he just made me race all over the place, and he also let me race some of his own bikes. As well as my RGV, I raced a bike that Dad built, which was a 750cc Ducati in a Harris frame. I did a 'Battle of the Twins' meeting with the Harris Ducati, but I couldn't tell you how I did in it.

I realise now that Dad was quietly but relentlessly building up my knowledge and understanding of circuits and bikes, which I think he saw as being the priority for me in the early years. I also think perhaps he thought, like I did for at least the first couple of years, that it was just a bit of fun and not much else.

In 1989, I only did a handful of meetings and shared my RGV with Dad. He actually used it at the TT for his last ever race there, but it blew to pieces. I was more gutted that I had to rebuild the engine after he'd finished with it. I always did my best not to blow engines up, and I wasn't one for crashing in those days because I was paying for it all myself. Crashing costs money, so that kept me upright most of the time.

I also knew how much crashing hurts, having watched Dad smash himself to bits over and over again. Seeing the damage he did to himself and the pain he suffered from crashes, especially his big one in 1985, never put me off racing but it did make me not want to crash. Genuinely, the only effect any of his suffering had on me was about the same as the prospect of having to spend any money on crash damage. Why wouldn't I race, when racing and not crashing seemed a perfectly achievable logical goal to me?

We followed the same pattern for 1990, but for the first time it was more Dad helping me than me tagging along with him. By then I'd started to get more confident and had begun to understand the bike too, in terms of basic stuff like gearing, suspension, carburetion and so on. I won a few club races here and there that year, and when I over-heard my mate Neil Bartlett speaking about me to someone else, I realised actually I'd stopped being last or nearly last. Neil said to this person, 'Yeah, Michael is really good, but I don't think he's ever going to make it to the top'. Even though he wasn't exactly bigging me up, the fact that he saw me as 'good' meant that he saw me as better than I saw myself. It was that moment that I realised I could win club races without falling off or blowing engines up, at pretty much any race-track in the UK.

At the end of the 1990 season, Suzuki updated the RGV, so I traded up to the new model for the 1991 season and, with help from Merry-down, entered my first championship with a view to having a go at winning it by doing all the rounds. Merrydown were a local bike club in Stourport that would sponsor local riders with stuff like entry fees and painting the bikes. They were brilliant.

The Superteens championship was where I first met John McGuin-ness; we effectively started our racing careers at the same time. He was on the 'Shell Oil scholarship' bike, which had all the bells and whistles, and I was on my Merrydown racing RGV250. I was pretty jealous of his team and what he had going on there, but I think it wasn't all it was cracked up to be. My RGV was brilliant, and I ran it on a shoestring to finish 3rd in the championship, in front of John. Beating him is something that, throughout my career, right up to present day, I've always taken that little bit of extra pleasure in doing, as I know he does when he beats me.

The top three in the championship were supposed to go for a test with a team called 'Team GB', which was a small 250cc Grand Prix race team part-funded by the ACU (Auto Cycle Union) to give up-and-coming riders a break into Grand Prix racing on the latest bikes. The 'Team GB' promise really pissed me off in the end, because I genuinely believed the hype, and when I finished third I was really excited about the chance to test a 250GP bike with a well funded team.

I didn't get a call to go to the test, probably because Dad had pissed so many of the wrong kinds of people off during his time, or maybe I didn't look good enough, or whatever. I always thought going back on their promise was bad enough, but not even to call to say that they didn't want me was really shitty. After all, I was still only nineteen years old, and quite naïve. As far as I recall, they just gave three random lads a day testing at Donington, and they chose James Haydon. I think he had the right look, the right family life and was fresh to racing. I think they also picked Jason Vincent.

Dad helped me loads initially when I first started racing. He was great to have around, and there's no doubt in my mind that he did me a massive favour by steering me away from trying to win races and championships from the word go, and instead focusing on learning tracks and bikes. He didn't have any money to fund me but he had tons of experience he could pass on to me, which was great – up to a certain point.

Later on, Dad started to become a hindrance – or, more specifically, the name Rutter did. He had pissed a lot of people off in his day, and

I have no doubt that in my early days this fact worked against me in more than a few situations with certain people, like the 'Team GB' lot. Equally, I'm sure it probably helped open a few doors sooner for me than they would have if I didn't have the name. What I didn't really appreciate at the time, which was probably a good thing, was the expectation by people in the paddock for me to do well, just because I was Tony Rutter's son. Sometimes the weight of the name was a burden, but most of the time I really didn't give a shit.

After the disappointment of getting snubbed by 'Team GB', for 1992 we decided to have a crack at the 250GP British Championship, so, via Neil Tuxworth at Honda Racing, Dad arranged to buy Phil McCallen's Honda RS250 GP bike, and off I went. The Honda was a proper race bike as opposed to a modified road bike, like my RGVs had been.

The season wasn't great, but there were one or two race meetings that went OK, usually in the rain. However, there were other things that happened in 1992 that stand out above everything else. I had my first big crash, a near-death experience in an Irish pub, my first-ever road race, and I had my first break that led to me packing my job in and turning professional the following year.

The crash itself was a fairly standard highside coming out of the Melbourne loop at Donington Park, except this one was massive. I went high up into the air and landed straight back down on the tarmac. It was like jumping out of a first-floor window face-first; I landed really hard and hit my head. It properly hurt, so I crawled to the side of the track, and suddenly my eyesight went. I went blind for about a minute and started panicking, sitting there on the side of the track in total darkness. Eventually my eyesight came back, but then I had to drive my van and caravan home. I remember getting in the van and then being at home, and nothing else about that journey. I didn't bother going to see a doctor – you didn't back then – but that bang on the head did shake me. It was the first time I got properly hurt in a race.

The thing about my Honda RS250 was that as nice as it was to look at it was in fact the biggest pile of shit in the world. Those RS250s are brilliant when they have the full-power, all-singing-all-dancing 'A-kit' on them, but if you've got standard kit, which mine did, they're actually really slow. The highest top speed I managed on it anywhere was 137mph flat out, which wasn't much faster than my RGV. I had some decent results on it in the championship, especially in the wet, mainly because it was easy to ride in the wet due to being so slow. I've never really had much to do with racing bikes with two-stroke engines since then.

Once I was racing somewhere in Ireland and was staying at a hotel near where Phil McCallen lives. He suggested that we should meet up for a drink after the race and he told me that he'd meet me in this pub in town, so off I went into town and walked into this pub that matched Phil's description. I kid you not, it was like a scene in a western movie. The whole bar just fell completely silent, and literally everyone stopped what they were doing and stared at me.

There I was, a twenty-year-old lad in an Irish pub in the middle of nowhere, not quite sure what was going on. I couldn't see Phil anywhere, so I went to the bar and asked for a pint, and the barman just looked at me and said, 'What the hell are you doing here?' and I explained that I'd come for a drink and was meeting someone. He said, 'I think you've got the wrong pub'. I had no idea what he was on about, so I just repeated what I'd said, that I was meeting someone for a beer.

Then the barman asked if I was a squaddie. It was a term I'd never heard in my life before, so I asked him what a squaddie was. Turns out that because I had short hair and an English accent they thought I was a soldier. The barman said that I really shouldn't stop in that pub, so even though I was at a total loss as to what he was on about, I did get the message that he wasn't messing about and that I wasn't welcome there. He was actually doing me a favour by giving me a chance to walk out under my own effort.

I went to another pub down the road, and Phil was waiting for me there. I told him what had happened and he was amazed that I got out of there in one piece. Obviously I'd gone to the wrong pub for someone that could be mistaken for an English soldier. I had no appreciation of the situation that was going on in Ireland back then. I was young, stupid and I never watched the news.

Another time that I put my foot in it with the Irish was the first time I went to the Ulster GP with Honda. I'd never been there with Dad, so it was my first time ever. When I got to the hotel that Honda put me up in, it was like new, everything was brand new and I thought Honda had really pushed the boat out and were treating me well. That evening, I had a few drinks in the bar and got talking to the barman and said how nice the hotel was, and I asked him if it was new. He said no, it's just that it had been blown up a few times recently by the IRA, so it was basically like new all the time due to constantly being re-decorated after being bombed.

A bloke called Malcolm Wheeler was without a doubt THE first person that stuck his neck out for me. He went on to be editor of *Classic Bike* magazine, but before that he used to race with my dad in F2, and at the time he worked for a fella called Hoss Elm, who was the importer for Ducati in the UK at the time. Hoss was sponsoring Carl Fogarty and James Whitham, and Malcolm was pestering him and Dad about getting me on a Ducati superbike for a couple of rides.

Hoss was a really nice, genuine bloke, but he was also the weirdest bloke in the world. He used to take the bikes apart so he could rest the engine parts in a dark room, then put it back together again and go racing. He would even miss race meetings to do it. Hoss would rock up in his Ferrari and bring us little gifts like a carbon fibre fuel filler cap, which at the time was unheard-of, and he'd be certain that it would make the bike faster.

Hoss has one leg, and I've never seen a bloke with one leg run so quick in my life as when Carl Fogarty won the North West 200 on one of Hoss's 888s. I was speaking to him one minute, then the next thing

39

I know he's running down the pit lane to celebrate with Foggy, and his leg couldn't keep up with him. It was an unbelievable sight.

I rode Hoss's 888 Ducati in a race at Snetterton, and it felt so different to anything I'd ridden before. It was so fast and I absolutely loved riding it. I knew straight away that superbikes was where I wanted to be, and I also worked out pretty quickly that I should start wearing earplugs if I was going to carry on racing.

The noise coming from the Ducati's intake just under the fuel tank was so loud that when I was in the tuck position and on full throttle (which is a lot at Snetterton) the noise physically hurt my eardrums; it was agony. I had to keep turning my head to the side in order to give an eardrum a break from the pain, then swap sides. I genuinely still can't hear properly to this day after that race; I'm sure that Hoss's Ducati did some permanent damage to my ears.

My couple of rides on the Ducati were enough to catch the eye of Stuart Hicken, who still runs a team in the British Superbikes (BSB) paddock today. He was helping Medd Kawasaki's rider at the time, Ray Stringer, and Stuart invited me to do the 'Stars of Darley' meeting towards the end of the 1992 season alongside Ray, and I beat him.

My time as an amateur racer lasted just three seasons, which to be fair is all it would have lasted anyway, because my nan's money had all but run out. However, Malcolm Wheeler and Stuart Hicken are the ones that I have to thank for giving me chance to turn pro.

5
1993–1996:
Turning Pro

During the 1992 season, I remember being in the car with Dad, and I said to him that racing was costing me a fortune, and I was thinking of packing it in. We weren't well off. Everyone thinks we were because of Dad's profile, but we weren't at all.

It was my nan on Dad's side who had left me the money I'd used for my amateur racing. She was a cook at a school in Wordsley, and I didn't want to end up with nothing left of what she had worked hard to give me. I figured that if I packed it in before it ran out, at least I would still have a bit of something from her that I could doing something with. I could just go back to working on bikes; I really enjoyed doing that, so I knew that I would be happy enough to pack in racing.

What I didn't know at the time was that Stuart Hicken at Medd Racing had noticed my results in '92 when I did a few one-off races for Hoss Elm. Medd Racing was a team owned by Stuart and Nick Medd, who had been around for a few years and even gone GP racing as privateers, so to ride for them was a really good opportunity.

The 1993 season was when I turned pro; it was the first season I got paid to race bikes. I really did feel incredibly lucky. By then, even though I'd only been racing for just three years, I had already seen plenty of people who were absolutely fantastic and who were a lot better than me but things just didn't quite go their way for whatever reason. They just weren't in the right place at the right time, and so they didn't go anywhere.

The other side of that is those people who weren't as good as me but kept getting the breaks and who ended up massive in the sport. You really do need some luck on your side for sure. Don't get me wrong – I've had my fair share of good luck. I know that there are plenty of people that would give anything for the breaks that I've had over the years. I mean, I've lasted thirty years in the sport and earned a decent living out of it.

I got my first wage packet for racing bikes in 1993. I remember sitting down with Roger Marshall and Stuart Medd and them offering me £100 a week to ride for them, and I felt like I'd won the lottery. I remembered Ray Stringer saying to me that I would get paid about £100 per week, and it blew my mind because at the time I was doing a YTS scheme at Phil's Motorcycles for £25 per week, and even then I still had money left over. I can't remember what I was earning at Motorcycle Mart, but it wasn't anywhere near that first wage packet as a pro racer.

Ray got £200 a week, but he did a lot of the engine work for the team. The bikes were Kawasaki ZXR750s, which at the time were a really popular choice of bike for private teams to use. Yamaha had just brought out their YZF750 so a lot of the top teams were switching to them, and the Ducati 888 was a pukka race bike that was winning in World Superbikes. By comparison, the ZXR was a little bit long in the tooth, but it was still a good package.

I remember just before a race at Mallory Park – I think it was the 'Race of the Year' – and we were trying some new parts on the ZXR. Ray said, 'C'mon, we need to run these parts in before the race'. He used to run parts in on the roads round where he lived by Kirkby Mallory and Stoke Golding, so he said to me it was OK, that he did it all the time, and to just follow him. So off we went, on the damp roads, on cold slick tyres. Within about half a mile of setting off, the police passed us going in the opposite direction. I looked over my shoulder to see them turning around to come after us, and when I turned back round Ray had gone off as fast as he could, so I followed him. The two of us were having massive slides, and nearly crashing with every touch of the throttle. Then suddenly, Ray turned into a field and I followed him, where my bike got stuck in the mud and then sank, so I jumped off it and hid in a bush. The police went past and we got away with it. By the time we dug the bikes out of the mud, we and the bikes were covered in it. There was a lot of that sort of thing with Ray; he was really good fun.

I moved up to Ashby-de-la-Zouch in Leicestershire and slept in the back of the race truck, which was kept at Tudor Motors, which was a car garage on the outskirts, under a bridge next to the M42 motorway. The nearest pub was about a mile away, in Ashby. I just sat there night after night, with no power, just a mobile phone that cost something like £200/month. It was one of those really early ones, so no social media, games or movies like the smartphones of today.

I would walk to the pub in Ashby, have a pint on my own, and then go back to the truck, then the next day I'd go to work for £100/week. The novelty soon wore off because there was nothing to do in the evenings, and all my mates were back home. It was the same thing day after day. Stuart and Roger used to say to me that I didn't realise how lucky I was, and I just thought, yeah, whatever. Peter Hickman did the same thing when he started out. He lived in a motorhome in the paddock at Cadwell Park, which is in the middle of nowhere.

Sometimes I would ride the fifty-or-so miles home on my little Suzuki TS125 learner bike, and then go racing at the weekend. The agony of riding so far, so slowly was worth it to not have to stay in that truck. On that subject, it was like a mini articulated truck that had six bunks and on race weekends we would all sleep in it. Luckily I could sleep anywhere, and I would sleep all the time if I could; I used to love sleep. I would usually just go and sleep in my bunk when we were driving to a race meeting.

On one trip to Brands Hatch, I went to sleep, and when we got to the circuit I got woken up by one of the mechanics. Then I saw Ray get up and walk along, then a mechanic. I thought, right, I'll get up – but I couldn't move a muscle. I was petrified; I couldn't move any part of my body. It was like that for maybe ten minutes. Everyone else was getting ready and talking, and I was lying there on the bunk, and I couldn't move a finger. Nothing. I thought I was paralysed. It scared the shit out of me. Before long, everyone noticed that I was awake, and they worked out that I couldn't speak or anything – but the bastards just laughed at me. Suddenly, out of nowhere, one finger moved and then the rest of my body woke up with a jolt. To this day I have no idea what that was about.

One of the biggest crashes I ever had was in 1993 at Cadwell Park. An engine breather pipe had fallen off after I came over the top of the Mountain, and it had blown a load of engine oil all over the place. As I went through the first part of Hall Bends, changing direction from right to left, the rev counter suddenly span right round, and I thought, that's weird. The next thing I know, I'm flying through the air before landing hard. I was in so much pain, and I got taken to Louth hospital. I had never been in hospital for anything like that before. I went for an X-ray and they said I'd broken a corner off my hip, and broken a few ribs, my collarbone and some other stuff.

I was lying in bed feeling sorry for myself in the hospital, and I could see all the people dotted around me. It was one of those old-fashioned hospitals, like in the *Carry On* films. There was one bloke who had broken his neck, and he was on one of those flip beds, upside down, looking at the floor. I don't know how that would help him, but there he was, in a bed, upside down. One night the comedian Jasper Carrot was on TV being really funny, and you know when you try not to laugh because you know it's going to hurt, which then just makes you want to laugh even more? Well, everyone else in the ward was pissing themselves laughing, and I was desperately trying not to laugh, but failing. What with all my broken ribs, and laughing so hard, I felt close to passing out because the pain was so intense. The bloke with the broken neck was spewing all over the floor just below him because he was in so much pain with laughter. The nurses had to switch the TV off to calm things down.

I was desperate to get out of that hospital, so the doctors said that as soon as I could get myself to the toilet, take a piss and get back to my bed, I could go home. Getting out of bed was one thing; with a broken hip, walking was obviously another thing entirely. They said they could help me by giving me some tablets, so I was right up for that, and said, yeah, let me have them. They produced a massive tablet the size of a cork, and I said, how am I supposed to swallow that? They said, you don't swallow it; it goes in the other end. All because an oil pipe on my bike had been glued instead of welded.

Eighteen years later, that was the same corner that Josh Brookes knocked me off when I was on the Ducati. That put me out of the top six shoot-out and left me massively out of pocket because I was on for a big bonus if I made it into the shoot-out. Hall Bends is where I had my biggest crash, and where I had my biggest loss of bonus money.

I was twenty-one years old when I was on the Medd Kawasaki in my first full season of superbike racing, and if I'm honest I was over the moon with finishing 7th overall because it was a really strong field that year; John Reynolds, Rob McElnea, James Whitham, Steve Hislop, Phil McCallen and David Jefferies were all on the grid.

I was the rookie, but I was still devastated when I got lapped at Knockhill, in the wet. I just couldn't ride it; it just felt like I was going to crash all the time. Then James Whitham came flying past me and I just thought, 'Balls to it', and tried to stay with him. I started to get more confidence towards the end of the race, so I actually passed

James back and un-lapped myself, which means technically I didn't finish the race as a lapped rider.

The wet weather tag was with me from the word go; it came from my Dad, who was brilliant in all conditions but especially the wet. He used to drum it into me that if it's raining, it's the same for everybody, so just try to enjoy it. If you enjoy something then you'll be good at it. He was very technical as well: the wheels had to be perfectly in line and the steering damper had to be just right. He taught me a lot of things that riders don't get taught now, gearing and stuff, and getting the base setup of a bike right. It really helped in my early years, having Dad to show me how to get a good basic setup of a bike.

In the wet the quicker you go, the easier it gets because the tyres get warmer. I was always one for trying new things. Dunlop always said there was no need for tyre warmers on wets, but I thought otherwise and got mine so hot that there would be steam coming off them on the grid. I used to be twenty seconds in front of everyone until their tyres got warm, then they'd start catching me – but the race would be over by then. The wet is a great leveller for all bikes. I always seemed to be on a bike that didn't have the same power as the front-runners, but when it's wet you can't use a horsepower advantage, so it levels the playing field. Today, there's electronic rider aids to help.

Ray and I entered the 1993 Superbike World Championship round at Brands Hatch as wild cards, and back then the grids in World Superbikes had forty-five people on them, more than twice what they have today. My bike featured Ray's clever addition of a '3 dog' gearbox which made it easier to select a gear and so saved time. I think I qualified two rows from the back, and Ray, who was a front-runner in BSB at the time, was about 19th. Our bikes were nothing like the WSB bikes, which were rockets, but in the race it started raining really hard and I got up to about 4th position. Just as I thought I was on for something special, Ray's fancy gearbox blew to pieces during a gearshift, and that was the end of my WSB debut.

I'd had some good races by the end of that first year, and was racing where I should have been, and we had some really good laughs at that team. There was a brilliant atmosphere, and I couldn't believe that I was getting paid so much money. Ray is a good lad; he is like a professor and would get so excited about the technical side of racing that he would work all night at the side of his mum and dad's house.

We used to go to the workshop in Ray's old Renault, a properly knackered old thing that took a real hammering from him. Ray used to get to a really steep humpback bridge just before Sutton Cheney near Mallory Park, and when it was dark he would turn the lights off to make sure nothing was coming the other way and just launch the car. The landings were so hard that the windscreen cracked; eventually it got to the point where the wing mirrors would fall off. Ray called me up at the end of the year and said, 'Yeah, Michael, about the Renault. You used it as much as me, and it needs about £500 spending on it to get it back to how it was'. I refused to pay, because it was always him that jumped it.

When Ray could tear himself away from working on the bikes, we would go to the pub and have a great time, and when we got back from the pub he would always make us toasted cheese sandwiches. Then we would both work on the bikes in the day. Ray took care of the engines because he was, and still is, really good at that, plus I think probably because he knew I shouldn't be let anywhere near them.

I was spray painting the bike's bodywork in Ray's mum and dad's garden one time, and his mum went absolutely mad at me because I was getting fluorescent orange paint all over her garden. It was everywhere – the grass, the patio furniture and her windows. There was more paint on Ray's mum's garden and house than on the bike's panels.

We had such a laugh, probably too much of a laugh, because Stuart and Nick got Roger Marshall in about halfway through the season to try and improve our results. Roger really dominated British racing in the eighties so knew a thing or two about winning. He was really

47

good at motivating the team in a way that a racer understands, which is another way of saying he took us to the pub a lot and got us drunk. He knew that happy racers are fast racers, and it worked. We both went 0.5 seconds faster without doing a thing to the bikes.

That said, I ended up getting sacked after that season because I wasn't doing well enough, even though I finished my rookie season in 7th overall. Medd switched to Hondas for the 1994 season and took James Haydon on. He brought money, and I was a cost.

It was a shame, but I understood why it happened, and it also turned out to be a blessing in disguise. The Honda RC45 was shit in 1994, and the Ducati 888 that I had was brilliant. Again, it just goes to show how much luck is involved. If I had stayed at Medd on the RC45 in 1994, it probably would have finished my career before it had got started. I look back on those moments and realise that they are all part of how I got to where I am thirty years later.

So in 1994 I did my own thing, with backing from a company called McCullough, who make gardening equipment. A fella called Barry Reakey from Bridgnorth, who worked for McCullough, managed to get about £20K worth of sponsorship from them towards the cost of £40K for the year. Barry used to know my dad through his bike shop and his racing, and he used to come and watch me race when I started. He was just one of those really good guys that became a friend of the family.

It was a fortune in one deal, and it really did a lot to put me on the map. I came up with the yellow colour scheme by copying the box from one of their chainsaws. There weren't any other bikes on the grid that were all yellow, so it stood out, and I thought it was stunning. Even today people still talk about it. At the time it was just me working on the bike with a bit of help from Dad, and an engine tuner called John Hackett preparing the engines. He runs a Ducati dealership in Coventry and specialises in tuning Ducati engines.

As well as riding the McCullough Ducati in BSB that year, Roger and Stuart from Medd called me to see if I wanted to do the TT with them as Robert Dunlop's teammate. I couldn't say no, and so 1994 was my first year at the TT as a racer. Obviously, because of my dad, I'd been going to the TT since I was born, so I already knew everything about the TT races, the upsides, the downsides – and it always seemed to be downsides on the radio. Hearing that someone else has died is what always stuck with me about the TT.

I bought myself an ex British Telecom van to sleep in and I got people to come and help me at the races. It was a brilliant season that started perfectly. The first round of the SuperCup championship that season was at Donington Park, and the Ducati World Superbike team entered the race with Carl Fogarty on their brand-new race bike, the 916. His teammate James Whitham was there too on the factory Ducati 888. They were really just using the meeting as a test before the first round of the world championship, which was also going to be at Donington Park a few weeks later. The 916 was big news then; it was like nothing anyone had ever seen at the time and would go on to become an icon, winning world and domestic championships for years. I was there on my yellow McCullough 888, and Fogarty and Whitham thought they had it won, which to be fair they did, but not before they got a scare from me.

Years later, James told me a story of how before the race he and Carl had agreed to make a show of it and pass each other here and there, and hadn't really thought about anyone else actually making a race of it. I got a really good start and got my head down to make the most of it, but it didn't take them long to catch me up and pass me, and I think they thought that would be the last they saw of me.

James said that he and Foggy were messing about as agreed and putting on a show, until he noticed his pit board said '+0', which is what the guys in the pits will put on for you if there is no gap between you and the person behind you. He turned around, and there I was, hanging on for dear life. I was riding so hard just to stay with them while they were just showboating. They both put their heads down and pulled away from me at the end, but James did admit years later

49

that it was his first time on the factory bikes, and I nearly spoiled the party for him.

Carl won the first of his four world championships that year. He won all of them for Ducati and went on to become a household name, and rightly so – a very wealthy man and their golden boy. It irritates me that my dad won the same amount of world championships for Ducati that Fogarty did and got nothing from them.

I know they were a different company when my dad was winning on their bikes. They were a fraction of the size that they were in the early nineties, never mind these days, and they were much less popular then with racers. Some say that Dad pretty much saved them. I don't know if that's entirely true but I do know that no one else would have anything to do with them at the time, and Dad was the only one bringing them any glory.

My path would cross Fogarty's again in 1995 but under much less glamorous circumstances. I was in my second season with McCullough, and we had switched from the 888 to the 916 after finishing 6th in the British championship the year before. I was having another good season. John Hackett knew this American character called Igor Gorodynski, who I think either bought a bike from John or had some engines tuned by him. Either way, he was desperate for me to go over and race his bike in the USA WSB round at Laguna Seca in California, which was, and still is, one of the most iconic racetracks in the world. I wasn't going to pass up the opportunity.

So, how mad is this? Igor's bike was already over there, but the front forks and yokes weren't anywhere near good enough to race with. John and I took the whole front suspension and steering out of my McCullough bike and, along with the swing arm, we took it all on the plane with us as hand luggage to America. When we got to Los Angeles, we met up with Igor, went to a bike shop and put my front end into his bike. Then we loaded it all up into a Hertz hire van and drove the 400 miles to Laguna Seca.

It was ace, because I had never really seen America before, and there was me, John and Igor driving this van through California. It felt like a proper foreign road trip with mates. I already felt like I was really lucky to have got to a third season as a pro racer, and that I was able to earn money from racing bikes, but this felt like a world away from Phil's bikes back home. I was buzzing with excitement over the whole thing. Three years previously, I was spending my days cleaning bikes and doing jobs about the place for money, and now here I was, driving through California to go and race at Laguna Seca in a world championship race.

We got to the circuit and pulled up to the gates, and eventually – after working out that in America they make you sign on outside the circuit before they let you in, which is different to the English system – we were in the paddock.

We had driven across America, and here we were in the WSB paddock in a hire van holding a road bike with my suspension put in the front of it, and we didn't have any tyre warmers or stands, and only a few tools. What's more, I'd never seen the place before, and was a world championship event, so there were no mugs out there. In fact, Freddie Spencer was there on a Ducati making a comeback – a guy that had won three Grand Prix World Championships, two of them in the same season. In 1985, he became the first and only person so far in history to win 250cc and 500cc championships in the same season; the man is a god. We were really onto a loser, but I did it because ... why not?

I had told Michelin that I was going, and they said that they would provide tyres for us, so the first job was to go and get tyres organised. They had a massive truck full of tyres, and I went up and introduced myself as Michael Rutter from the UK, and they said, 'Who?' I told them that Michelin UK had said everything was arranged, but apparently this lot hadn't heard anything from them. So, I called England when the time was right – we were seven hours behind UK time so it was a right ball ache. I had to go through AT+T exchanges and all sorts. Eventually I got to speak to the right people in the UK and explained that there weren't any tyres for me. They said, 'No, there are. Michelin is waiting for you'.

It turned out that there was a Michelin truck there for me, but it wasn't the massive truck; it was about the size of a transit van with a tail lift, manned by a massive fat bloke sitting on a deck chair, smoking, his feet up on the tyres. I doubt he'd ever sold a tyre in his life. He was the tyre man for the local AMA series or something. I said to him that I'd come to pick some tyres up, and he drawled, 'Ahh yeah man', gave me a pile of tyres for the weekend, and disappeared. I had never seen the tyres before, and none of the codes matched anything I'd raced before, so I was thinking I'd been tucked up with some tyres that had sat in the corner of this bloke's unit for years.

Desperate for some tyre warmers, I wandered around but no one was about – and then I spotted Fogarty and his missus walking down the paddock. He shouted over to me, 'Alright, Michael? What you doing here?' I told him the story about John and Igor, and suddenly I thought perhaps he could help me out. I said, 'Carl, I'm in the shit. Is there any chance you could see if I can borrow a set of tyre warmers?' and he just looked at me and said '. . . No', and walked off.

I couldn't believe it. He was a god then, at the height of his powers, and he just dismissed me like I was nobody. Then I looked down and I was wearing a Carl Fogarty T-shirt, which was a freebie from a magazine. I felt like such a dickhead.

In one of the practice sessions I was right behind Freddie Spencer, and I had a massive crash coming out of the first corner when I highsided really hard. A highside is when the rear of the bike breaks away then suddenly grips. You get flicked off the bike vertically, and how high you get fired into the air depends on how suddenly and violently the rear breaks away and grips again. This one was massive; it felt like I was airborne for ages and when I hit the tarmac I thought I had broken a whole load of ribs.

The medical support in America was light years ahead of the UK scene's support at the time, so I walked in to the medical centre and told them I thought I'd broken some ribs and it bloody hurt, so they scanned me, and much to my surprise they said that I'd only cracked one rib. The doctor also asked if I had been drinking Coca-Cola, which I had been; I used to drink it all the time then. I asked how he knew, and he showed me the X-ray of my ribs, and there was a ball of gas where my stomach was. He said it was from drinking Coca-Cola, and he said it stains, so it's really good for X-rays. I don't know if that's true or not, but I looked at the massive ball of gas in my stomach and didn't like what I saw. I've never touched fizzy drinks since.

I did the races and got thrashed, but I finished them both. I had to use a different helmet for the races because I'd smashed mine up in practice, but at least I can say I've raced at Laguna Seca.

I did another race for Igor later the same year at New Hampshire racetrack, and I was doing really well in the race but crashed again. I flew over the handlebars and hit the ground hard; then the bike caught fire, so I picked myself up and grabbed a fire extinguisher, putting the fire out. The bike was destroyed, and I hurt like hell and felt really sorry for myself when I went back to the hotel.

The hotel was in a ski resort and because it was summer it was surrounded by woodland. I was in so much pain that night that I couldn't sleep, so I decided to go out for a walk down this path out the back of the hotel. I found a seat to sit down on, and then I saw something in the corner of my eye – there was this bloody bear coming at me out of the woods. I couldn't believe it. I thought, this is how it's going to end – the day just keeps getting worse.

Then a miracle occurred. When the bear started running towards me, all the pain disappeared and I was able to jump up and run flat out. I swear I've never run as fast before or since. Luckily I wasn't too far from the resort, so I made it back to safety before the bear caught me, and I just ran straight into my room. It's amazing how everything feels fine and your body suddenly becomes pain-free and starts working fine when a bear is chasing you.

I've never been back to America, which is something I can't say about Macau. As well as Laguna Seca, 1994 was also my first year at the Macau Grand Prix on the Ducati. John built a trick engine for me, which lasted about 250 metres then shat itself, so I ended up just watching. My Macau Grand Prix debut was so low-key and so short-lived that it is hard to believe what I would end up going on to achieve there.

It was a really good laugh though. Phillip McCallen took me out, and I'd never ever been anywhere on my own so far away from home, and I tell you, I learned so much. Dad was supposed to race at Macau twice, but both times something cropped up and he couldn't make it out there.

I hung round with Phillip, Simon Beck, Lee Pullan, Steve Hislop, Mike Edwards and Dave Goodley. It was carnage. I have never laughed as much in my life. Every day was mad. There was only one pub that everyone went to, and there were only two restaurants that I would go to: McDonald's or Pizza Hut. It was brilliant. The guys took me to some places full of women with numbers on them, and you could choose which one you wanted. I'd never seen anything like that in my life, and being of a young age, it was a massive shock to me.

We went to a nightclub with Philip, and without knowing that it was £10 a pint he got the first round in, and the bill was over £100. He couldn't afford it, so he suddenly said 'Run!', and I ran as fast as I could. All I could hear behind me was some sort of commotion, so I stopped to have a look at what was going on. Phil was there, and he'd had his shirt ripped off him when some of the bouncers had got hold of him. He came walking across the road towards me with just one arm on his shirt, like everything was normal. He was a properly hard bastard.

Talking of hard men in racing, and Phil in particular, I remember – in 1997 I think – going down the straight at the North West 200 leading the race on the 600. He came alongside me really close at some crazy speed and gave me a nudge with his elbow. We were that close. I remember thinking, 'What the hell is he doing?' and I just instinctively gave him a nudge back, but harder. After that, he was OK with me. A lot of people were really intimidated by him and others like him, but while I knew those guys had reputations, I really made a point of not allowing myself to get intimidated. The guys who have reputations for being hardmen beat lots of racers on reputation alone before they even get on the bike.

Jim Moodie was another one. There was no one harder than Jim at racing. No one. You wouldn't want to fight him off the track, and on the track he was just as bad. I remember in 1995 at Donington Park seeing him up ahead; he was on the Castrol Honda in second place, and I was on my McCullough Ducati. We were coming up to the Old Hairpin and it was wet on the inside line, where I needed to go to be able to pass him. I knew it would be risky, but I thought I'd just go for it, so I went through and on to the wet patch where I had a big slide. I don't know how I stopped on, probably because I hit Jim. Somehow I got through, but it was really messy, then something went in my head going up to McLeans, probably regret.

A few corners later as I was accelerating out of Melbourne loop, I took a look behind me, and Jim wasn't there. I decided that I must have knocked him off, which I wasn't very proud of, but most of all I was shitting myself about what he might do to me after the race. I finished in 2nd place, and I remember seeing Jim from the top of the garages walking down flat out towards the podium finishers' enclosure where I was, and he was covered in mud.

I was sure that I was in big trouble, so decided to just stand there and take what was coming to me. He came right up to my face and said, 'It's a good job I like you'. Straight away I started apologising to him for knocking him off and braced myself for the worst, when he said, 'No, no you didn't. When you passed me I was so angry that when I got to the next corner I crashed all on my own'. I was so happy that it wasn't me who knocked him off – not only because Jim was the last person you'd want to do that to, but also because I have always tried to race cleanly. I'd hate a reputation as a racer who put fellow competitors' lives at risk.

Castrol Honda got me to test their bike in 1995 at Donington Park and it went well, so they asked me if I wanted to ride the bike at the Ulster GP. Of course, I said yes. They sent the bike over and Steve Hislop lent me a set of his Castrol Honda leathers for the meeting. My bike developed a problem and couldn't be raced, so Joey, who was there racing too but wasn't fully fit, told Honda to give me his bike to race. I couldn't believe the gesture, but Honda said no, so neither bike raced. I never really understood that.

Apart from being chased by a wild bear, another thing that properly shit me up when I was on the McCullough bike was one time at Mallory Park. I'd done the meeting, and the truck was parked at the top of the paddock, which is on a hill. The battery had gone flat, so I got someone to jump start it and then leave it there on tick over to charge the battery up. I had wandered off and was probably about a hundred metres from it when out the corner of my eye I saw it moving.

Before I got a jump-start for it, I had tried to bump-start it, so I'd taken the air brake off and hadn't put it back on. It turned out that the truck had been sat there, ticking over with the airbrake off, slowly creeping forward to the edge of the hill. Now it was starting to roll down the hill towards the paddock café.

I started running flat out straight away and reached it by the time it was about halfway to the café. It was lucky that I'd left the door open, because it had accelerated to the speed where I couldn't catch it anymore, so I had one shot to grab the door and try to get in. I just managed it, and with a stroke of luck the door actually swung me into the cab. I hit the brakes, and everything in the back shot forward and slammed into the bulkhead behind the cab, making a noise so loud that it was like a bomb going off. To be fair I was quite a bit away from the café still, but if I hadn't caught it at that first attempt it would have got away from me and gone all the way through the café, out the other side and into the lake.

The McCullough deal was only meant to be for one year but we got three years out of it, after which I was looking to go up to the next step. The McCullough deal had reached its natural conclusion by the end of 1996, and because I had a good TT that year, finishing 3rd, Honda had started to show interest in me. Their interest was mainly for road racing but I managed to persuade them to run me in the British championship in 1997 too. Even though there were also offers from WSB and BSB for 1997, they were all bikes that I didn't think could win. The Honda team and bikes were the best that were on offer. It was a no-brainer for me.

Those first four seasons after turning pro had everything packed into them. They were amazing. I finished my first four British championships in 7th, 6th, 5th and 4th place, raced in my first TT, my first North West 200 and my first Macau Grand Prix. I'd also raced in a World Superbike race at Laguna Seca – and I was just twenty-four years old. I had already been lucky enough to do more in four years than most don't get to do in a lifetime, and I had a contract with Honda Racing in my pocket. I really didn't know it at the time, but I was only getting started.

6
1994:
My First TT

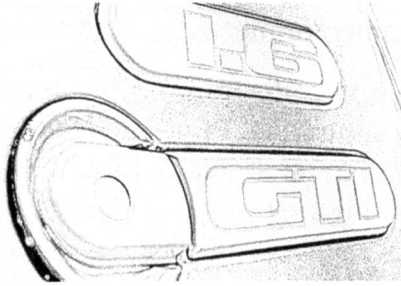

I used to think everyone dreamed of racing at the TT, but I worked out fairly quickly that it was just me. I was really nervous about doing it because I knew what could happen, but there isn't a single time in my life that I can ever remember not wanting to race at the TT; it was such a massive thing in my family. I used to love going to the Isle of Man with my dad, a place full of so many childhood memories for me. It was two weeks in the year that I used to look forward to more than anything else, and I would be devastated when they were over and we had to come home. It is such a special place.

Like I said, Medd dropped me from their BSB team at the end of the 1993 season to make way for James Haydon, and they switched from Kawasakis to the Honda RC45 while I was riding the McCullough Ducati in BSB for my second season. I was delighted when Stuart Medd got in touch and asked if I wanted to ride their Honda RC45 at the TT alongside Robert Dunlop.

Robert was Joey Dunlop's brother, and between the two of them they dominated road racing in the eighties and nineties. There are a few people who say Robert was the better of the two, but I don't know, and it's not really fair to compare. They were both incredible and had huge fan bases. They were both so popular in road racing and for good reason: they were completely dedicated to it, and so humble with all the success that they had. Tragically, they would both die while racing, Joey in 2000 at a race in Estonia and Robert at the North West 200 in 2008.

Years later, I would also be teammates with Robert's son, Michael, at the Honda TT Legends World Endurance Championship team in 2013. He is a very nice lad, and really talented. I like him a lot. At a test for the Honda team in France, we shared a hotel room and got on really well. I broke my leg at that test, and Michael helped me to get dressed, and generally got me out and about until I was back home. I think perhaps I've ended up good mates with Michael because I knew his dad really well and got on with him. Who knows?

I didn't know Michael's brother William as well, but I do believe that if Michael had stuck at short circuit racing, he would have been right there for championships. He is properly fast now on the roads, but I tell you, no one would have seen which way he went if he was still on short circuits. Whatever it was the Dunlops had for breakfast that made them all so fast, Michael had gone back for seconds. I just don't think he enjoys the short circuits, which I understand. I have grown up with both road racing and short circuits, and they're two completely different mindsets and cultures.

So, early in 1994, well before the TT, I wanted to learn the course properly, so I went there with fellow racer Mick Boddice Jnr, and my mate Andrew Oakes. We took my Peugeot 205GTi, which was the smaller 1.6 litre engine because I couldn't afford the 1.9, and we must have done twenty laps, listening to the BeeGees on the radio, talking and going to pubs. My god, it was hilarious. We went round and tried to learn the track but just ended up talking and getting pissed. It was great fun, but as preparation for my TT debut it was a total waste of time and petrol.

Back then they didn't have the system that they do today for bringing newcomers along. These days, all newcomers go through a really intensive and thorough induction. Basically the race organisers will hand-pick riders who they want to race at the TT and who they feel would be up to it. They only take on people who are competing at a high level, either domestically or internationally, and even then they get them over for really full-on coaching sessions with a couple of former competitors, John Barton and Richard 'Milky' Quayle. John and Milky are known as TT Rider Liaison Officers, and the pair work really closely with the newcomers from the very first idea of racing at the TT right up to and including their first race meeting. Nowadays, it can take years before newcomers are let loose on the course, even experienced pro racers.

So, come practice week I turned up with my novice's orange bib that all the newcomers have to wear and a Honda RC45 which, contrary to the myth, was pretty much the worst-handling bike known to man at the time, but I thought nothing of it, because it was normal. That was just how it was then.

The bigwigs at Honda thought it would be a good idea to send me out in a car with their star riders for a lesson on which way the course goes, so I got put in a car with Robert Dunlop, Steve Hislop and Phil McCallen to learn the track. They were three of the biggest names of TT racing at the time. Between them they had 18 TT wins and all of them would go on to win more. Phil McCallen, in particular, had won just three of his eventual eleven wins. Three years later in 1996, he won four TTs in one week, which was a record that stood until 2010, when Ian Hutchinson won five.

The three of them were told to take me, a twenty-two-year-old novice, out for a lap and show me the ropes. I was in the front with Steve driving, and Robert and Phil were in the back. Phil was going, 'This is a left here', and Steve was saying, 'No, it's a flat out right-hander here'. Basically, as far as I could tell, Phil didn't have a clue, literally no idea, what was coming next. I was shocked that the three of them had three totally different ideas of the circuit.

It was as pointless as it was hilarious. These three legends were all arguing amongst themselves over what corner comes next when they were supposed to be teaching me. Robert was laughing his head off so much that I did wonder if they were just winding me up.

Between that lap with so-called experts and the laps with Andrew and Mick Boddice Jnr earlier in the year, I still hadn't got a clue – but I realised years later that I should have listened to Steve Hislop: he knew where every single bump was, and his knowledge of the course was photographic. It was extraordinary.

In the hours leading up to my first-ever practice session, all I can remember is that it was pitch-black when I woke up, and it was really cold. I walked out of the hotel and it was eerily quiet apart from the seagulls starting to squawk. I could even hear a van door closing in the distance.

It must have been 4.30 in the morning when I walked up the hill to the paddock, and soon after it just started to get a bit light. The sky started to turn from that jet black to a sort of inky deep blue. Then by the time I was on the bike, waiting on the grid, it was starting to get dusky, so not yet light. As soon as the sun appeared over the horizon, they started setting bikes off in pairs. It was surreal and almost impossible to describe.

I was so nervous that really the only thing I remember is my surroundings going from pitch-black and deathly quiet when I was walking to the paddock, to sunrise and feeling nothing but nerves. all in the space of a few hours. I hadn't got a clue what to expect. Nowadays there are so many videos online and games that newcomers can watch and play that they know what is coming, but I had no idea. Some newcomers today probably know more about the course than I do now.

All we had was *V for Victory* by Joey Dunlop, and the track had changed since they made that, and anyway, I wouldn't watch it because that would be like doing homework. I was listening to John

McGuinness recently, and he was saying that he'd been watching an on-board video of Peter Hickman's lap-record lap, trying to work out where he was going quicker, and what he had to do to beat him. I was thinking to myself that I'd never watched an on-board lap of the course in my entire life for the purpose of picking up tips or working out where I can go faster. Maybe I should have, but it's probably a bit late for that now. It's just a bit too much like homework for me, so that's where you really do have to take your hat off to people like John. I remember Peter Hickman going to Phillip Island with us recently, and he said that he had been watching videos of the track and what it does, and I had to bluff my way out of the conversation and pretend that I'd done the same.

It wasn't the first time I'd been to a morning practice. I'd always gone up with my dad when he did them. They were always really weird: the contrast of silence, darkness and calmness just before the noise and colour of race bikes at sunrise. Dad would go off down Bray Hill, and then I would go and have a coffee in the Mike Hailwood Centre and wait twenty minutes before wandering over to the pit lane to see if Dad would go through or come in, then go and have another coffee.

Then when it was all over, Dad and I would go and have some breakfast at the hotel and then go back to bed. When it was a nice day, it was an amazing atmosphere and feeling, but it was also the most dangerous thing in the world. I mean, how do you make something already really dangerous even more dangerous? Answer: make people get up at 4.30 in the morning to do it. That said, I am really glad I did the morning practices before they stopped them in 2003; they were such a mad part of the TT's history that will never happen again. There were no spectators out, and hardly any marshals. You just wouldn't get away with it these days.

Finally the moment arrived for me to do my first-ever closed-roads lap of the TT course, and I will never forget going off down Bray Hill for the first time. It's really steep in places, and the bike just accelerated as fast as I could change gear. The acceleration is brutal as the bike powers through all six gears down a hill that gets steeper the further down you go.

Bray Hill is about a 6% gradient at the top half, which is bloody steep – but then just as you're in 5th or 6th gear, depending on the bike, the gradient increases to about 12%, which is about the same as a ramp in a multi-storey car park. It goes on for about half a mile, flanked by houses and all the while snaking from left to right by enough to make perfect positioning of the bike on the road absolutely critical. You go from the relative calm of the start line straight into that. The road flattens out at some crossroads, and that is the bottom of Bray Hill.

You reach the bottom of Bray Hill after just a few seconds, which are without a doubt by far the single most intense seconds you could ever experience doing anything. It is an intoxicating experience; there is simply nothing like it. Nothing. I wish I could say that it lived up to my expectations in that first practice, but the truth is that I was so focused on trying to work out which way it was all going that it sort of passed me by. These days the whole Bray Hill experience hits me every time, but back then, on my first-ever lap, honestly, I don't remember it. I was just trying to think about what was next.

After the bottom of Bray Hill, you go over a couple of jumps in 6th gear and slow down for Quarterbridge, which is a tight right-hander. After that, I accelerated out onto a fairly long straight and suddenly thought, 'Oh shit, where am I?' I was completely lost; I had no clue where I was going. The whole learning-the-track thing had counted for exactly nothing. Mick Lofthouse passed me on a 125, and he pointed to me to follow him, so I followed him for about a mile, but I couldn't keep up and he just went off into the distance. I really didn't have a clue where I was going. Not one.

Eventually I got to Ballacraine, which is about 7 miles into the lap, by using the road signs that they put out with the corner names on to show which way the course went. I had seen the sign for Ballacraine, telling riders to turn right, so I thought I'd start slowing down as the corner wasn't too far away. I went for the brake lever and I thought, this doesn't feel right, and no sooner did I have the thought than it just fell off. My front brake lever just disappeared.

Luckily I was going so slowly that it didn't matter too much. I didn't really know what I had to do if I needed to stop on track – no one had told me – so I just carried on really slowly and used the rear brake to try and slow the bike down. On an RC45 the rear brake caliper is about the size of a 10p piece; it's total shit. So, inevitably, with about 3 or 4 miles still to go, on the way down the Mountain to the Creg-ny-Baa, it was having to work so hard that the brake fluid had boiled up to the point that I had no rear brake either.

Eventually, when I got back to the pits after something ridiculous like an hour after setting off, Roger Marshall, who was our boss, came up to me, and he was raging. He said, 'What's happened? Where have you been?' So I told him that the front brake lever fell off, and I rode the thing not really knowing where I was going, and with no rear brake for the last few miles. Once he'd heard that, he calmed down.

Even though I would have much preferred to have had my front brake lever, in some ways not having it and being forced to have to ride really slowly probably did me a favour, because I didn't know where I was going. If it hadn't have fallen off, I would have been riding much faster and just hanging onto the bike, distracted by its power. I'd never usually suggest that having no front brakes is ever safer than having them, but on that occasion it might just have been. The punchline was that the lever fell off straight into the fairing, so it was still there. We didn't even lose it.

Steve Hislop told me that the quicker you go down Bray Hill, the safer it is. He gave me some tips, like to pull on the handlebars when the bike goes into a wobble at a certain point, and to give the bars a good yank at another place to try and lift the front wheel. He explained to me that at the TT it is much more than position on the roads, turn-in points, and lines through corners. You have to provoke the bike to do things that you don't on smooth short circuits. In some places the bumps are so bad that it's smoother – and therefore faster – to be wheelying. It's a bit like the difference between two-dimensional riding and three-dimensional riding.

Steve promised me that if I could do all the things that he'd told me to do at the exact places he told me to do them, I'd be able to go down Bray Hill flat out no problem. All through practice week I was going down there with the bike shaking so much that the handlebars were thrashing from full left lock to full right lock every time, and I wasn't even close to flat out.

Of course, Steve was right though, because as I got faster and better at timing everything, I got better and better overall. I soon realised that the quicker you go at the TT, not just Bray Hill, the easier it is; the bike sort of jumps and skips everywhere. The bikes then were lethal – they didn't handle – and so getting them to skip along the track made them easier to ride. The less they were in contact with the ground, the better.

Back then, if by some miracle you could get one to handle, you would be untouchable. It changed in the late nineties with the Yamaha R1, and since then all bikes are so good that if they don't handle then there's something major wrong with it, and there will be a fault.

For the race, I went off as number 54, miles behind Robert, obviously. He went off much further up the start order; in the top ten. During the first lap, I caught and passed quite a few people, but not because I was doing anything special. I was on a really fast bike, starting amongst all the other newcomers, who were on more sensible bikes that were a lot slower than mine, and there's me on a missile in the middle of them.

I finished the first lap and the bike was handling like shit, but I thought it was just me and got stuck in to lap two. I still really didn't know where I was going so just concentrated on remembering the bits that I could. By then I had got a few laps under my belt and was starting to pick stuff up.

When I got to Ballaugh on the second lap, the marshals were waving yellow flags at me, which is a warning that there is a problem up ahead, so you need to slow down. There is a small humpback bridge in Ballaugh that makes the bikes jump quite high. Soon after going over the jump, I saw Robert lying on the floor, motionless, with his bike pointing towards me, with no rear wheel in it. I thought, 'Ahh, no way'. It looked like a mess.

I had been coming to the TT since I was a baby, and I'd lost count of overhearing conversations between my dad and other riders about who had died, which always really upset me. I had always heard about accidents at the TT, but Robert's was the first aftermath of an accident hat I had seen first-hand. I was shocked at just what a mess the bike was in, and at seeing him lying there obviously in a really bad way. I was worried that he was dead.

At the end of that second lap, I pulled into the pits for fuel and a new rear tyre, and I said to my pit crew that Robert had had a really nasty accident, and they knew already. They told me that he was OK, which was sort of a relief, but I had seen him and knew that if he was alive then he wasn't in a good way.

The bike handled much better for the next two laps, and I started to feel a bit more like I was getting into a rhythm with the course. To this day I couldn't tell you what my position was in the race, or what my lap times were; I was just trying to remember where I was going and get around without any problems.

At the end of lap four, I pitted again for fuel and another tyre, and went out again for the last two laps of the race, and that's when the bike started handling worse than ever. It was bad for the first two laps when the steering wouldn't stop shaking, but now it was horrendous, especially when I was on the throttle, accelerating. I thought that the rear shock absorber had lost all its fluid and was just bouncing on the spring, with no damping for it. I decided that it didn't matter anyway, because I was hardly at lap-record pace.

Then after the Gooseneck, which is a slow first-gear hairpin, you start to climb up the side of Mount Snaefell, and there are two quick left-handers that must be 140mph at least, and the bike was dragging its foot pegs on the floor through the corners, which it hadn't done before. I just put it down to the rear of the bike being much lower than it should be due to the rear shock absorber packing up.

I finished the race in 17th place and first newcomer. I pulled in and asked the team how Robert was, but there wasn't any more news on him. They were asking me how the race was and they seemed quite pleased with my result. I told them that the rear shock had gone in the last few laps, so one of the guys checked to see how bad it was and pushed down on the rear of the bike to see how much damping had been lost. He said it felt OK, and that was that.

Then they noticed that my rear wheel only had three spokes out of ten still connected to the hub – you could literally grab the rear wheel and pull it from side to side. I reckon if I pulled on it hard enough then I could have pulled the whole wheel clean off with my bare hands.

Robert wasn't as lucky as me. His rear wheel had the same fault and had collapsed after the Ballaugh Bridge jump. We had been sharing wheels, and with Robert that much quicker than me, and therefore putting much more stress through his wheels, they just couldn't take it and his rear wheel fell apart while mine only had three spokes holding it together. Mine must have only been moments away from collapsing too. They pulled the team from the meeting after that; Nick Medd said there were no more wheels for me to carry on with, and I wasn't doing anything anyway.

It took Robert a couple of years to recover from the accident and he lost a lot of the function in his right hand. He was never quite the same again, but he did come back to racing and he won races with a modified brake lever so he could brake with his left hand. However, the big superbikes were too much for him after that. He won a court case against the team for damages, who in turn won a case against the wheel manufacturer.

It was a pretty full-on debut. I only did the one race – which will always be remembered for Robert's accident – but what with my brake lever falling off in practice and seven out of ten spokes on my rear wheel breaking in the race, I can honestly say that someone was looking down on me.

Looking back, riding that RC45 for my first TT was absolutely insane. I should never have gone out on something like that for my debut – it was far too fast for me. Normally a newcomer would start out on a 250, which would have been a much better option. I only did it because they asked me to do it. It never occurred to me that it could be such a stupid thing to do for my first time; I didn't think beyond the chance to go and race at the TT.

Dad really didn't say much to me after the race; he pretty much left me to it. I think maybe he knew that learning the course was something I would need to figure out for myself. There isn't a right way or wrong way to learn the course, but you do have to do the miles. There is simply no other way. We all learn it differently: some guys learn it in sections, some from corner to corner, some by the surroundings, and that is the bit you have to figure out for yourself.

First I started to remember the sections that I enjoyed the most and the sections that I least enjoyed. Then over time I started joining them up, and eventually, without really realising it, after a few years I stopped thinking about where I was going, and I just knew. Once you get to that stage, if you find yourself having to think about where you are then you're in big trouble, because you're lost and disorientated, and you'll be a lot more committed to a line at that point than you are when you're learning.

Despite all the lucky escapes and not having a clue where I was going, I did learn a massive amount of stuff that you can only learn if you race at the TT, but I felt like I had barely scratched the surface, and I knew I could do much better. I also picked up some TT superstitions. For instance, I had heard people say that if your bike doesn't want to start then it is someone telling you that you're not meant to be going out. Mark Farmer's bike wouldn't start that year, and they were trying for ages to get it going. Someone said to me that if it is that hard to get going, just park it and try again the next day. Eventually they got his bike going, and within an hour Mark was dead.

1994 was the year that I went from being a lifelong TT spectator to a TT racer. It's funny – I was so familiar with the place, and I had been going there since I could remember, but at that first meeting I knew nothing about anything. I knew that I had to go back though. I had a taste of it from the other side of the barrier, and I wanted more. Randomly, John McGuinness told me that he was a spectator that year, and he said to me that he remembered spotting some idiot on a trick RC45 with an orange bib coming wobbling past him. Years later, he realised that idiot was me.

7
1997–1998:
Honda –
Job for Life

came into the 1997 season with a real feeling that I had arrived. I'd had a great start to my career with Medd and McCullough, and I'd caught Honda's eye. They wanted me to be part of their setup 'for life', which, considering just four years earlier I'd nearly run out of the bit of money Nan had left me and I was about to pack it in, was unheard-of. The 'job for life' angle and bikes built and prepared direct from the Honda factory (factory bikes) with support direct from the factory was enough for me to turn down offers in World Superbikes and British Superbikes, which if I'm honest I probably would have taken a year earlier. It was my first proper contract.

Honda commissioned a tuning company called V&M to run the team on the ground. They're a proper bunch of guys and highly respected by the whole racing community for tuning engines and preparing bikes to a high standard. In the nineties, they were the kiddies. Jack Valentine and Steve Mellor founded the company in the late eighties, and they quickly became the go-to place for the who's who of road racing and British championship racing for fast engines. Honda UK were no different, and so they appointed V&M to run the team in 1997.

The V&M colours were yellow and red, and they looked so cool on the factory RC45; it was beautiful. However, I'm going to say something that I know will upset quite a few people, because I know the RC45 is held in high regard all over the world. I think it is probably the worst bike I ever rode; it handled so badly. I remember saying to Simon Beck when he got one in 1999 for the TT that they were evil. The next day he was dead.

Simon was a great rider who had plugged away for years with really good results, and he was over the moon to have finally broken through to one of the top teams, which was exactly how I felt at the start of 1997. I'm in no way suggesting that the RC45's handling was to blame for his accident at the TT that took his life; I'm only making the point that sometimes all that glitters isn't gold.

The main problem with the RC45 was that I never knew what it was going to do. The geometry of the bike was set so they were really light on the rear, with a lot of the weight biased to the front, which made it really nervous, and hyper responsive to some setup changes and totally non-responsive to others. I suppose if you rode one all the time and knew what they were going to do then they were good.

As well as them being evil, you've got the pressure from Honda to do well. The RC45 engine was a masterpiece though; it had tractable power, and lots of it, which it needed as the Ducatis were coming on strong with their much larger capacity engines.

It ended up being a frustrating TT in 1997, a tale of 'so close, yet so far'. I'd stepped on the podium for the first time the year before on my McCullough Ducati, and felt like I really made a breakthrough with the course. I really was starting to understand it after my first clueless laps in 1994 and it was all starting to make sense to me. Now that I had factory Hondas and a really experienced team around me, I went to the TT daring to dream for the first time that maybe, just maybe, a win could be on the cards.

I started that TT with a second-place finish to Phil McCallen in the F1 race, which, to be fair, considering he was virtually unbeatable at the time, I wasn't too down about. Unless he had some sort of machine problem or physical problem he was always the favourite for the race win.

In between the F1 and Senior race, Phil crashed in the 250cc race and knocked himself about a bit, so he wasn't at his best for the Senior race. I thought maybe I'd have a chance, and sure enough, I'd caught Phil on the road on the first lap of the Senior and was leading the race. Then towards the end of the second lap, at Signpost Corner, which is only a couple of miles from the end of the lap, I crashed.

The bike had cracked a piston and was spraying oil all over the front tyre, which dumped me on my arse. I was really lucky that Signpost Corner is one of the TT's slowest corners. I can't imagine how big an accident that would have been if the oil leak happened somewhere like Brandish, which is only a couple of corners before and is properly fast. I was told after the race that the pistons should have been changed before the race but the team hadn't done it.

It's not the TT or any of the British championship racing that I did on the RC45 with V&M colours that people remember. People still talk about the World Superbike race at Brands Hatch, which I entered as a wild card.

At the start of the weekend we were all joking, because we had been shoved right at the very far end of the pit lane, under the podium. The walkway to the podium was right next to us, and all the trophies were sitting there on a table outside our garage. Ian Simpson – who was my teammate – and I joked that wouldn't it be nice to get one of them, as if we stood any chance at all against the very, very best superbikes and superbike riders in the world . . .

Carl Fogarty, John Kocinski, Aaron Slight, Colin Edwards, Pierfrancesco Chili, Scott Russell, Akira Yanagawa and Simon Crafar were all absolute giants of the sport then, at the top of their game. The budgets that the teams and factories had were like nothing else. If we were one of the top teams of the British Superbike paddock, we were definitely the plebs in the World Superbike paddock.

The first race was OK. I finished 11th, which we were all pretty pleased with, so as far as we were concerned the weekend was going well, and everything was fine. Then came the second race, which, as I said, I had no idea at the time that all these years later people would still remember me for.

The first part of race 2 was dry, until it started raining, so it got stopped. I don't know where I was, but in those situations they restart the race with grid positions determined by where you were in the race when it was stopped. They make you race the remaining laps to make up the total race distance with an aggregate time. In a lot of ways, it's a bit like racing at the TT in as much as you might not actually be racing the bloke in front of you on the course. At the TT, if you've caught him, you've already passed him on corrected time, having set off ten seconds after him. In an aggregate race in short circuit racing, there is a subtle difference in as much as you might catch someone, have to pass them AND pull away by an amount of time before you actually pass him on corrected time. It's a nightmare, and to be honest whenever it happens I don't really worry about it; I just ride my own race, and whatever happens happens.

Sitting on the grid in the rain for the second part of the race, Rob McElnea came up to me and said to just take it easy and if I did, I'd do well, which I thought was odd coming from Rob at the time, as he was managing the Cadbury's Boost Yamaha team so was a rival of ours. Anyway, I got an OK launch and settled down, doing my own thing. Then after a few laps I looked at my pit board and it said I was P4; I thought it must have been a mistake.

73

Then on the next lap it said I was in second position, and I'd caught up to the back of Fogarty, who was leading on the road. I thought, what do I do? I was so confused by everything that was going on. One minute I was riding round invisible in 11th place in race 1, and now I had cruised up to the back of the greatest superbike rider of a generation with total ease. I was miles faster than him, which I just couldn't get my head round. Luckily, I had raced in the wet at Brands Hatch not long before the WSB race, so I had a good setup already for my bike, so it wasn't all down to skill; we had a bit of luck as well.

There was a sea of people there all for Carl; I've never seen so many people at Brands Hatch in my life, before or since. Apparently, there were 100,000 people there, all for him, and I believe it. I thought if I take him out then I'm not getting out alive. So, while I worked out what to do, and dealt with the dilemma that I really wasn't expecting to deal with that weekend, I followed him for two laps. Then I thought sod it, and I passed him, and got my head down.

In all the stress and worry about taking Carl out, I had actually forgotten that it was an aggregate race and was thinking that because I was now leading on the road that I was leading the race, and I was concentrating on not crashing. If I knew then what I know now, I'd have pushed much harder to pull away, and overturn the gap that Carl had on me in the first part of the race when it got stopped. It didn't help that my pit board didn't have the corrected time gap, so for all the world, in my head I was leading a WSB race by miles, and it was so easy that I was doing wheelies on the last lap, messing about and showing off.

I finished 3rd overall, but I nearly didn't get that due to dicking about on the last lap. Yanagawa was only 1.3 seconds behind me on corrected time, even though he was miles behind me on track. I was 11 seconds behind Kocisinki and 15 seconds behind Carl on corrected time. I don't know if I could have pulled away even more to overturn their advantages but I do know that I really wasn't trying that hard. Anyway, I'll always be able to say that in that one wet race I crossed the line first, even though I was third.

After the race, Carl didn't say much apart from well done, and that's about it; he was just busy entertaining the crowd. Kocinski never went to the podium because there was some trouble between him and Carl, so it was just me and Carl on the podium. The whole thing just kept getting weirder all the time – I mean, we were the poor relations of the paddock, and there I was, standing on the podium with just Carl Fogarty and tens of thousands of people as far as the eye could see, all cheering and waving Union Jacks. Obviously they were all there for Carl, but I was there on that podium on merit.

The madness of the situation kept going though. After the podium, they put us in this convertible car to do a lap so all the fans all the way round the circuit could get a look at the riders. So it was just me, Carl and Carl's wife Michaela. I was just a snotty kid, but there I was, sat on top of this car, waving at everyone. The crowd was going mad for Fogarty. It was incredible. I didn't even exist, but I was there!

The press conference was hilarious too. John Kocinski had to go to that – there's no way you can get out of going to a press conference; it's a big no-no. All the British press were winding him up by asking him if he wished he had a V&M Honda. Kocinski was the factory Honda World Superbike rider that season, and the number-one rider in the team, so basically he was the top dog, and he'd just got whipped by a bloke that he had never heard of, on the same bike as his but with a much lower specification. He really didn't like that.

When I met him later in 1999 during my season in Grand Prix, I found him to be a really nice bloke, and he made me feel really welcome. It's well documented that he is as mad as a hatter, and it's all true. Whenever I parked next to his motorhome in the paddock, my girlfriend and I used to watch him setting up his.

Sandrine was the lucky lady at the time, and we went everywhere together. We now have two children together, Juliette and Cecilia, who are all grown up now. Anyway, Kocinski had this cleaning obsession, and he would brush his helmet out with his hand onto a mat and then spend half an hour just cleaning that. He also sacked his motorhome driver because he used the toilet in it once. Everything had to be perfect. I remember at one of the meetings someone was trying to piss Kocinski off, so they chucked bread on top of his motorhome so the birds would shit on his roof, knowing that would send him into a meltdown.

The strange thing is once I'd finished a race, even a massive one like the Brands Hatch WSB with all the hype that followed it, almost immediately after I'd be thinking, that's done, what's next? I had beaten the world's best riders, and in the moment I was genuinely surprised myself; I was absolutely peaking, especially when none of us expected it, but you move straight onto the next thing.

I got a couple of offers in WSB from some smaller teams, but I never took them; I was getting paid well and I didn't want to end up with nothing. I knew a few people who went to WSB with small teams and it ruined them, so I thought it was best to just carry on as I was, unless I got offered a factory ride. Obviously, I would have taken a factory ride in WSB, but I was never really good enough for that, or at least I didn't see myself as good enough.

I remember speaking to Dad about not doing WSB. He never used to talk about any of his achievements, or doing well, or that he won this and won that, with one interesting exception: he told me that he wished he'd had stuck at Grand Prix racing. He said he thought he would have done well at it, and that's as much as Dad ever said to me that revealed how he saw himself and his abilities.

I wish I'd done a year in WSB, but I'm not hung up about it. I wish I'd done a season in Grand Prix on a decent bike and had a proper go at it, but it was what it was. I wish I'd won a British championship, but I didn't. Having said that, if I'd done a season in WSB then I would have competed in all classes of road racing by now.

The 1997 season overall wasn't too bad. I'd been quick at the TT, quick enough to feel robbed of at least one win, and I'd had my moment of glory at Brands Hatch WSB, and I finished 3rd in the British championship. The grid that season was made up of four trick Ducati 916s ridden by shit-hot riders John Reynolds, Sean Emmett, Troy Bayliss and Matt Llewellyn, and a pair of factory Yamaha YZF750s ridden by the world-class Niall Mackenzie and Steve Hislop, so for me to pinch 3rd place overall was OK. That said, it was clear to me that the Ducati in particular was emerging as the bike to have, and the RC45 was starting to show its age.

For 1998, Honda wanted the team to look more corporate because it was their fiftieth anniversary at the TT, so the yellow and red V&M paintwork that was on the bikes in 1997, and which everyone recognised, was swapped for the corporate red and black of Honda Racing back then. Jack Valentine still ran the team until Honda decided to take over from him after I threatened to quit about a month before the TT. I wanted to use Showa suspension, but Jack made us use Penske, which wasn't as good, so I just said that they should carry on without me. I still think there was more to it than just me stamping my feet over suspension and tyres. I didn't know it at the time but I'd be back with V&M in 2000.

Ian Simpson and I had factory Honda engines, and standard chassis. There were different spec 'factory' engines but we had one each of the best spec you could get. Unfortunately, one of the engines seized up with me on it at Donington Park because one of the mechanics forgot to put the oil cooler on it, and this brand-new factory engine shat itself pretty much as soon as I left the pit lane. I had only got to the top of Craner Curves and had turned around to see if anyone was behind me, when it locked up solid and down I went.

That left us with one pukka factory engine between us for the rest of the year. We were supposed to share it but I made sure that I had it most of the time. When we got to the North West 200, Simmo was keen to get his hands on it, because the track is so fast and the straights are so long there that having more power is an advantage, or at least perceived wisdom says so. As you can imagine, we both wanted the more powerful factory engine for the race, so I suggested that we flipped a coin. Simmo won, and all I could say was 'Bastard'. He was sure to win the race.

When the race came, Simmo and I were leading, and I was just about managing to sit in his slipstream, which is the pocket of still air created by the rider or riders at the front. In effect, because the air is still behind the rider in front, the bike behind needs less power to make the same speed as the bike in front, which is having to work harder to push through the denser air in front of it. Some people call it slipstreaming and it's one of the oldest tricks in the racing book, especially if you're at a power disadvantage.

I was tucked in behind Simmo, and I was giggling like hell because I could just about hold on to him in a straight line, and we were about the same on the rest of the track. I knew it would be irritating him that he couldn't drop me. Don't get me wrong: hanging on to him was one thing; passing him would be a whole different thing. Plus, if I so much as dropped out of his slipstream by even a foot, that would be it; there would be no getting back in it. He'd be gone, and I'd drop back like a stone.

Then I saw this little curl of smoke coming from his rear tyre, like you sometimes see a vortex of smoke coming from an aeroplane's wing tip. His tyre was overheating due to that extra bit of power that he had, and I knew that his rear tyre wasn't going to last. Once they get so hot that they are giving off curls of smoke, it's game over. His tyre fell apart, and ironically my having less power meant that I won the race, proving that luck isn't always obvious at the time. If I had the faster engine, I wouldn't have been able to help myself either and I would have done the same as Simmo and ridden as hard as I could to shake him off. Losing that coin toss meant that I won the race.

The RC45s we got for the TT were completely different to the ones we were using in BSB. They were full-factory RC45s that were meant for Phillip McCallen, but he had been injured so we got his bikes. Even so, they were still handling badly, and at the TT, the fact that the RC45 was so lairy on the route's bumpy ground meant that my contact lenses moved about. My eye prescription was -5; in other words, it was properly shit if I didn't wear contact lenses.

In the F1 race, the first superbike race of the week, my contact lenses were all over the place, and whenever I blinked, sometimes they'd come back into the right place on my eyeball, and sometimes they wouldn't. One lens moved on my eye, and no matter how many times I blinked it wouldn't come back, so for about 3 miles I couldn't see anything out of one eye. I was leading the race by about twenty seconds with visibility in just one eye, then I blinked again, and the other one actually fell out while I was going up the Mountain.

I was really in the shit because I couldn't see anything and I was just starting to think about pulling over and retiring when I blinked and the remaining one came back. This was on lap four, so I was due to come into the pits anyway. During the pit stop, I put another one in and got going again, still leading, then on the last lap one lens fell out again, and I did most of the last lap with one eye shut, praying that the one lens that was still OK didn't also fall out. I lost the race by around thirty seconds to Ian Simpson.

For the second superbike race of the week (the Senior), I sealed up my visor a lot better to cut out as much draught as possible from inside my helmet, and it was better but my lenses were still moving around. I was leading on the first lap, and caught Simmo on the road so I knew I was ten seconds up on him. After the start of the second lap, I hit the compression at the bottom of Bray Hill harder and faster than ever before, and I heard a 'skrshhh' and thought, what's that? Then when I tipped into Quarterbridge about half a mile later I thought it didn't feel right. Then at the next corner at Braddan Bridge it felt worse, like something was broken. I got all the way to Glen Helen about five miles or so later and I pulled up by the commentary box to have a look at it. The bloody thing had a flat tyre.

It seems the force of the bump at the bottom of Bray Hill had blown some air out of the tyre, so I rode the rest of the lap, about another 25 miles or so, with an underinflated front tyre until I got back to the pits.

They changed the wheel, and the bike felt OK again, but I'd lost so much time cruising round for 25 miles that I only finished 13th.

I was gutted. I'd been comfortably leading both superbike races that week, and, purely down to bad luck, I'd missed out on winning both. There was some good news from the 1998 TT though ...

I got my first TT win on the Motorcycle-City-sponsored Honda CBR600. I was very lucky to even get into that team. Apart from the RC45 for the superbike I didn't really have anything else for the TT that year. Phil McCallen had a crash at Snetterton and had damaged his back, so as well as getting upgraded to his factory RC45 for the superbike races I also got his Fireblade for the Production race and his 600 for the Supersport race – or the 'Junior' as it was called then.

The 600 race was before the Production race and was one of those dodgy races that would have been stopped these days. It started off dry, and I was number four on the road while Ian Simpson, who was on the other Motorcycle City bike, started at number fifteen, I think. Ian and Jim were my biggest rivals for that race, but Jim retired from the race quite early on, so it was between me and Ian for the win.

On the last lap, it started to rain when I was somewhere near the Creg-ny-Baa, so I only had a few miles left and back then they didn't stop the race for rain. I remember thinking that the rain was good for me, because Ian was a lot further back on the road, so he was going to get more of the rain than me. I still think it was a lucky win in a way, but I'll take it all the same; after all, I missed out on a few wins due to bad luck before – and since – that race.

I'd been knocking at the door for a while with some second and third places, but to get a win was so special. I never dreamed that I'd get on the podium, so standing on the top step wasn't something I'd really even thought about. I always tended to prepare to be disappointed so that I wouldn't get too down if things didn't come off. I would look at the guys riding at the front at the time, like Joey Dunlop, Jim Moodie, Phil McCallen, Steve Hislop and Nick Jefferies when I started, and be in awe, never really believing that I could compete with them. But then I started chipping away, and I'd get a bit gutted with finishing second, but if I'm completely honest, I really didn't think I'd ever do it, especially against those guys. It was amazing, and of course Dad was there, which was great.

My first TT win was Honda's 99th, so the race that they really wanted me to win more than any was the next race a few days later – the Production race on their Fireblade. Yamaha had just brought out their YZF-R1, which would go on to dominate the TT for a long time, and I think Honda knew then that the Production race in 1998 would be the Fireblade's last chance to win a race for a while. Plus, Honda didn't want to wait another year for their 100th win. On the start line, Dave Hancock, who is basically the main test rider at Honda for all their new bikes including the Fireblade, came up to me and put a bit of pressure on me by saying that I needed to win this race.

I tell you, that Fireblade was like a missile. It went off the line and the wheel didn't touch the floor until I got to the top of Bray Hill. Almost straight away, the oil warning light came on and I didn't really know whether to go flat out and hope for the best or hold back a bit and go easy on the engine. To be honest, I was slightly relieved when Jim Moodie, who was also on a Fireblade, passed me on the road. I knew he would be leading the race, and I was second, so Honda would get their 100th win one way or another, and I didn't have to risk a retirement. To be fair, to beat Jim round there on the same kit then would have taken a massive effort and I'd have had to put a big strain on my engine. Even so, Jim made me look stupid; he was more on it than I was, even though I was being careful. Under the circumstances I was happy enough with second place.

Even though he wasn't riding, Phil McCallen was there, working for the team, and I remember vividly how brilliant he was with me. It was amazing how he had everything ready for me; he was so professional and constantly one step ahead of me. He knew exactly what I'd want next before I'd even thought of it. He was the perfect crew chief for me, which is a role I'm trying to do well in now that I'm running my own team.

The 1998 TT nearly didn't happen at all due to a superstition that I picked up a few years earlier. 27 was my race number at Medd Kawasaki; I'd actually wanted number 26 but someone else had it in 1993. I had number 26 when I raced my RGV because I had seen a picture of Dad taken at Mansfield Corner at Cadwell Park on his Yamaha TZ350 with the number 26. I always thought it was a cool photo, which is why I wanted to stick with number 26 on the Medd Kawasaki.

I was OK with the number 27 – until someone told me that it's unlucky. Most of me thought it was a load of rubbish, but once someone says something like that to you then you start seeing it. I sold a car, and the bloke paid with £50 notes, and about half of them were fake, and all the serial numbers on them were 27. I started seeing 27 all the time whenever people were having bad luck.

When we got to the 1998 TT, the weather was rubbish – cold and drizzly – and out of curiosity I asked what pit we were in, and they said 27. Straight away I said I wouldn't ride and sent someone to the control tower to get another pit. They wouldn't move us, but I was deadly serious: I wasn't going to race. Eventually they did manage to change me to pit number 26. All through my career I've avoided the number 27; if there are 27 minutes left in a session, I won't go out. But I'm not superstitious.

It was amazing to get my first TT win that year, but I couldn't ignore the fact that I lost the F1 race purely due to my contact lenses falling out, and I'd had problems with them falling out in the British championship a few times too. They were costing me results, so I thought I should get my eyes lasered. It was the best thing I ever had done, but I should have read the pamphlet beforehand. The plan was to do both eyes together; they don't normally do that, but I needed them done before the start of the next season and there wasn't enough time to get them done one after the other.

IOM, Villa Marina.

Suzuka 8 hours race.

Dad's bike shop.

IOM TT parade lap.

North West 200.

TT podium, 1997 F1 race.

Me and dad have never been far apart

Me and dad lapping the TT course on our Ducatis in 2008 for a parade lap. I thought it would be boring following him after so many years away, but he still knew his way around. It was brilliant.

Mum, Dad and me just after Dad won one of his TTs.

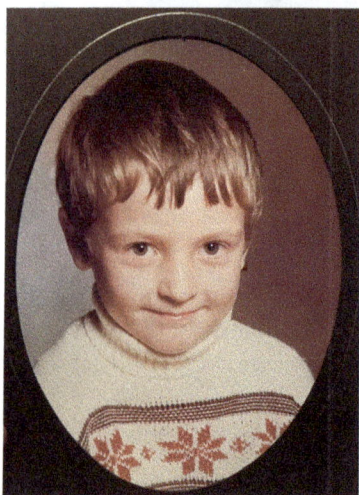

School and I didn't really get along. It was mutual.

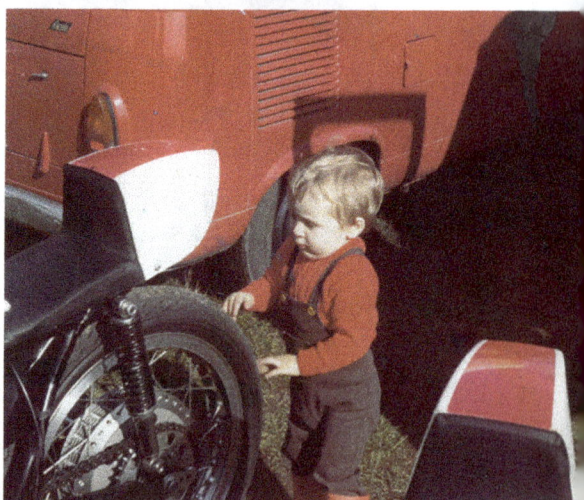

I've been around race bikes since before I can remember.

I must have done hundreds of miles on this bike imagining I was a motorbike racer.

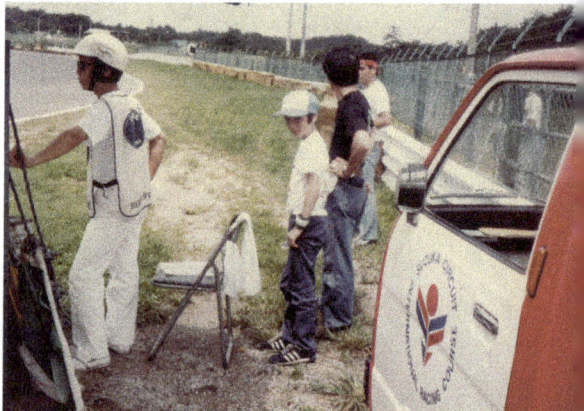

Hanging around with some marshalls at Suzuka while Dad was on track.

ad's bike shop. Obviously I loved spending time there. There
as a sweet shop across the road too.

Model aeroplanes were my other thing.

At the startline of the 1988 Senior TT with Dad.

Dad's bike after his crash at Montjuic Park.

Me and Fred Corbett. He was one of Dad's mechanics.

Racing Simon Le Bon's bike.

The invoice for my first ever race bike.

My first ride as a pro in 1993. I still don't have anything to do with the number 27.

One my two races at the Ulster Grand Prix. I'm wearing a set of Steve Hislop's leathers because I didn't have any Castrol branded ones.

The Kushitani suit that Steve Hislop lent me for th the Ulster Grand Prix, and let me keep.

d's last ever TT in 1991, on my Suzuki RGV250. broke down.

My TT debut in 1994. Start number 54, orange newcomers bib, it's raining, I'm on a Honda RC45 with slick tyres and have no clue where I'm going.

My first Macau Grand Prix in 1994 lasted about 300 yards.

u can see the stone that got caught on my front tyre and ripped e mud guard off. I very nearly crashed at Mallory Park.

At Laguna Seca WSB in 1995 in California with John Hackett.

John Hackett and Igor Gorodynski with Igor's road bike at Laguna Seca.

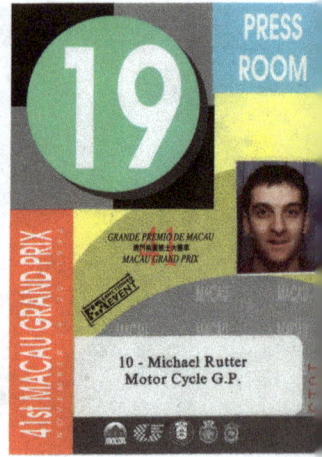

My Press Room pass for my first Macau Grand Prix in 1994.

Crashing out of the lead of 1997 Senior TT at Signpost Corner. A piston had cracke and sprayed oil all over my front tyre.

Me, Carl Fogarty and Michaela Fogarty in "that" dress after my WSB podium in 1997.

At the 1998 North West 200. Ian Simpson won the rig to use the one full factory engine the team had, on th flip of a coin. Ironically, my lower spec engine was th one to have, and I won.

The Honda RC45 was a really hard bike to ride at the TT. I'm also riding with just one contact lens in this picture.

My first TT win.

On my way to my first TT win in 1998. The next piston-powered one would be 19 years later.

The V&M Team in 2000, the second time I raced in their colours.

THAT race with Joey Dunlop during the 2000 Senior TT. We raced each other so hard. Sadly, they were his last ever laps of the TT.

Second place to David Jefferies and in front of Joey Dunlop. What a podium to be part of. Sadly, neither of them are with us anymore.

Me and David Jefferies. He was in another league at the 2000 TT.

My two years at Renegade in 2002 and 2003 were my first real shots at the BSB title.

Steve Hislop was never far away in 2002. He was never far away throughout my whole career.

I went in and got them lasered, and the doctor asked who was picking me up, because I had two patches on my eyes and obviously couldn't drive. So I told him that Sandrine was doing the driving. Then I got the worst headache ever, and when I told the doctor he asked if I had read the pamphlet. I admitted that I hadn't, to which he said that if I had, I would have known to take strong headache tablets before the procedure, and that now he couldn't give me any because I was in hospital (which I've never really understood).

On the way home, I was in absolute agony and with two patches on my eyes, and my daughter Juliette was crying in the car, which made the whole situation worse. When we eventually got home, I couldn't resist taking the patches off, even though the doctor said not to. I really wanted to see if I could see. Well, I couldn't see a bloody thing, so I was shitting myself. I was sure the doctor had just made them worse and that this was the end of my racing career.

Eventually I went to sleep and woke up at 5 am to be at the hospital for 7 am, and I couldn't believe it; my eyesight was perfect, so I drove to the hospital myself, put the patches back on, and sat in the waiting room. The doctor led me to his room and asked if I was ready, and to prepare myself for a big surprise. When he pulled the patches off, I had to pretend that it was the first time and fake being amazed at the transformation.

About halfway through the 1998 BSB season at Snetterton, after qualifying on the Saturday, I went for something to eat and drink with Sandrine at a nearby pub. Honda had given me a company car that year which we used to take to all the races. Coming back from the pub later that night, I was messing about in the car, and when you turn off the road into the circuit, it's a really long drive to the entrance along a strip of tarmac that used to be a runway. I was trying to get the car to go flat out.

Unbeknown to me, while we were out having dinner the organisers had put out all the barriers that they use to filter the public cars when they turn up for race day. I was absolutely flat out in this Honda company car when suddenly out of the dark I see the barriers all there right in front of me. I shat myself at the thought of ploughing through them all at about 70mph and wrecking the car, so my instinct was to yank the steering wheel to try and go round them, but the tarmac there was so grippy because it used to be a runway, and the car just rolled over a few times and ended up in a ditch on its side. It was totally destroyed.

Sandrine was knocked out and when she started to come round she said that she couldn't move, so I got out of the car in the pitch-black, with just the car's indicators flashing. I tried to push the car back onto its wheels because her arm had been flung out the smashed window and had got trapped under the door. I was shitting myself, and no matter how hard I pushed I just couldn't push it back onto its wheels to get to Sandrine, but I did manage to move it enough to free her arm.

I didn't know what to do. The paddock was still way in the distance, and no one there knew where we were and that we were in trouble, so I decided to run for help. As I started running, in a complete stroke of luck I kicked my phone, which had been flung out of the car and was on the floor. It lit up in the dark as it span across the tarmac. I grabbed it and called Jim Moodie and Niall Mackenzie, who both came out to us straight away, and then I called an ambulance. I don't know what would have happened if I hadn't kicked that phone by accident.

Sandrine was alright, but the car had a shock absorber in the back that had flown out the rear window and smashed it. To this day I think that the shock absorber is still in the grass somewhere. There were bits of Honda's car everywhere, right in front of the main entrance of Snetterton, in the early hours of race day, and all the Honda bosses were coming to the race. By that time, dawn was just starting to break, so I paid this local bloke an extortionate amount of money to get rid of the car and I would deal with it all after the race. When he came out and picked it up, I said to him to just take it away and that I wasn't bothered where, just anywhere but here. So he took it away, and I never heard from him again.

However, about two days later I got a call from Honda saying that some bloke had dropped my company car off literally right outside the main doors of Honda headquarters in Slough, and that it looked like it had been in a massive accident. Apparently it had been there for two days before Honda called me to find out what it was doing there. I 'fessed up, and they were OK about it, but despite the whole 'job for life' thing they let me go at the end of the season, which may or may not be related to me writing off one of their cars.

8
1999: Grand Prix

I won the last race of the last round of the 1998 season on the Honda RC45, which means I was the last person to win a race in the UK on one, but it wasn't enough to stop Honda giving me the flick at the end of 1998. I was shocked; it was a massive punch in the stomach.

I had naively bought in to the whole 'job for life' thing that they had sold me, only for them to announce out of the blue that they weren't going to race in the UK in 1999 at all. They didn't tell me until the November, so all the rides in BSB had already gone. I said, 'But you told me I've got a job for life', and they just said, 'Err, sorry. Bye.'

On reflection, I get why Honda decided not to keep racing the RC45 to almost certain mediocrity in 1999. It was reaching the end of the line as a competitive bike. Ducati had moved the game on with their near 1000cc V-twin engines and were starting to dominate. It was becoming clear that to make a 750cc four-cylinder bike competitive against the Ducatis would be hugely expensive.

Honda put all their resources into running the 750cc RC45 for one more year, just in World Superbikes with Aaron Slight and Colin

Edwards as their riders, and Colin finished runner-up in the championship, which was bloody impressive. That said, he was something mad like 120 points behind Fogarty, who won his fourth and final championship that year. In 2000 Honda made their own version of a 1000cc V-twin, called the SP-1, and Colin won the championship with it first time out.

It was a massive wake-up call for me, and a hard but valuable lesson. It was November 1998, and I had nothing for the next season. I was really panicking because I'd had a couple of really good years with Honda on the RC45 and really felt like I was ready to go for the title in 1999.

Then Mike Trimby, who was the bloke who ran GPs at the time, heard that I didn't have a ride for 1999 and got in touch. Mike still runs the International Race Teams Association (IRTA), which represents all MotoGP teams so that they can all speak with one voice to the FIM (Fédération Internationale de Motocyclisme), which is the overall governing body for all motorcycle racing at world level. He said I should have a go at GPs, so he put me in touch with this guy called Joe Miller who he knew from the Macau GP that Mike organised. Joe owned a haulage company and sponsored loads of people, including Jeremy McWilliams in 250cc Grand Prix races. The team really wanted an English rider, so I said I would do it but wanted paying. They paid me £40,000, which was OK, but the condition was that I had to find sponsorship to repay the money.

So in 1999 I rode in GPs, which is probably the worst thing I could have done for my career, but I'm so glad that I did. The team had a customer spec Honda NSR500V, which in basic terms was a twin-cylinder version of the FOUR-CYLINDER and much more powerful NSR500. That was the bike you needed if you wanted to win races or even to get into the top ten. The idea was to take advantage of the lower weight limit allowed for twin-cylinder bikes, and produce a bike that privateer teams like ours could afford to buy and run. In theory, what it lost out on the straights it should make up in the corners.

Sete Gibernau had one as part of the full-factory HRC Repsol-sponsored team. His was bloody fast, but all the customer ones were about the same – beautiful but really slow. To make it worse, 1999 was when Grand Prix bikes had to switch to unleaded fuel from proper race fuel and the V-twin just didn't like the stuff. It probably made 130bhp, which is less power than my RC45 from the previous season, but it only weighed 103Kg, which is basically nothing. In comparison, the V4 NSR weighed 130Kg but by 1999 was making a reputed 200bhp. We were hopelessly outclassed.

Before the first round of the season, there was a test at Jerez in Spain, and there was a riders' meeting that I had to go to. Being the new boy, I got there first, dead keen, sitting on the table in my new branded leathers. The next person who walked into the room was Mick Doohan, basically a god amongst men. He had won five world championships by then and was so dominant in the nineties that apparently he was the first motorcycle racer ever to command an EIGHT-figure salary. He was untouchable, and there was me, a pasty bloke from the Black Country who's never raced outside the UK.

I was too afraid to even say hello to Doohan. He sat on the table behind me and totally ignored me. I'm glad he did because I was so nervous that I probably would have said something really stupid. So just the two of us were sat in silence in this empty room for what felt like ages. It was so awkward, but then everyone else started coming in and broke the silence up. Later on, Jeremy McWilliams told me that if you upset Doohan, he would give you such a hard time on track. I didn't think much of it at the time but his words would plague me until we came back to Jerez for the third round of the season. The test came and went without much of a hitch. I did what I did, and then we went on the best adventure ever.

The first meeting was at Sepang in Malaysia. It was the first time the circuit had been used for a motorcycle Grand Prix, so no one really knew what to expect. It has been the home of the Malaysian round of MotoGP, as it is known these days, ever since. I was shitting myself; I didn't really know where I was going, I was on a really slow bike, and the straights at Sepang are really long. I was coming down the start/finish straight in the first practice session, and I was looking over my shoulder every few seconds because I didn't want to get in anyone's way. I was looking behind me so much and was so worried that I probably could have done with some mirrors on the bike.

Suddenly Doohan was there, right behind me. I thought, 'Ahh shit', so I pulled over into the first corner, miles off the racing line, and well out of his way. He came past me, waving his hand in the air, all pissed off at me, and I thought, 'Bloody hell, I'll just have to try harder to keep out of his way'. I really didn't want a reputation for always being the bloke who gets in the way of the front-runners or knocks them off. The job prospects with other teams in the paddock wouldn't be great if I was causing their superstar riders headaches.

Every time I went out in that first session, Doohan would bloody find me. He was always there, probably thinking to himself, 'Oh my god, look at this bellend wobbling around'. I saw him somewhere else on the track, and he went off on one again, and I really was trying to keep out of his way.

In the second practice session I was going down the start/finish straight again, and I see he is about five or six bike lengths behind me again. This time I thought, 'I've had enough. He's going to have a tantrum whatever I do, so I might as well do my own thing, and give him something to really moan about.' I tipped into the first corner, which is a long, really tight right-hander that then flicks left. Suddenly, I thought, 'Oh Michael, just leave it and pull out of the way and leave him to it', so I turn around to see where he is, and all I see is him spinning around on his arse. He'd overdone his corner speed, which caused his front tyre to lose grip and dump him on the ground. It's called a low side. He never touched me, but for a moment I thought I was properly in the shit.

In another session the next day, it was pouring down with rain. The area is notorious for epic downpours at certain times of the day during the 'rainy season'. I was always OK in the rain, but this was lethal. It was like nothing I'd ever ridden in before. In the dry, my bike was 37mph down on the rest, which sort of becomes an advantage in the wet conditions as the top teams can't use their massive power advantage because their bikes would just spin the rear tyre everywhere, in every gear. Nowadays it's no longer a problem as they use electronics to control the bike's torque, power delivery, throttle response and traction control. None of that stuff existed then, so I really didn't mind the rain.

I was coming up to the last corner, and there he was again. Carrying on the habit from the previous day's practice sessions, I had once again found Doohan out on track, only this time he was in front of me, and I was catching him. The last corner is a left-hand hairpin at the end of a long straight, so it has a big braking zone which I thought would give me enough time to outbrake him. I waited for him to hit the brakes, hesitated, then hit mine when I was alongside him. I caught a glimpse in the corner of my eye of him looking across at me, probably expecting to see one of his regular rivals. Then I swear he did a double take, and looked across at me again.

I got in front of him on the classic inside line, and only just stopped on the bike, but I made it round. Then I looked behind me and he had pulled off into the pits, which at Sepang you do at the end of the braking zone, before you turn in to the corner, so he never actually followed me round the turn, but he was definitely trying on the brakes and I totally did him. It was only once, in one session, but I'm classing that as a completed pass on the greatest motorcycle racer of the era, Mick Doohan.

Two rounds later, at Jerez in Spain I was behind Doohan when his incredible career ended. It was first or second practice and, as was becoming normal, he found me on track, so I decided to try and get a tow off him in the few corners where I could see him. I was following him as close as I could when his rear tyre just touched the white line which marks the edge of the track. It was still damp after some rain from earlier in the day, so as soon as his rear slick tyre touched it, the rear of the bike came round on him and fired him straight over the top of the bike, really high in the air.

I reckon it would have been about a 100mph corner, and he went down really hard, and that was him done. He broke the same leg that he'd nearly lost in 1992, plus a load of other bones. It is ironic that – after all the shit he had given me on track, and considering I never had anything to do with him at all and he probably didn't even know my name – I got the front-row seat for the end of his career. It was a sad way for him to go out. None of us wants to finish our careers on a stretcher, especially on a fairly simple mistake. He was a god and he knew it, but that day he was unlucky. I never saw him again.

Doohan's crash wasn't the only one that year that I nearly got tangled up in. James Whitham was also riding in GPs that year on a Modenas KR3, which was a three-cylinder thing, sort of a halfway house between what I had and the full-fat V4s that the top teams had. It was only slightly better than ours and also was never going to beat a V4. At Brno in the Czech Republic, Whitham had a massive crash that made a right mess of him and the bike.

Like Doohan, his crash was a big highside, causing the fuel tank to split and burst into flames. The fireball was like nothing I'd ever seen before. It was like a scene from a disaster movie. I was right behind him when it happened, so I had no choice but to ride through the middle of it. I had nowhere else to go. The heat was really intense because that much fuel had been sprayed all over the place. Even the tyre wall at the far side of the gravel trap set alight. The tarmac melted too. James was bloody lucky not to end up in the middle of the fire. He had broken his pelvis really badly, so he would have struggled to get himself out of there. He would have been in real trouble.

The V4 GP bikes were phenomenal. They would just come on to the straight, squat down, and disappear into the distance. I remember at the Paul Ricard circuit in France going down the start/finish straight, just starting a qualifying lap. I had my head down, buried behind the screen, properly gritting my teeth. Those qualifying laps are the best time to ride a bike on track: the bike's hardly got any fuel in it so it is as light as it can be, and the rear tyre is the stickiest one available for the most grip, and you're riding the thing as fast as it can possibly go. Everything is on the absolute limit to try and get the best possible lap time. It is a proper rush.

As I headed down to turn 1, past the pit exit, Kenny Roberts Jnr came out of the pits on his full-factory V4 Suzuki RGV500 to cruise round on a steady out lap before he started a qualifying lap. I had aced the first few corners and was on the back straight in the middle of my qualifying lap when Roberts passed me bolt upright, only holding on with one hand and fiddling with his helmet visor with the other.

It was so demoralising for everyone, and I thought to myself, 'What's the point?' It was only round four of a sixteen-round season, and people started to give up and just go through the motions. Our bike was just stupidly slow. Fifteen years later, I got the chance to ride the exact same bike that a one-handed Roberts had used to overtake me for a feature for *Performance Bikes* magazine. It was a real eye-opener for me because I always knew we had showed up to a gunfight with a knife, but spending an afternoon riding it years later made me realise that we didn't even bring a knife: we had brought a spud gun, at best.

When we got to Italy, I said, 'Right, if we're going to carry on like this, we need better suspension, better this, better that, and I wanted my old crew chief from Honda' – a bloke called Bill Simpson, who is Ian Simpson's dad. I had worked with him previously at Honda on the RC45 and he was really good at everything, so I paid him to come along and try to move the job forward a bit.

Bill doesn't drink and was that bit older than the rest of us. Mark Woodage and John Moat were my mechanics then, and they still work in the British Superbike paddock, so you get an idea of how young all of us in the team were back then. They were only kids really, and they were running a MotoGP team – how mad is that? They did a good job for their age but we really needed someone with some experience in the garage to help.

So, Bill came aboard at the San Marino GP, and one morning I was walking down the garages to get to our garage, which was was right in between the factory Honda and factory Suzuki garages, which were simply incredible: fully decked out with boards, tool chests, ramps, the whole shooting match. When I got to our garage, there was Bill, lying asleep on the floor, with his head on his briefcase, and two bits of blue workshop tissue rolled up and stuffed into his ears because of the noise. I walked in and said to Mark and John, 'What's wrong with him?' They confessed that they had got Bill really pissed the night before. I couldn't believe it; for the first time in his life Bill had got absolutely pissed out of his head. Just when I needed a steady hand in the garage, he was written off.

Hardly anyone spoke to us. We were absolutely nothing in that paddock; we were invisible. Tadayuki 'Taddy' Okada was on the factory Honda along with teammate Alex Criville, who won the world championship that year. Taddy finished third in the championship, so he was a really big deal. Despite the massive gulf between our statuses, he and I hit it off straight away and we got on really well. I didn't realise at the time, but he would feature a lot in my career years later. He was really funny, and because he wasn't allowed to be seen drinking he would hang around with us, out of the way, and have a few drinks.

It wasn't all bad though: the British GP at Donington Park was fantastic. I know it can sound cheesy when you hear riders at their home Grand Prix saying how special it all is, and how all the support really does help, but, even though I only rode at my home Grand Prix the once, I can say that it really is a properly special weekend. John and Mark were a bit gutted to be at Donington, to be honest. They were having the time of their lives travelling the world and going to new places. When we were racing in Europe, they would base themselves with the truck in Italy at a really popular party destination next to a beach, so when they got to Donington there was nothing special about it for them and it was a bit of an anti-climax. It was the same place they had been going to for years, the same garages, the same bloke on the gate, and the same food in the canteen.

On track, I don't think anyone even knew I was there, or that there were any British riders in the race, but there was definitely something in the air, and it was good to actually know which way the track went, and where the pit entry was. The other thing that was fantastic about the meeting was that it was the only round I scored points at all season – five points to be exact, for finishing eleventh … out of eleven finishers.

Basically, everyone else broke down, crashed or didn't start the race. Doohan was already done, and Sete Gibernau had a big-off in warm-up that ruled him out from starting. It was carnage. Twenty-three people qualified for the race, and only eleven finished. 'To finish first, first you must finish' is a phrase that was never more relevant than at the 1999 British Grand Prix.

I qualified in 20th – ahead of John McGuinness, even though his bike was 4mph faster than mine on the main straight. Mind you, Alex Criville, who was on pole position for Honda, was 15mph faster than me – and it isn't even a long straight. At Donington Park, my bike was slower than Valentino Rossi's 250cc bike in the support race.

Inevitably, my bike started playing up in the race with two laps to go. The rear was handling really badly, and it was unbelievably hard to ride, even slowly. I knew I was in 11th place, so I rode round with it like that because I knew I might never get another chance to get some points. As soon as I took the flag, I pulled over at the exit of pit lane and leaned the bike up against the wall to have a look at what was up with the rear end.

The V-twin 500 had a single-sided swing arm, so the rear wheel is fixed to it with a single nut and there is a circlip that acts as a failsafe so the nut can't fall off. I could see that the circlip had done its job but that the wheel nut had unwound itself right out to it, so the wheel didn't fall off completely but it was just hanging there. The only thing stopping the rear wheel just falling off completely was a 50p circlip. Even so, it was a brilliant weekend that I'll never forget.

At the South African round, we got to the circuit at Welkom, which no one had been to before. It was a brand-new circuit and it wasn't really finished, so there was dust everywhere; it was really bad and looked like a bombsite. Everyone was saying that it wasn't safe to ride on because of all the dust. It was way too slippery, so the organiser got a load of builders and locals and gave them sweeping brushes, but they obviously weren't interested.

Some bright spark got thirty hire cars for all the GP riders to drive round the track and clear the dust. Obviously I was a GP rider, so I got one of the thirty brand-new Mercedes Benz cars. You could cram as many people as you wanted from other classes into the car with you, but I still can't believe that they set us all off onto a dusty, slippery racetrack in these brand-new cars. I remember a car passing me at one point and looking across, and seeing Rossi in its passenger seat, pissing himself laughing. The organisers stopped it after ten laps to clear the mess up. There were cars everywhere and all of them were ruined: crashed, blown up, stuck in gravel traps, you name it. Every single one got written off in under thirty minutes. They should have televised that as the race.

Obviously, during the season I was looking round for a better bike, and I got an invitation from MuZ to test their bike after the Czech GP. The MuZ wasn't on the same level as Honda, Yamaha or Suzuki, but it was a V4 and a lot faster than my Honda. (Then again, everything was faster than my Honda.) They were getting through riders like nothing else. I couldn't keep up with who was riding for them from one race to the next. I think they had five or six people ride for them that year – Simon Crafar, Luca Cadalora, Anthony Gobert, some Japanese fella and Jurgen van de Goorbergh, maybe more – but that didn't put me off; I really wanted a shot on a V4.

95

I got to the circuit as instructed, and I sat there all on my own, waiting. They said they were going to give me a test for the whole day too, which I thought was really important and a sign that they weren't messing. After waiting all day, I found a phone and called them up, only for them to say that they had cancelled. I thought it was strange because they were all well up for it. Later on, I was told that Rob McElnea, who was managing Chris Walker, wanted to get his guy on the bike and told them not to go near me. I never had a manager, which, looking back, was probably a mistake.

I also had a chance of going on the Red Bull Yamaha YZR500 V4 in place of Garry McCoy, because he had crashed. Peter Clifford, who ran the team was dead keen to give me a try, but it never came to anything. I think Red Bull got involved and, for whatever reason, overruled Peter and it never happened. I also think the fact that I was already in GPs was a factor. If I had got the Red Bull ride then there would still be an empty seat on the grid. If I could have just got on one of those Yamahas, I reckon I could have gone well on it, but any racer would say the same thing.

In 1999, I didn't just ride GPs; I also rode for Lester Harris on a Suzuki at Macau that year, which wasn't a big deal because the GP season was over by then. The TT was a different matter. That was a mistake.

It clashed with the Italian GP in Mugello, so during the GP weekend I flew back and forth between Italy and the Isle of Man about four times. That's four 3,000-mile round trips, each one with three flights and a couple of hours' drive, during a weekend, while qualifying and racing in the Italian GP and practising for the TT. It was madness, and for the life of me I can't remember why I agreed to it. I had no idea where I was or what time of day it was.

I also rode this mad Fireblade that Honda had commissioned RS Performance to build and homologate as a way of competing with the Yamaha R1 in the Production class. It was called the EVO Blade. It was really fast and stable, but I did struggle to get it to turn. I really didn't like it, so I rode a Honda V-twin 500 for Paul Bird instead, but that blew its gearbox.

I also agreed to ride the TT that year on a Daily Star-sponsored Honda CBR600. It was the one time I thought I was going to die there. I was all over the place on it, really trying but doing rubbish. I just couldn't concentrate; my head was full of anything other than what I was supposed to be doing. Then I ran wide at Glen Helen and thought, 'Shit, that was so close'. I didn't hit anything, just ran in too hot, and off-line, which is all it takes over there. The margin for error is tiny, and I was miles off-line and going far too fast. I genuinely thought that was the end for me. It scared the shit out of me.

When I'm on it at the TT, I do things without thinking, and it all flows, but at that meeting my head was all over the place, and I just wasn't concentrating. It happened just before the commentary box at about 100mph, at the exact same spot where Rob Holden got killed three years earlier.

I remembered that year, just before morning practice, speaking to him and having a great chat with him. He passed me on the way to Balla-craine, and he waved at me. He was in great form and going well, so I followed him for a bit, and then he just went out of sight at the last bit of the Glen Helen section, on the last right just before you go up the hill. He had crashed on the left. He had just gone out of sight, and all I saw was people running up the side of the road. I went past him and I knew he was dead. You could just tell by how he was lying there. He was the first person I saw die.

At the time, when people asked what I saw, I said what I had seen. I went to bed that day after morning practice had finished, and I remember just getting to sleep and then being woken by the police. They came to the hotel to get me to go and give a statement, so I said all I saw was him going out of sight, and that I didn't see the crash. Then I had to go to a coroner's hearing. That was awful, seeing all his grieving family and friends there, and it didn't matter what I said; it didn't change anything for them. I did it because I thought it was the right thing to do, but I'm not sure it was. Maybe I'm wrong, but now unless I see something that could help, I just say I didn't see anything.

The season was so bad that, unsurprisingly, no one wanted to sponsor us, so at the end of the season Joe Miller asked me when I was going to give him his £40K back. He seemed really surprised when I told him that we didn't get any sponsors because it was so bad, so I couldn't give him his money back. Joe was OK about the money; I think he understood how bad the whole episode was for everyone.

I'm glad I did the year, but it was probably the worst thing for my career because no one wanted me when I got back to the UK for the 2000 season, except my old mate Ray Stringer. Ray had got a massive sponsorship deal from Level 3, the company that laid the internet cable between America and Europe. They had so much money that it wasn't even funny; they didn't know what to do with it all. I can't remember the exact figure, but it was massive – something like a £700,000 budget for the race team.

Ray wanted to run the brand-new Yamaha R7, and because of his big sponsor he offered me really good money to ride for him – and to be fair I like Ray anyway and we get on really well, so I thought why not? There was a lot of hype around the R7, and the official Yamaha team, run by Rob McElnea, had got a big sponsor in too – Virgin – but we would be the first ones to win on it.

9
2000:
Joey & DJ

The 2000 season was my first year back in the UK after being away in GPs. I was doing OK on the Yamaha R7, and I actually became the first person to win a race on it anywhere in the world, but for me that BSB season was all about getting my career back on track. I had dropped off every team's shopping list, apart from my old mate Ray Stringer, who put together the Level 3 team with the R7 which, as good as it was, wasn't really up to the job.

The 2000 BSB season will always be best remembered for the title battle between Neil Hodgson and Chris Walker. Those two boys were really going at it; their teams had properly sorted trick bikes from Suzuki and Ducati and they were both riding brilliantly. The championship got decided at the final round at Donington Park, and all Chris had to do was finish fourth in the race to take the title. Normally this would have been a doddle for Chris, but his engine blew up and Hodgson took the title right out from under Walker's nose. It was epic, and pretty much everyone remembers the 2000 season finale for the image of Walker in tears as he trudged back to the pits.

What is less well known about that race is that it was Niall Macken-zie's last one as a pro. He had been racing since the eighties, when my dad was still racing, and he'd won the BSB title three times. Earlier in his career he raced in GPs for twelve years and he got seven podium finishes in Grand Prix, then he came to BSB and dominated it for ages. He was a really big deal then, and I always thought the Walker/Hodgson rivalry overshadowed his retirement from the sport, but that's racing. People only give a shit about you when you're winning; as soon as you're not, you're invisible.

I got a last-minute call to take Ian Simpson's place at the 2000 TT because he'd had a nasty crash at Knockhill. I actually didn't have a ride for the TT that year, and now I was David Jefferies' teammate on a Yamaha R71, which was the same R7 chassis as my 750cc BSB bike but with the bigger 1000cc engine from Yamaha's R1. I'd beaten David at the North West 200 in every race a couple of weeks earlier – I think I won all four that year – so I got to the TT and was full of confidence.

The last time I rode a big bike at the TT was in 1998. I did do the TT in 1999 when I was doing GPs but it was on a 600cc Supersport bike and my head was all over the place, and in 1998 I rode a factory-built Honda RC45, the red and black one, but it was the end of an era for that old-school genre of bikes. The steering would shake so violently all the time at the TT so I used to have to pump the brake lever on the straights just to get the brake pads to return to the discs ready for the next time I'd need to use them.

From the start line at top of Bray Hill to Quarterbridge a mile or so later, the steering would shake so violently that sometimes I'd have to pull on the brake lever ten times just to regain enough pressure in the system to stop for Quarterbridge. Even going from Quarterbridge on the short, smooth run to Braddan Bridge, I would have to pump the brake lever three or four times. They were frightening bikes to ride, just horrible.

Everything changed when Yamaha launched the R1 in 1998. It was a massive step forward for chassis design, and the 2000 TT was my first

100

time on this new generation of bike. I was absolutely blown away by how much easier the R1 was to ride than my RC45 had been.

For the first practice lap on the first day I followed David, and when I came in at the end of the lap the team asked me what I reckoned. I said I had no chance of beating him. He passed me going out of Ramsey, going up to May Hill, and the way he tipped in and got the rear tyre spinning up halfway through the corner, sliding the bike all the way from kerb to kerb, was like nothing I'd ever seen before. He was perfect, not even slightly ragged or out of control; it was beautiful to watch. I said to the team, 'He has already beaten me, and everyone else for that matter'. I said to the them that I couldn't do what I had just seen David do.

He rode that way the whole time. It wasn't a show to try and play mind games on me; he wasn't like that. David was so confident, and he was physically big and strong so he could manhandle the bike in a way that us smaller riders couldn't. It was like a toy to him. For me, the Superbike is a big bike and I really have to think about what I'm doing on it, but he could just pick one up and put it where he wanted. The combination of his strength and incredible talent was something else, but when you add in the fact that he simply loved riding bikes as fast as he possibly could, it's easy to see how he became a force of nature.

David got caught out in 2003. I wasn't racing at the TT that year because I was on Red Bull Ducatis in BSB that season, and they just kept blowing up. I remember seeing him at the Knockhill round of BSB just before the TT fortnight. He was leaving the circuit after the meeting had finished to go straight to the Isle of Man. I said, 'David, good luck mate', and he replied in his broad Yorkshire accent, 'Ahh yeah, I bet you're gutted that you're not going'. I said of course I was, and told him to be careful, and the last thing he ever said to me was 'Yeah, we'll give a good go at it this year'. He wasn't having a great season that year, but the last time I saw him he was his usual larger-than-life self and really looking forward to going to the TT.

I was sitting in the garden at home and listening to the practice session on the radio when I heard something had happened. I knew that it was David because of where he was on the split times. His dad Tony was telling me that he had been struggling with the bike setup but was working his way through it. He also said that he knew that the last time he saw his son alive was when David went past the pits to start the lap that he would later die on. Tony told me that he knew David was enjoying himself, and that is the only thing that helps him deal with it. I don't know what went wrong for David, whether he made a mistake, or if there was oil on the course, but he never came back.

David was a very colourful character; he was a really nice, genuine bloke who would do anything for you. The same age as me, he started racing at the TT a few years after I did, but he came through it so fast; he was so naturally gifted. Like me, he also had a dad called Tony who was a successful bike racer in his day. Tony won three TTs in the early seventies and achieved most of his success on Triumphs; he was a real hotshot in the day. The whole Jefferies family are so lovely – Tony, Louise, all of them. They are beautiful people who were hit hard by David's death; the whole sport was hit hard by it.

But that sad event was still three years away as I prepared for the 2000 TT. The first race of the week was the F1 race, and the course was still wet, or at least damp, in places. I was riding round bolt upright and shitting myself because the conditions were so sketchy. Joey Dunlop had started behind me on the road, and he passed me on his factory Honda SP-1 just before Ramsey, flat out and fully committed on slick tyres. I thought, fair play to him.

The next thing I saw was that David's bike had broken down and it was parked up on the side of the road. With David out of the race, there was a chance for the win, so I thought I'd try and chase Joey down, but he had just disappeared, and I wasn't committed enough to go with him. Joey was on a mission in that race and went on to win it, recording his 24th TT victory. He won two more that week in the Ultra-Lightweight and Lightweight TTs to get to his eventual final tally of twenty-six wins, which to this day is still more than anyone else. The first podium of the week was Joey in first place, me in second place and John McGuinness in third. It was a good start to the week.

The Production TT was the last time I raced in the TT in the rain. I think two people died in that race. I finished 3rd behind Milky Quayle and David. The rain was bouncing off the road, and I was aquaplaning all over the place. On the approach to Quarterbridge I shut the throttle and the bike just went sideways onto the steerings lockstop. Somehow I just held it there, upright but in this massive sideways slide all the way down the hill, just hanging onto it. I rode round so slow but still ended up 3rd on the R1. In the Production class we had to use road tyres that have no tread to speak of, which is fine on the dry but lethal in the wet.

For the Senior race I thought, I'll have a go, but I knew deep down that I wasn't going to beat David; he was in a different race to us. If he finished, we all knew where he was going to finish. Having said that, after my second place in the F1 race I'd had another podium in the Production TT, and a fifth place in the Junior TT, so I knew I was in the hunt.

The starting order was different for the Senior race, and I started behind Joey. I was really up for paying him back for when he caught me up in the F1 race and disappeared up the road. I got straight down to business from the very start, with the sole intention of catching Joey on the road. Eventually I caught him up, which meant I knew I was on for a good result.

I passed Joey, and I thought, I'm not seeing that silly old bastard again. He was forty-eight then, and to me he seemed really old – I mean, my dad used to race against him. Now look at me: I'm the silly old bastard out there, only a year younger than he was then at the time of writing this book. So, there I was, past Joey with a nice empty road in front of me, and I was flat out on my R1 minding my own business, mile after mile, then out of nowhere this Honda came hurtling past me, missing me by millimetres. I was thinking, where the bloody hell has he come from? I couldn't believe it and thought, no, not again. He must have made twenty seconds back on me and he was riding like his hair was on fire. I was so pissed off that he had caught me back up and re-passed me.

For the second time in a week, he made me feel like a novice. I decided that even though I was behind him on the road, I was still actually beating him on corrected time; he wasn't going to beat me on the road. Obviously, he'd had a similar thought and decided to put some manners on me again. We must have passed each other five or six times on that one lap, neither of us prepared to follow the other.

The pair of us would come up to some corners and I would think to myself, 'Tell you what, fair play to you'. Joey was so incredibly fast that he made me feel like a novice club racer. Then, to make matters worse, we would get to some corners where I was sure that I would be quicker than him – those you find on short circuits that are smooth, open and fast, the sort of corner where I had more experience than him – and he'd be even quicker. I couldn't believe it was the same person that I'd made up thirty seconds on, on the road. It was weird how different our paces were in different places. There were sections where he was unbelievably quick, and some places where I thought he would be really quick but it would turn out that I was the quicker of the two of us and be all over him.

I'd decided where I was going to pass him. It would have to be on the last lap, on the run down to the Creg-ny-Baa pub. There is always a massive crowd there, and it is one of the most iconic parts of the course – I mean, how many chances in a lifetime am I ever going to get to pass Joey Dunlop on the last lap of the Senior TT, at the end of an epic race on the road? It had to be at the Creg. It just had to be. He was so neat in the way he sat on the bike and it never looked like he was trying. He was going so fast yet it looked effortless for him. I pulled up alongside of him out of his draught and I thought, I'll have him here, I'll show him, but he hit the brakes so late that I thought, I'm not going to stop, and he isn't going to stop either.

I had gone from a picture in my mind of the most perfect overtake imaginable for a bike racer to one where both of us end up in a heap on the floor of the pub car park. Somehow we both just about got it stopped and round the corner. He had outbraked me, and I was supposed to be the big-shot short-circuit racer who was nearly half his age. I thought, bloody hell, that is amazing.

Joey was fighting me the whole way, even though there was nothing in it for him at this point because I could follow him for the last couple of miles and even drop back by up to thirty seconds and I'd still have beaten him in the race. Something must have happened to him that made him keep pushing. The result was a truly fantastic four laps of us knocking lumps of shit out of each other for nothing more than the pride. He was so determined to stay in front of me that we'd got into a one-on-one, old-fashioned race to the line.

I thought, right, what am I gonna do now? I was still behind him, and his Honda was quick, with its full-factory World Superbike spec engine, which Honda had flown in especially for him. The last few miles of the course are really quick and really narrow, so I wasn't sure where, or if at all, I was going to be able to pass him. I thought he's going to bloody beat me, I couldn't believe it, the old bastard is going to do me.

We went through Signpost Corner, and I was right on his back wheel, then we drove down towards Governor's, which is the very last place you can try and make a pass on anyone by outbraking them before the end of the lap.

He must have known that I was right behind him because he messed up a little bit. He braked so hard that – no word of a lie – his rear wheel was feet into the air; the bike must have been at 45 degrees, on its nose. He had to let the brake off or he was going to go right over his handlebars. I could tell he didn't want to but he had no choice. You can see it on the race highlights footage: by the time he comes into shot his rear wheel is actually coming back down because he has already let the brake off, but you'll have to take my word for just how

105

high his rear wheel was – way higher than what you see on the footage.

He ran on and missed his turn-in point for the corner, which was enough for me to nip through, and I passed him within sight of the finish line. We were virtually touching going into the Nook, which is basically a shortcut that links Governor's to the Glencrutchery Road (the start/finish straight, by any other name), and when we went over the line I was screaming 'Yesssssss!' into my helmet. I was over the moon.

Obviously, I would have preferred to win the race, but racing that hard with such a massive legend for so long, on the greatest racetrack on the planet, went some way towards making up for not winning the overall race. Anyway, true to form, David was miles up the road from all of us, and we were all racing for second place. After we finished the race, Joey and I shook hands, but he never said anything to me; not a word. I was absolutely buzzing but I had no idea if he enjoyed it or not. It was impossible to tell.

After the podium, I was in the press room with all the journalists. It was packed and there was so much going on in the room, and so many people there, all with questions. It's hard enough at the best of times to collect your thoughts, and on that occasion I was still just trying to digest the head-to-head race that Joey and I had just had, and why Joey didn't say anything to me.

I was talking to a journalist called Norrie White from *Motorcycle News* when this arm came over my shoulder with a massive Honda logo on it and handed me a pint of beer. It was Joey, and he said, 'There you are. I really enjoyed that', to which I said, 'Ahh cheers Joey', and we sat there and the two of us drank a beer and relived the race.

That gesture still makes me tingle to this day. I was like, wow, did all that really happen? Joey had never said a word to me until then; I did try speaking to him before but couldn't understand anything he said and I couldn't tell if he liked me or not. But there we were: he had bought me a pint and said he enjoyed his race with me, and we sat and drank our pints together.

Joey used to race against my dad, so for me to race against him at all was cool, and for that race to be a proper full-on race, not a couple of polite passes here and there, made it really special. The last three laps of the race when we were together, I never knew where he was going to come back and pass me, but I knew he was going to. He must have really trusted me, because it was clean racing. Realising that someone of Joey's stature trusted me and was happy to race that hard with me really does make the hair on the back of my neck stand up. What an honour.

He would come really close with some of the passes on the straights, and I would do the same. I can still see him now, in his yellow helmet and his bike's two exhausts sticking out the back, and his bike just wobbling a bit. It was incredible. It's a picture that I alone have in my mind, and I tell you, it's pin-sharp. I still can't believe that he got the bike turned in to Governors.

It was one special moment and easily rates as one of my all-time TT highlights ... and then a few weeks later Joey was dead.

He died at a small race in Estonia, which sums him up – he was just as happy racing in a tiny race in the middle of nowhere as he was in the biggest race of them all. He didn't care, just as long as he was riding his race bikes.

I was the last one to race with him at the TT. I was with him for his last-ever laps of his beloved TT course that he had raced at for so many years. As it turned out, that last lap was also his fastest ever lap of the course, so even though I didn't know it at the time, not only did I get a front-row seat for his last-ever lap but also his fastest-ever lap.

I don't know if Joey's record of twenty-six wins will ever be beaten, but either way his status as an icon of the TT will last forever. You need a lot of luck to finish a TT race and even more to win, but who knows – records are there to be broken.

The experience of racing that close with him made me wonder how fast he must have been when he was thirty. He must have been incredibly fast – I know I was faster when I was younger. He must have been unbelievable in his prime. I know he had good bikes but he also had his fair share of shit bikes, and they all still need riding, good or bad, and he did it for so long.

David won the race, I was second, and Joey was third. I was standing with two of the greatest riders the TT has ever seen. What a podium to be on. What a time to be alive.

10

2001, 2007 and 2012: Right Bike, Wrong Time

It's a complete coincidence that whenever I've raced a Kawasaki it's always been the right bike, right team, but wrong time. Apart from my rookie season in 1993 with Medd, I raced a Kawasaki ZX-7RR in 2001, and a ZX-10R in 2007 and 2012. There was nothing wrong with the bikes at the time; they'd just had their day when I raced them.

2001 was the last season before 1000cc four-cylinder bikes were allowed to compete against the 1000cc twin-cylinder Ducatis in 2002, but by then pretty much every team with any ambition of winning had already abandoned the 750cc bikes in favour of the Ducati – except my team. They had a big-money sponsor called Transatlantic

Finance, really trick bikes from Kawasaki, and me and Steve Plater. It would have been perfect a couple of years before.

The Transatlantic Finance money never came through, so the team folded after a couple of meetings and so I did a few meetings with Stuart Hicken's Hawk Racing team, and I think I did OK. Then, with some help from my personal sponsors and Kawasaki, we sorted the finances out, and I was back on the original Kawasaki, with Ray Stringer running the garage. That season, James Haydon was the only other 750cc rider who was bothering the Ducatis. He did really well and beat me in the championship. He finished fourth and I finished sixth, but I did win at Rockingham that year, which meant I was the only person that year to win a race on a four-cylinder bike; twenty-five out of the twenty-six races that season were won by a Ducati. That win also meant that I was the last person to ever win a superbike race on a 750cc bike anywhere in the world.

I had a couple of 'biggies' on the Kawasaki in 2001 that I was really lucky to be able to walk away from. We were using some fancy six-piston brake calipers that the team got for free, but they were rubbish. We had all sorts of problems with them having a mind of their own. At Donington Park during morning warm-up I hit the brakes for Redgate, which is the corner at the end of the start/finish straight, and nothing happened. It's a really fast part of the lap, and it felt like an eternity before I decided to jump off the back of the bike. It ploughed through the catch fence at basically full speed and just got obliterated. I raced the spare bike after that because there was pretty much nothing left of my number-one bike.

Then, at Snetterton I was coming out the chicane at the start/finish straight and accelerated through first, second, third gear, with the bike wheelying, then as soon as the front wheel came back down and touched the tarmac it locked and I went straight over the handlebars. Somehow the front brakes had locked while the front wheel was in the air. The bike went one side of the pit entrance wall and I went the other side. A few feet to the right and I would have been a mess; there was no air fencing or anything back then.

When I left Paul Bird's team after the 2006 season (more of that later), I hit a bad patch. I felt my career was going downhill and just dying. Once you have ridden a factory bike, you are spoiled forever, and everything else after that just feels like you are on your way out. I felt like I was past my prime. Once you know what the best is like, nothing else comes close, and the season at Birdy's was just not what I expected or hoped for.

A fella called Nick Morgan contacted me about riding for his team in 2007 after he decided to move into the superbike class following some decent success in the 600cc Supersport class that his team had. I get on really well with Nick, and he was realistic with what was possible with the Kawasaki superbike that year, so there was less pressure. Nick's background is racing and tuning, having set up MSS Performance ages ago. Basically, he's one of the go-to people if you want a fast Kawasaki.

Nick got support from Kawasaki UK in the late nineties, so when he asked if I'd like to be part of his move into superbikes, I knew it would be a tall order to be competitive. For one, Nick had never raced in superbikes before and had a lot to learn, and we only had about half the budget of the teams at the front. Plus, in 2007 the ZX-10R wasn't the weapon of choice.

HRC were still ploughing millions into the Fireblade with Johnny Rea and Ryuichi Kiyonari, Ducati were there with million-pound full-factory 999 F06s and Gregorio Lavilla and Leon Haslam, while Suzuki had Cal Crutchlow and Chris Walker on their trick GSXRs, Virgin Yamaha had Tommy Hill and James Haydon, and there were other Fireblades being ridden by Shane Byrne, Tom Sykes, Leon Camier, Karl Harris and Guy Martin. I was the only one on the whole grid on a Kawasaki ZX-10R, in arguably one of the most competitive grids that BSB has ever seen in terms of talent and machinery. I brought all my experience to the team, and they made me feel like I was part of the project.

So the team was me on the Superbike, and Stuart Easton on the 600. The superbike engines came from a place in France called Akira and cost a fortune, but they weren't very suited to BSB tracks. They just wouldn't pull off the corners, the power delivery was more suited to the faster, flowing tracks that you typically get in Europe, so we struggled with acceleration off the slower corners that you tend to get at our tracks in the UK. The bike didn't handle brilliantly either because there was a lot of weight up high on it which affects where its centre of gravity is, which in turn affects the fundamentals of the way it handles, and the weight distribution wasn't great. The ZX-10R was an OK bike, but it just didn't do anything particularly special to be a race bike, and, with Nick's connection with Kawasaki, we couldn't really drop it for something else.

As well as a bike that wasn't quite up to the job, I wasn't quite myself for half the season either. During my career, I've never missed a race for being ill, only when I've been physically hurt, but the closest I got to it was that year at Silverstone. I had got to Silverstone with my caravan, parked it and went to wind its legs down, and as I was doing that, I got a really bad migraine. I don't get many, but this was a really bad one which made my eyesight go.

I felt terrible the next day and my eyesight still wasn't great, and the headache never went away. I went ahead and raced and did my job, but I wasn't anywhere near as good as I should have been. When I got home, I remember looking at people and not being able to see their faces. There was something going on that I hadn't experienced before, so I went to see a doctor and he gave me tablets for a migraine that seemed to make it better.

Then a few days later I was lying in bed, and there was this ringing noise in my ear. It started off quiet and got louder and louder, so I called the doctor the next day, who said it was probably tinnitus and that there was nothing they could do as it was permanent. After a few weeks it got to the point where I couldn't sleep, or I would wake up at night and think that I can't handle it any more. The noise was so loud, and the more worked up I got, the worse it got. I thought, if this goes on, I can't carry on. I really was getting to a point where I thought I couldn't live with it anymore. It was driving me insane.

I went to the Motorcycle Show at the NEC in Birmingham and was talking to the boss of Datatag, and telling him about it, saying I couldn't sleep and couldn't handle it. Straight away, he told me that he had it too. He said his was so bad that he couldn't even hear the show. I immediately felt loads better. It gave me some hope, and even just knowing that other people suffer with the same thing helps. I can't be sure but I do think that it has a lot to do with my neck injury from the time Shakey knocked me off at Snetterton in 2002. I still have a stiff neck from that one. I was feeling a lot of stress at that time too, because racing was going downhill a bit, and I split up with Sandrine not long after having our babies. I think it all got on top of me, but I reckon it's a physical damage thing, so most probably the racing has something to do with it, either the noise or all the bangs to my head. That was a massive low for me, and I genuinely struggled at times to cope with it. I still have it now, but it's not nearly as bad.

On the subject of splitting up with Sandrine, after I moved out of our house in Kirkby Mallory, I moved back home with Mum and Dad. I needed somewhere to live until I got sorted, so when I arrived with my bag, Mum and Dad were on the settee watching the TV and I just went in and sat down. After a little while, the TV volume started creeping up until it was flat out, and I literally couldn't hear anything. I told Dad that the TV volume was flat out and to turn it down – turns out he was sitting on the controller. So he turned it back down to normal. Then it happened again, and after the third time in less than an hour I couldn't take it any more. I grabbed my bag, which was still in the hallway, and said, 'I'm off', and went to my motorhome and drove it to my mate's house. I knew moving back in with Mum and Dad would be tricky, but even I didn't think that I'd only last two hours.

We decided to do the TT in 2007 too, and I hadn't been there for seven years. It was cancelled in 2001 due to the foot-and-mouth disease outbreak, and the other teams that I'd ridden for had said to choose BSB or TT but not both. To be fair, Birdy didn't want to do the TT in 2006 when I was riding for him and said I could go and ride for

113

another team at the TT if I wanted, but there wasn't anything available or good enough to race and win on, so I gave 2006 a miss. By 2007 I was desperate to go back and be part of the centenary of the TT. I was really missing the place, and my last race there in 2000 with Joey was such a high, I just had to go back.

Back then, the TT didn't have as high a stature as it does now. Since then, Paul Phillips has really turned it around. Paul was employed by the Isle of Man government in 2006 as TT Business Development Manager and tasked with bringing the event up to date, attract more riders, and obviously visitors. He's been brilliant at talking to the riders and teams to see what we all want, and addressing all the things that were wrong. The event today is barely recognisable to how it used to be before he got involved.

Before the TT, we went to the North West 200, and it was OK. The 600 was a brilliant bike, and I got a third on it behind Bruce Anstey and John McGuinness, which I was pretty pleased with after getting held up in qualifying. I only qualified in 11th. In contrast, I got pole position on the superbike, with Guy Martin and John McGuinness on the front row with me. I finished 5th and 3rd in the two races, which set us up nicely for the TT, then I went to do the Snetterton round of BSB the week before the TT ...

I qualified OK on the third row and finished just outside the top ten in race 1, then in race 2 I highsided while coming out of the chicane that comes on to the start/finish straight and landed really hard. I knew straight away that I'd broken my scaphoid – that's one of the wristbones – because it was so painful; but I was getting paid a lot to go to the TT, and we'd put so much effort into preparing for it that I decided to just ignore it. Luckily, it was my clutch hand, so it wasn't too bad. There's about three or four points on the TT course where I knew it would give me gyp, but the rest of the time it would be OK, so I couldn't use it as an excuse.

Things nearly went from bad to worse for me after the Snetterton meeting. Ian Hutchinson, John McGuinness and I were all going to the TT straight from Snetterton in our motorhomes, and after leaving the circuit we pulled into the first petrol station to fill up with fuel before the drive across to the ferry. I was in absolute agony and quite distracted by the pain in my wrist.

We pulled up at the pumps with me first in the line, then John in his £250K motorhome, and then Hutchy pulled up behind the two of us. I jumped out, and it was like that time at Mallory Park in 1994 all over again: I was just about to start filling the tank when I looked at it and realised it was bloody moving backwards (towards John's motorhome), so I jumped back in and, in my panic, floored the accelerator. I must have left it in reverse because I started speeding towards John.

I could see John in the mirror, bracing for impact, but just in time I hit the brakes hard and stopped inches away from his motorhome. However, every single plate, mug, glass, knife, fork that was in the cupboards fell out and smashed all over my floor. John was white as a sheet because it would have totally written off the front of his motorhome, and he'd have hit Hutchy's in turn too. As it was, I'd ended the day with a broken wrist, and the contents of my motorhome smashed on the floor, heading to the Isle of Man for two weeks' racing at the TT for the first time in seven years. What was I thinking?

The last bike I raced at the TT was a Yamaha R1, when I got a pair of second places to Joey and DJ. My comeback didn't go anything like as well; the whole experience was a massive shock to me. I didn't expect to be winning or anything, but I did think I'd go there and it'd all be OK because I knew where I was going.

On the first day of practice, I got on the 600, which was different to my usual routine (I usually like to go out on the superbike first to get it out of the way), but the 600 felt as fast as the last superbike that I rode there. The track was really different too: it was loads smoother compared to when I last rode on it. I was frightened to death because I knew it was going to be very different to how I remembered it, and I told myself it was going to be a shock, but those first laps on the 600, on that smooth surface, just blew my mind.

The number-one thing I needed to get back up to speed on was doing lots of laps, and I just wasn't getting them because the superbike kept stopping all the time, and when it *was* running I was more worried about it blowing up and crashing. It was nothing to do with Nick; it was just the tune of the engine not really being suited to the TT course which has long periods on an open throttle. Since all the 600s were tuned the same, none of them were lasting. A load of top brass from Kawasaki in Japan came to the TT to watch their bike, but I only passed them once, and that was all they saw. The 600 was really good and really quick but it also kept blowing up. It wasn't the comeback I'd hoped for. It was probably the TT that I stopped the most times at. Pretty much every time I got to Ballacraine, whichever bike I was on stopped or blew up.

For the superbike race, we put another engine in and it just lasted to Glen Helen, which is about seven or eight miles into the lap, I guess. After that, we decided to put a standard road-bike engine in for the Senior race, just to try and get a finish, which we did. I finished in 8th behind McGuinness, Guy Martin and Hutchy, who were the top three, and Ian Lougher, Adrian Archibald, Conor Cummins and Steve Plater, also in front of me. It didn't feel like much of a result but it was good just to finish; plus we were the first Kawasaki, which sort of gave us something to be cheerful about.

The only really good thing about the 2007 TT was starting at number 1. The organisers asked what number I wanted, and I thought it would be quite cool to be first on the road. It's the only time I've ever started at number 1, and to be honest, I can't really comment if it was worth it or not because I just kept stopping – although it was quite cool setting off first, knowing that all the attention is on you, even if it's just until the next rider starts. Everyone has been waiting during the build up to the race, so when you start number 1 on the road, you start the race for everyone watching.

After the TT and back in BSB, the rest of 2007 was hard-going. The bike was reliable on the short circuits but it was fundamentally the wrong layout, and the engine tune wasn't right. We got through that year, but the bottom line is that it just wasn't the bike to be on at that time. Fair play to Nick, but there's only so much he could do with it. It was only a one-year deal with Nick, and it was a tough season for everyone, but no one fell out, plus I'd got an offer to ride a Ducati in 2008, which was a much more competitive bike at the time. I finished the 2007 championship in 12th position on 118 points. The following year, on the Ducati, I was back to winning races and finished 6th.

2007 finished with a trip to Macau; we got a sponsorship deal for the race from Aviva so used the exact same bike and painted it all in Aviva's yellow. It looked rank, but I put it on pole through sheer bloody bravery. The pole lap was probably one of the riskiest laps I've done at Macau; I took a lot more chances than I normally would on a qualifying lap, but I really wanted to salvage something from the season for the team and me. Plus, if I won the race then I would have become the most successful rider at Macau, so I was well up for it.

In the race, I was in a battle for 3rd with Thomas Hinterreiter, thinking to myself that some foreigner who I'd never heard of couldn't beat me, and I started getting frustrated and desperate. I'd put a few really hard laps together and had just started to drop him and catch Steve Plater and John McGuinness at the front, when I overshot my braking marker for Lisboa Bend and ran on up the slip road. I had to turn the bike around and get back on the track. I finished 11th in the end, but even though I was catching the front two before I messed up, I don't think I could have won on that bike; I was having to try so hard and be perfect every corner on every lap just to keep them in sight.

I was forty in 2012, which by all accounts was already over the hill, but I had still wanted to race, and I still felt like I could. Batham's brewery were sponsoring me personally by then (more on that later), and they were starting to get properly bitten by the bug. It was around then that they first started having ideas about running their own team. Having their sponsorship meant that I was on more teams' shopping lists for the 2012 season.

117

I went back with Nick Morgan, who by then had a few more super-bikes seasons under his belt than when I rode for him during his superbikes debut. The 2012 rule change – to reduce dependency on electronics by making all teams use a spec ECU – had meant that small teams like his should have been able to save a lot of money.

The latest ZX-10R was fantastic – what a bike that was. Nick told me that it was a contender, and when I jumped on it at the first test I was blown away by how good it was. The team was very small for BSB, and Nick also signed Peter Hickman, who was an up-and-coming rookie back then, and Nick also put out a couple of superstock bikes. Looking back, it was madness, and with the best will in the world, for such a small team, he really did overstretch his resources.

The season got off to a good start when I finished in third position at the first race of the season. I didn't know it at the time, but not only was that as good as it would get all season but that was my last ever podium in BSB. We had some half-decent results, but there were a lot of retirements too, and as the season went on I think Nick decided he wasn't going to keep going with his own team in BSB at the end of the season, so it all just fizzled out.

The high point was winning the superstock race at the North West 200. We actually had a really good North West where as well as the win I got a 2nd and 4th in the superbike races. So we went off to the TT feeling pretty good, but it was there that the tone for the rest of the season was set, with a 7th in the superstock race, retirement from the superbike race, and the Senior getting cancelled for the first time in history due to bad weather.

Peter got himself sacked because he rode a Suzuki in World Super-bikes in a one-off race. He asked Nick if he could, and he'd said no, but Peter wasn't doing great in BSB then so he went and rode the Suzuki anyway. Unsurprisingly, Kawasaki weren't happy and he got the sack. Nick replaced him with another young rookie called Danny Buchan, who's doing the business today in superbikes, still on bikes prepared by Nick and MSS Performance.

Nick announced in 2013 that he would be taking a break from BSB but carrying on with running Kawasaki UK's road-racing programme. I've got a lot of time for Nick and his passion for racing. His technical knowledge and understanding of race bike preparation make him pretty unique as a team boss. He has been loyal to Kawasaki over the years and has become a real specialist. It's no surprise that Kawasaki have kept him for so long.

I really had hoped the 2012 season would be better. All the ingredients were there, but I do believe that the team was spread too thin. While there is no arguing with the fact that Shakey won the title that year on a ZX-10R, he was in a team that was completely focused on him, and with a budget far bigger than basically everyone else's in the paddock, never mind ours.

By the end of the season, I was struggling to get into the points, let alone get on the podium. It wasn't really until a couple of seasons later, in 2014, that the ZX-10RR really became the weapon of choice. Up until then, it was only Paul Bird's team and Shakey that could get the best from it. The Honda was still the bike to be on then, as I would find out at the 2012 Macau GP.

I raced a Honda Fireblade prepared by SMT Racing at Macau at the end of 2012. It was a strange race because it was almost dark by the end of it. The race had been shortened due to delays because of all sorts of crashes in the car races, and bad weather. By the end of the race, it was so late at night that the street lights were coming on while I was still racing; it was really spooky.

The bike was brilliant, and I just clicked with it from the very first practice session. I got pole position and led the whole race from start to finish to take my eighth win there. I haven't won the Macau GP since 2012; I've been on the podium every time and got close to another couple of wins since, but at the time of writing, the win tally there is still eight, which is still the record for most wins there by anyone.

It's probably just a coincidence that for those three seasons where I ended up on perfectly good bikes but just at the wrong time, all three bikes happened to be Kawasakis. I still managed to make a little bit of history in 2001 by being the only and last four-cylinder bike to win a superbike race before the 1000cc bikes came, and a bit of my own in 2012 when I stood on a BSB podium for the last time. I was wearing green on both occasions.

11
2002 & 2003:
Renegade

After a few lean years in British Superbikes following my GP season in 1999, 2002 was to be the beginning of four incredible seasons for me in BSB. The sport in general was going through a really popular period. The crowds at the race meetings were massive, the bikes were really trick, and tyres weren't controlled by rules designed to keep costs down. Looking back now, I probably didn't realise it at the time but the early to mid-noughties were probably BSB's best period in terms of fans, hardware and tyres.

Stuart Higgs, who runs BSB these days, introduced a new rule in 2008 which made everyone use control tyres supplied by Pirelli. The rule was designed to close the gap between the top teams, who had access to trick tyres, and the rest of the grid in order to make the racing closer.

Stuart always has one eye on the show and selling tickets, so I get that his priorities are different to mine, but along with a lot of the other riders and teams, I really did think it was a shit idea. Racing should be the best riders on the best bikes with the best tyres, riding flat out, breaking lap records to beat each other, not artificially evened out in the name of entertainment. Then again, I *would* think that, because I was lucky to have had the best tyres; if you didn't, you were nowhere.

Back in 2002, I knew Dunlop well, and because I was road racing and short circuit racing, I had a strong connection with the Dunlop factory in Birmingham and I got on with all of them. I was always really interested in tyre development too, and if you're interested then you can find out loads about it, and influence it. A lot of the time I ended up with A-grade tyres, and Stuart took that away from me in 2008.

Deep down, I know it was right in a way, but I did have one of my advantages taken from me through no reason or fault of my own. To ride on a tyre that gives you maximum grip and feel is so rewarding; getting the best out of a really grippy tyre on the best bike is an incredible feeling. When we were all forced to use the same Pirellis, the thrill and challenge of making the most of the best tyres that a massive company like Dunlop can make was gone.

Pirelli were told to make tyres that anyone could ride on, and the easiest way to do that was to make them with a really soft and pliable carcass that generates loads of movement and feel in the tyre. In contrast, the Dunlops that I was getting in 2002 and the Michelins that I had at Honda in 2004/05 had really hard carcasses, so I had to push them really hard to get them to work. The more you pushed them, the better they were. I could feel them sliding in plenty of time, and they would maintain their profile at all lean angles – no matter how hard I braked. The challenge was being able to push them hard enough to get that feeling. There weren't many riders who could, but it did mean that those of us who could were able to go properly fast.

If I rode on the Pirellis the same way that I could on the Dunlop or Michelins, I'd crash straight away; they just couldn't cope with the forces that I had got used to being able to inflict on the Dunlops. At first, I'd hit the brakes and the Pirelli front tyre would just collapse, like a flat tyre, and the rear would start sliding under power before it felt like I was even getting going. I had to use really high front tyre pressures to try and get the tyre to stop collapsing when I was braking.

Adapting to the control tyres in 2008 was difficult for me because I was really hard on the front end – in fact I still am really hard on front tyres – but credit where it is due: since 2008 Pirelli have moved up massively, and now there isn't much difference between today's tyres and the mega tyres of the early noughties.

The standard of riding was unreal too. Steve Hislop was riding for Paul Bird on a factory Ducati sponsored by MonsterMob, and in 2002 he famously broke Valentino Rossi's lap record at Donington Park. Imagine a British superbike beating a lap record set by Marc Marquez these days! It just wouldn't happen, not even close, but that's how trick all the hardware was then, and how hard we were riding then.

Compared to now, BSB was seriously big business, and BSB is bloody expensive now. To run a single-bike BSB team these days – one that's good enough to compete at the front of the grid – takes maybe £400,000 a year. That was my Michelin tyre bill for one season when I was at Honda in 2004.

It was another era, barely recognisable nowadays. If you look at photos or video footage of the races, the racetracks were packed with tens of thousands of people all the way round for a BSB round, and sponsors and manufacturers knew it. BSB was absolutely massive. There is no doubt that this was BSB's golden era, and, luckily for me, I had done enough in 2001 to make a name for myself again and was back on the shopping lists for a few of the big teams then.

A guy called Mark Griffiths got in touch to say he was setting up a team called Renegade Racing, and he had full-factory Ducatis, and a pile of money from Highland Springs, and his own company, which sold CDs, DVDs and videos (remember those?). It was quite a big company called MVC, but, as with all those sorts of music retailers, it ended up dying with the rise of digital music. Mark also managed a few footballers, and he was the flashiest person I ever knew. He would say to me that he was going to do this and that, and everything he said he was going to do, he did – and it was always gold-plated. Basically, he was one of those characters that you get from time to time in bike racing who are really into bikes and racing, have a few quid, and just decide to give it a go.

He signed me and Shane 'Shakey' Byrne, who was an up-and-coming lad back then and who'd done really well as a privateer the year before and was definitely going places. It was a really smart move by Mark to sign Shakey, but sometimes I do think that signing someone as fast and hungry as him ironically contributed to Mark and me missing out on the title that year. Shakey was so damn fast, and then there was the Snetterton round when he took the pair of us out when he collided with me at the end of the really fast Revett Straight. It was a massive accident; I still have a stiff neck to this day from it, and it cost my run at the championship dearly. The repair bill for both bikes was massive.

Shakey is a character, and it would be impossible to write this book and not mention him. He has done so well for himself and has become the most successful rider in the history of the BSB series, but back then he was just starting out. He was one of a few really shit-hot teammates that I've had over the years.

I remember in 2005 speaking to Johnny Rea at Oulton Park, when he was at Red Bull Honda and I was at HM Plant – basically the same team but different colours. He was asking me what I thought he should do for the following year, because he was already hot property by then, and already getting offers from all over the world. I told him to make as much money as he could right now, because I'd seen what had happened to my dad. He had won so many races and world championships, yet all he had to show for it was a Rover 300 at the end. I always said to myself that I didn't want to end up like that.

Luckily, Johnny didn't take my advice, and he stayed with Red Bull, where he was earning nothing but getting good kit. He took the gamble of decent kit over no money and risked waiting for a massive payday further down the line that might never come. Just look at Johnny now: he's unreal. Sometimes I do think that I should have been a bit like that and played a longer game like my dad did, and ridden for free on the good kit, but I just couldn't bring myself to do it.

I remember Honda speaking to me at Castle Combe, when I had broken my collarbone. Johnny had taken my ride, and Honda said they wanted me to have a word with him about his general behaviour and about calming things down a bit off-track. I asked, how could I have a word with him – why would he listen to me? They said that, for some reason, he looked up to me as the team leader.

So there was me, Havier Beltram and Neil Tuxworth with a teenage Johnny Rea sat in front of us. I blurted out a load of old nonsense and added, 'Oh, and another thing, get rid of that stupid baseball cap and sunglasses. You look like a dick'. Again, luckily for him, he totally ignored me. He already had a better grasp on image and how to make money in other ways than I did. Clever kid.

I remember a similar situation but with me as the rookie, starting out in the early nineties, getting advice and learning about earning potential from people like Jim Moodie, Ian Simpson and Niall Mackenzie. Those guys in particular had a big influence on me in the early days of my career.

I was at a short circuit race in Northern Ireland in about 1993 – it might have been Kirkistown or Bishopscourt but I can't be sure – and I was sitting in a truck with them. Jim asked me how much I was getting paid to be there. I told him I wasn't getting paid anything, so Jim, Ian and Niall all started telling me that I needed to start realising my value, and to stop letting organisers and promoters take the piss out of me.

It was like a big bell went off, and suddenly I remembered overhearing conversations that my dad would have with race organisers trying to bullshit him about how many spectators had turned up, and Dad arguing with them. Dad hardly ever got paid; he got a bit here and there but not much. So I went to the organisers there and then and said I wanted £500, and straight away they said OK, and gave me £500! I couldn't believe it was that easy, and back then £500 was a fortune. I had no concept of my value to the promoters back then, but those three guys changed everything for me, and my god, they were on such a good deal.

I never understood why during a race Ian would suddenly race with me really hard on certain laps, then ease off and ride round. I found out later that they would go through all the paperwork for the meeting and find the details, like there would be extra prize money for leading on certain laps. I never used to look at the paperwork; I couldn't read it anyway. Any time I asked him why he would race really hard with me to get by on some laps then cruise around on others, he would dodge the question, so while no doubt Ian, Jim and Niall were really good with helping me to earn money from the organisers, they didn't let me in on all their secrets!

There was never a dull moment when Shakey was around. He was like a little puppy dog without a care in the world. He'd got his big break with the Renegade team and was going to enjoy every single moment of it. Before the 2002 season started we were testing the new bikes at Almeria in southern Spain, and everything was going OK. Shakey and I went out to get some food for everyone at lunchtime, but Shakey, being Shakey, couldn't just do that: he drove the hire car all the way to the nearest village with the handbrake on.

It was a six-seater people carrier, meaning that there was no weight in the back when they're empty, so it was fairly easy for him to do a two-mile-long skid at about 60mph. Then we got to a T-junction, and he slammed it into 1st gear and made it rev so hard that the needle on the rev counter went right the way round and stayed there until the car more or less came to a stop. He literally couldn't even drive to the shop to get some sandwiches without some form of action or drama.

He was so much fun to be around and had that knack of getting everyone, from the fans to the team, behind him.

We got back to the circuit, finished the test, loaded the truck up with everything, and then everyone got back into the car with their bags. Shakey and I were on the back seat, and Mark and the mechanics were all up in the front. I can't remember who was driving, but when they pulled away the car made this 'duh duh duh' noise, and Mark said, 'Stop, stop, stop, there's something wrong with the car', so he got out, had a look over it, but couldn't see anything, and got back in. We pulled away and got going again and the same noise came back, and Mark again shouted, 'Stop, stop, stop, there must be something wrong'. He got out again and this time checked the tyres to find a massive flat spot in the rear ones. They were a write-off.

Mark was furious, and there wasn't a sound in the car all the way back to the hotel, except for Shakey and me giggling in the back of the car like a pair of kids. It was just like a family holiday, with the grumpy parents up front, naughty kids in the back and a really bad atmosphere. It got worse though, because the car wouldn't go past 28mph thanks to Shakey having blown up the turbo. Everyone in the car was so pissed off with us. It had been a long day, the hotel was miles away, and the car would only do 28mph while the tyres made a really loud humming noise.

When we eventually got back to the hotel Mark was still really angry with Shakey and vowed to make him pay for the damage to the car. I'm not sure if he ever did get the money out of him, but it was worth every penny all the same.

At the start, Shakey didn't have a clue though. He was at the bottom of his learning curve with us, and during testing he had loads of big crashes. I reckon he properly wrote off his bike three times at Guadix and Almeria before the season even started, but he was fast from day one – really fast. It didn't take him long to stop crashing, and after that he never looked back. Five British Superbike titles, World Superbike race wins and a few seasons in MotoGP don't happen by accident.

At the end of the year, Paul Bird came to me and asked me to ride for him, but I couldn't really see why I should change. I had a brilliant team and I was used to them, so I turned him down. Then he approached Shakey and did the deal with him before the last round at Donington Park. I think Shakey finished quite low down in that race, while I was up front racing with Steve Hislop. I actually did the double that day to claim second in the championship.

When I got back from the podium the team asked if I had seen Shakey's bike. I asked if he had fallen off, and they said he might as well have. His bike was stood in the garage without any bodywork on it, and it had water and oil coming out of all the wrong places and tyre debris all over it. It was a state.

It turns out that after the race Shakey decided to put on a bit of a show for the fans and did a series of huge burnouts for them, and then he stripped the bodywork off it and threw it into the crowd. We aren't talking about cheap fairings either; they were the pukka Ducati 'Corsa' carbon fibre fairings, which cost thousands of pounds. Mark was just standing there in his Prada trousers, speechless and looking at it in a state of shock. Nothing came of it, but he was devastated.

Steve Hislop took the 2002 title for the second time in his career. It was a really strange season for him. He would be untouchable one race, and nowhere at the next. Even though he won the title for Paul Bird that season on the MonsterMob Ducati, I think his hot/cold nature infuriated Paul, who fired him at the end of the season to make way for Shakey.

Earlier that season I followed Steve at Cadwell Park; it was the second race of the day that had been stopped while I was leading. Steve had won the first race, and I was leading the first part of the second race. He got a better start than me, so I got in behind him and thought there was no way he was going to beat me. Even though I was actually third in the championship at the time, Sean Emmett, who was in second, was pretty much out of it having had to swap teams mid-season, so the championship was effectively between Steve and me. I tried so hard to stay with him, but he just put his head down for two laps and disappeared into the distance. He made me look stupid, while at the same time looking like he was out on a Sunday afternoon plod.

After the race I got talking to Colin Edwards, who was watching on the bank. At the time, he was on his way to winning his second Super-bike World Championship for Honda and was there because Honda's team was only based up the road from Cadwell, in Louth. He tried to help me feel a bit better by saying that he'd never seen riding like it before, and that no one was going to beat him that day. It didn't help much; the bottom line was that, along with the rest of the grid, Steve annihilated me.

Then he would have a shocker at the next meeting and be nowhere. I remember lapping him in Thruxton, thinking, that's the end of Steve, we won't see him again – and then at Knockhill he won the race. He could be like stocks and shares: the lows were really low for him, and the highs were so high, he was amazing.

It was the 2002 season when I wiped Steve out at his home race at Knockhill, Scotland. He had beaten me in the first race, and on the last lap of race two I was telling myself that he wasn't going to beat me again. On the last lap, I was right behind him going into the hairpin, which is the last corner, and I braked so late and so hard that my rear wheel came right up off the ground. I thought, 'Oh no, I ain't gonna stop now', because to get the back wheel back on the ground you have to release the brake a bit, which means an already bad situation is only going to get worse.

I thought 'no, no, no, no' and shut my eyes just as I saw his rear wheel right in front of me, and then 'SKRSHHHH', I was on my arse, sliding down the road into the gravel trap. A second before, I was going for the win on the last lap, and now I was face-down in the gravel. It was all slow motion, and I was gutted. I took a look round and remember thinking that at least I didn't hit Steve and take him into the gravel with me. In my book, that's the worst thing you can do to a fellow competitor; it's one of my pet hates.

I was there in the middle of the gravel trap, picking myself up and relieved that it was just me that crashed, then next thing I noticed was that there were about ten marshals pushing Steve up the road to get him going again. If I was gutted before about chucking the points away, now I was mortified that I'd taken Steve out, and it was in front of his home crowd. Needless to say, once the marshals got Steve going again, they didn't exactly rush to help me; they just left me there in the gravel trap. No help. Steve still finished seventh.

The other thing about the hairpin at Knockhill is that it's about the only place on the whole lap with a grandstand, so the crowd there is huge. While I was waiting there for the race to finish, there were loads of people booing me and chucking things at me. Literally everyone hated me. It felt like ages before Steve came round on his cool-down lap, and as soon as I saw him coming I stood in the middle of the track to go and say sorry. He pulled up and straight away told me to get on the back, and he took me back to the pits. I said, 'Oh I'm so sorry Steve', and he just said, Don't worry about it. It's OK'. Turns out he broke his collarbone in the accident, but he never once complained to me about costing him the win and breaking his collarbone. I got out of Knockhill so quickly that day.

Steve was so good to me when I started at the TT. He seemed so old to me then, and now look at me! I really liked him; he'd raced against Dad in F2 years ago in certain races here and there, which is hard to believe now. I was standing next to his RVF750 that Honda had brought to the TT for him in 1991. Steve got one, Joey Dunlop got one, and Carl Fogarty got one.

The RVFs were almost mythical at the time; they were like nothing else I'd ever seen, and because the 1991 TT was some sort of celebration for Yamaha, Honda wanted to make sure they pissed on Yamaha's parade. The RVFs became the biggest talking points of the TT that year. I felt so lucky just to be stood next to them while I was warming up Dad's bike. At the same time, the Honda mechanics were warming Steve's RVF up; it just went 'wop wop wop'; they were amazing.

Steve was great with everyone, and generous to a fault. In 1994 when I did the Ulster GP for Castrol Honda I told them that I didn't have any Castrol leathers, so Steve gave me a set of his gorgeous factory Kushitani leathers to use, which fitted me perfectly. I couldn't believe how nice they were. I put some tape over the 'Hislop' name on the arse and did the race. When I went to give them back to him after, he said, 'Nah, just keep 'em'. I've still got them to this day. They're probably one of my most prized possessions. What a bloke.

Steve was forty-one when he died in a helicopter accident. He was so incredibly fast at the TT that he could win it on anything. He even won on the uncompetitive Norton in 1992. I'll never know how he did that on that bike, but Steve was very fast, and very clever. He knew every single bump on the course; he knew it all. He was amazing. If he was still alive, who knows how many he could have gone on to win on top of the eleven that he did. If you raced against him, you would know this. I remember the last time I saw him, he was having a real bad time on the Yamaha; he died on a real downer.

I think Mark's first season as a team owner in BSB blew his mind at just how much it costs, so the next year he scaled it back a bit, but we did have a really good year and got really close to the title again. Shakey was off to replace Steve at MonsterMob Ducati, and Sean Emmett was on the market and came with a load of sponsorship from Red Bull, so the bikes got changed from the red Highland Springs colours to the blue of Red Bull. I really hated Sean because I was jealous of him for getting a GP ride on Kevin Schwantz's bike in the mid-nineties, and that narked me. I just thought there were more deserving people than him for that ride. Plus in BSB he was always in the way, hanging around for a tow from faster riders in order to get a better lap time, which used to piss me off. I just didn't like him and thought he wasn't my cup of tea.

Sean turned up at the first meeting, and I thought, this is going to be the worst year ever. I'd got on so well with Shakey the year before, and I thought Sean was just going to pile in with a massive ego, being

131

that he was an ex-GP rider and darling of Red Bull. But in the end it was a hilarious year and would be one of the most memorable seasons of my career – not for the racing but for Sean's antics. We ended up getting on really well, which I never thought we would.

We were all banned from drinking, but Sean was a party animal. I was quite good, but he led me astray. We would sneak out and go to the pub for a few drinks, but he would always take it to another level and get so unbelievably drunk.

At the first round at Silverstone, I was in my motorhome at about 11 pm, going to bed, and Sean was constantly calling me and Leon Haslam to go around to his for a party. (Leon was in the team that year too, riding in the Supersport class.) Sean was still calling me at 3 am.

The next morning, I went into his motorhome and it was covered in empty beer cans and bottles, absolutely everywhere. It looked like he'd had dozens of people in his motorhome that night, including Leon. It was a mess. He went out in the warm-up session that morning and, on something like the second lap, he wrote off the bike, so he didn't even get a practice session in. On top of that, he didn't finish either race. Then the Supersport lads were out next, and Leon puked up inside his crash helmet just after he'd put it on. The two of them were a mess.

All three of us were testing at Cadwell Park during the season, Leon on his Supersport bike, Sean and me on our Superbikes. I was messing about, winding Leon up by riding alongside him on the start/finish straight, flicking the "Vs" at him. Bear in mind that he was flat out, looking at me, and I was more or less cruising on my Superbike. Then I thought I'd better start braking for the first corner, which is way past his braking point, so he went straight on, onto the grass as I peeled off to the left.

After the left there's a pair of right-handers that bring you on to the back straight, and I could see Haslam was still on his bike, bouncing along the grass like a rag doll, feet off the foot pegs, just hanging on and heading for the same back straight that I was on. Basically, he'd taken a massive shortcut at well over 100mph off-road. We were on a collision course, and he came flying off the top of this really high drop, and re-joined the track. I have no idea how he stayed on. His dad went mad at him for messing about, and Leon made it worse by trying to say he lost the brakes, but his dad knew he hadn't. Leon was so easily led astray.

Sean is so unbelievably naturally talented and a really nice bloke but he just didn't know when to stop. Every now and then you get those characters like that. They that come along and just have so much talent that it seems easy for them, so they don't feel like they need to focus or work at it. Anthony Gobert is another one like Sean. He also could do the seemingly impossible on a bike with virtually no effort, which meant he also lost his way. The ones that have that level of talent AND a single-minded focus on racing are the ones that make it to the very top and stay there – like Doohan, Rossi, Marquez, and so on.

Sean just didn't give a shit. At Thruxton he had a brand-new BMW car, which we took to the pub. There is this back lane into the track, and he drove the BMW down it. It's little more than a dirt-track and is barely as wide as the car at the start, and then it narrows. He was going down the track with the hedges scraping both sides of the car, and he kept going faster and faster, until he blew the tyres off the rims. He pulled up at the pub and I said, 'Bloody hell, Sean. Look at your new car', and all he did was say, 'Ahh, doesn't matter', and he just left it there. He just wasn't bothered. That's how he lived.

Later that season, he gave me a lift to Brands Hatch, and at the gates the security guard asked for his name, and Sean told him. The fella on the gate then told Sean that he wasn't allowed to bring his car in, so as soon as the guard turned away, Sean just drove through the gate. A full-on car chase ensued, all through the Brands Hatch site and right down to the bottom paddock, where his motorhome was. When we pulled up, three security guards came round, and a lass called Jane –

who worked for BSB and looked after the paddock parking and stuff – was there too. Everyone was going mental while we were still inside the car, then Sean shouted out the window, 'Look, my name is John Reynolds. If there is a problem, just fuck off'. He just didn't care. Jane calmed it all down and fixed everything up.

Unsurprisingly, by that stage Mark was getting really pissed off at constantly dealing with Sean's lifestyle, so he got very strict on going drinking. At that same Brands Hatch meeting, Mark said that he wanted us to be at the morning autograph sessions ten minutes before they started. He said if either of us were late, we would get sacked. So, I got up early and went to Sean's motorhome twenty minutes before the autograph session with the scooter that we had to share, and said, 'C'mon Sean, we've got to go'.

As usual, he was in a state, and in no hurry, so I said, 'Sod it, I'm going'. He tried to get me to stay and wait for him, but I knew he was never going to be ready, so I left him there. I got to the autograph session fine, and Sean turned up ten minutes late because he'd had to walk. Mark went mad at him, and because Sean didn't give a shit about any consequences to his actions, he started fighting with Mark right there in the garage. Obviously, he got sacked after that, and that was the end of Sean.

The two years with Renegade were brilliant. BSB was so competitive, the machinery was so trick, and the crowds were massive. It was a brilliant time to be a BSB rider. We got so close to the title in 2002 and weren't that far off in 2003, when we suffered from a few reliability problems.

On top of that, the team entered all four World Superbike rounds that took place in the UK as 'wild card' entries during those two years. I qualified on the front row at Brands Hatch in 2002, right there alongside world champions like Troy Bayliss and Colin Edwards. Admittedly, the Dunlop qualifying tyres that we had were great and helped get me up there, but the race tyre wasn't as good as the Michelin that everyone else was running. I started eight WSB races in 2002 and 2003 as a wild card, crashed out of three, and finished in the top ten in four of them.

When Mark Griffiths set up Renegade, he wanted to do it right – which he did. He packed a lot into two seasons and spent a fortune. Maybe if we hadn't have done the World Superbike rounds and instead spent the money on parts for the BSB challenge, I might have picked up at least one title in that spell, but that's racing; you never know. Mark offered me the chance to race for him in WSB, but by then I was already in new colours; I'd done enough to get a call from Honda Racing Corporation ...

12
2004 & 2005: HRC – Full Factory

HONDA RACING

In 2004, Honda came out with a new generation of their top-of-the-range sports bike, the Fireblade. The big news was that its engine capacity was now going to be 1000cc, which meant that it could compete in superbike racing. Previous generations of Fireblades were all around 900cc, which meant they simply weren't competitive. The 2004 Fireblade was something altogether different and benefited a lot from technology and lessons learned from their MotoGP team.

The other significant thing that happened in 2004 was that the World Superbike series switched to a control tyre, so all teams had to use the same brand of tyres: Pirellis. That didn't sit well with Honda; their default is always to produce the best race bike that they can, and then put it on the best tyres that they can. Being dictated to by the series organiser for World Superbikes on what tyres they could or couldn't use on their bike meant that Honda looked for a competitive Superbike series that didn't have a control tyre rule. The result was that Honda chose the British Superbike Championship to give their new Fireblade its world debut, and the dedicated racing division of Honda would run the team.

Honda Racing Corporation (HRC) is about as serious as it gets. They aren't a Honda-supported team, not a subsidiary; they ARE Honda. HRC handle all of Honda's global racing and research and development of racing motorcycle parts for all disciplines – Grand Prix racing, Superbike racing, off-road, motocross and trail riding.

In motorcycle racing, it really doesn't get bigger than riding for HRC, so when Neil Tuxworth from Honda got in touch and asked if I'd be up for racing the new Fireblade for HRC, I simply couldn't say no. I had made friends with Taddy Okada when I did GPs in 1999 when he was their rider, but now he was HRC's team manager for the Fireblade project.

For the first test, we went to Almeria racetrack in southern Spain; it's really popular with race teams for testing because the area is so dry, so you are virtually guaranteed good weather all year round. Someone once told me that it is Europe's only officially classified desert due its very low level of annual rainfall.

The team only brought one bike to the test, and I had never seen anything like it. There must have been at least ten mechanics for this one bike and they were all dressed in black, and so neat. Everything was so perfect. They pulled the bike out of the van and, oh my god, it was stunning, and there in front of me was a hand-built, full-factory Honda Fireblade. It was the very first one in existence and, as it turned out, was also the only one in existence. As I was looking it over, in complete awe of the finish and build quality, I was getting lectured not to crash it, or damage it in any way. I was told not to over-rev it, or mistreat it in any way – nothing.

I remember arriving at the airport and being met by Adrian Gorst, who was my new teammate's mechanic, and he said to me that I'd have an easy season. He said that my teammate was some unknown bloke called Ryuichi Kiyonari from Japan, who no one had heard of. We decided fairly early on that his name was too much of a mouthful, so we called him Kiyo. When he turned up and I met him for the first time, I'll be honest and tell you that I did think it would be a nice easy year. He hadn't seen any of the tracks before, whereas I had grown up at them. He is such a softly spoken bloke with incredible manners and humility, and at the time that made me think, this is gonna be OK. I decided that I had him whipped.

The team told me that Kiyo had been testing the bike in Japan, and they wanted to send him out first so he could get up to speed on the Michelin tyres. They were brand-new factory Michelin tyres, and we didn't know how they were going to work, so because Kiyo had some experience with the bike already he went first on the new tyres.

We all sat on the pit wall and waited for him to come round to start his first lap, and when he came out of the last left-hander that comes onto the start/finish straight in to view, he was totally sideways with smoke pouring off the rear tyre, and in complete control. I had never seen anything like it before; he was so fast, despite never having seen the place before. All he had ever done at Almeria was that outlap. I was stunned. We all looked at each other and all at the same time said, 'Oh shit, this is gonna be a difficult year'.

It was the first day of a four-day test, and when Kiyo came in at the end of his first run we were all stood there with our jaws on the floor. He did his debrief with the Japanese mechanics, and then they said it was my turn. I still had the lecture about not crashing the bike because it was the only one in existence fresh in my head, so I decided to be really careful.

They kept in the Michelins that Kiyo had been using, and the team said they wanted me to go out for fifteen laps. After about five laps, the rear tyre that was already in a state at the start of my run was totally destroyed, but when Honda say you have to stay out for fifteen laps, you have to stay out for fifteen laps and that's it, you don't come in. I made it to the last lap, and by then it was spinning out of control everywhere. Then, when I was turning into the first corner on a shut throttle, there was so little grip that the rear couldn't even hold the lateral G-force that comes from turning a bike, and the rear just came round on me and highsided me off.

This one-of-a-kind, hand-built bike that had been flown all the way to Spain from Japan went cartwheeling into the gravel trap and tyre wall, with bits flying off it everywhere. It was a mess. The swing arm was bent, and they didn't have a spare, so, as best they could, they straightened it out and repaired the rest of it with what spares they had. I had just got the dream ticket, on the best superbike in the world, with a full-factory team, with full-factory tyres, and I'd destroyed their one-and-only prototype on my first time out on it on the first day of a four-day test. I was so embarrassed. We did the rest of the test with the bike patched up like that.

At the end of that test, the team asked me what I wanted doing to my bike, which they would build and bring back in a month's time for a second test. I said I wanted a thumb-operated rear brake under the left handlebar and a few other things, like the handlebars' specific placement, length and thickness, the seat and foot pegs' position – basic stuff. I have always preferred using a thumb-operated rear brake instead of the usual rear brake lever that you operate with your right foot. Getting one added to my British Superbike was no problem, but Honda told me that if I wanted a thumb-operated rear brake for my Suzuka bike then I would get dropped from the Suzuka 8 Hours team.

The Suzuka 8 Hours race is a massive deal for the Japanese factories, especially Honda, who own the Suzuka racetrack that the race takes place on. It is an 8-hour-long endurance race that is the highlight of the year for the Japanese fans. It means everything to the factories to win at Suzuka, so they build the trickest bikes possible and get their star Grand Prix riders to ride at the race. Honda even made Valentino Rossi race in it for them twice when he was riding for them in MotoGP, which is madness when you think about it.

139

The race takes place midway through the GP season, and Rossi was their man who was best placed to win the Grand Prix World Championship – but they plonk him on a superbike to race flat out for 200 or more laps, with just one other teammate to share the riding. It's so easy to pick up an injury there, and that's it, your GP season is over. But the fact that they are prepared to put a dead-cert MotoGP World Championship at risk to win just shows how much it means to the factories to win the Suzuka 8 Hours. As a rider, a Suzuka 8 Hours race win means you're basically set up for life. It is huge.

Back to the thumb-operated rear brake lever. Honda said to me that either I wanted to ride at Suzuka, or I didn't. I thought they were taking the piss, so I said, well I can't ride without a thumb brake. The result was that I ended up getting dropped from the team, missing the chance to ride in the Suzuka 8 Hours race on a factory Honda. What a prize twat. It was a massive mistake. I should have just used a normal brake like the one Kiyo used.

One of the Japanese test riders took my place, and the team won. They wouldn't put the brake lever on for me because in endurance racing it's another thing on the bike that can break and may need repairing and therefore a potential problem. If it isn't absolutely essential, it doesn't go on the bike. My thumb-operated rear brake wasn't essential because the other two riders didn't want one, so why should they put it on just for me? This was one of those occasions where I really could have done with a manager. I really needed someone to say to me, 'Don't be a dick. Ride the bike with a normal back brake, and win the Suzuka 8 Hours', but I was too up my own arse, and thought, if they won't put a thumb brake on for me then sod them. A manager would have made me do it.

We went back to Almeria again for the next test, and this time there were two bikes – Kiyo's and mine. It was a big test for a full week: three days in Almeria, and then up the road to Guadix for another three days. The mechanics pulled these two bikes out of the truck, and they were things of absolute beauty. It was amazing seeing how the

Japanese worked. Now we had a bike each, there were two teams within the team. There was Kiyo's team with Adrian on one side of the garage, and my team with Les Pearson, who was my crew chief, on the other side.

They left us to it, and we started going through the bike. However, Honda want you to go a certain way with setup, like geometry, wheelbase and so on, which Kiyo did, but I'm a different rider to him, so I wanted a different setup to him. When you go off their script, the HRC guys don't say anything or make a big deal out of it; they just move over to the other side of the garage and leave you to it until you work it out for yourself and end up back at the setup that they know works.

They let us work it out for ourselves, which I thought at the time was really strange but I now think was actually a sign of confidence and trust in us. Too often in teams you get mechanics and crew chiefs not trusting their rider, and imposing their ideas on the setup, and letting egos get in the way. The HRC guys weren't being biased towards their guy; they were actually backing us by letting us figure it out for ourselves. Once we start going the way they want us to go with setup, they all come back to our side of the garage, because of course they were right!

A factory team is much more than just the bike. It is the people; they are all the best at what they do, and they only do that. The culture is different; it is incredibly focused and businesslike. The whole approach to the task of racing is different at the very top of the food chain from the bottom. Racing is a business. It's right there, in their name: it's Honda Racing Corporation, not Honda Racing Team.

At the end of the three days at Almeria, Taddy said that Kiyo and I were to have a race to round off the three days. At that time, Kiyo was miles faster than me, so we went to the grid, and I was thinking, 'This is stupid' – I knew I was going to get thrashed. Before the race, the team said we could choose our favourite tyre from the list of 200 fronts and 170 rears that they had. It was mind-bending; the choice of tyres was endless.

The funny thing is that after testing all those tyres I found a front tyre that I loved and would go on to always use because it had a really hard carcass and compound that I liked. According to Michelin, there was only one other of their riders in the world who also liked that front tyre and also used it all the time: Valentino Rossi. Without a doubt, that is the only thing I've got in common with Rossi.

So there I was, with my 'Rossi-spec' front tyre fitted, lined up on the grid, just Kiyo and me, with the whole team on the pit wall watching, and a load of people from other teams who had arrived to do some testing after we had gone. No pressure, then. It was to be a twenty-lap race, and you can imagine just how much we both really wanted to beat each other in our first head-to-head race. It was crazy for Honda to do, because it was only bragging rights at stake, and I didn't really want to do it. We had done about 9 million laps, and it was the end of the last day, and the last thing I wanted to do was have a race that I knew I was gonna get spanked in.

The clutches on those Fireblades were terrible; they were really grabby and not at all smooth, so when we went off the line, both clutches grabbed and pumped, which made the bikes immediately rear up into massive wheelies. We both hit each other mid-wheelie, and Kiyo went onto the grass on one side of the track, and I went on to the grass on the other side. We sorted ourselves out, and I led into the first corner. I was thinking, 'The bastard ain't gonna pass me. I'll crash before he passes me'.

Then, about two thirds of the way round the first lap, I came out of a corner, gave it too much throttle, and had a massive slide. I got kicked right out of the seat, so high that my feet were above my head! How I stayed on I'll never know. Kiyo didn't pass me until the next corner, and when he did he just cleared off. He made me look stupid.

At the end of the race, I came in and Kiyo was dead serious; I remember looking at his side of the garage and they all looked really fed up; it didn't make any sense to me. They had won the race, but even then there was no celebrating, just straight into a debrief., The atmosphere between everyone was actually really good; it was just a level of professionalism that I wasn't used to.

The team were all dead serious until about 8 pm on the last day of the Almeria part of the test, but then when the red wine came out they all transformed into joking, laughing, proper party animals, and I tell you, those boys can't take their drink. They would make me and Kiyo stand on a chair and have drinking races against each other with big glasses of red wine full to the top. I won that race.

They were out of control, and we were supposed to be testing two days later in Guadix. I'm not joking when I tell you that every single one of the Japanese guys were throwing the red wine down their throats like they'd never had it before. Plenty of the English team members were at it too; it was like all this pent-up stress and tension just got let off in one night by everyone and they couldn't get enough of the red wine.

Inevitably, they all started puking all over the place. It was a mess and everyone was just written off. One of the main Japanese mechanics that was such a nice bloke was so pissed that he was just lying on a chair in the bar. While I was stood there laughing at him, he was sick out of his mouth – and somehow he sucked it all back in before it got on his brand-new HRC uniform that he was still wearing. He properly puked up, and not a drop of it got on his clothes – it was amazing in a grim sort of way. Then I found one of them passed out in the toilet, just lying against the bog, completely out of it, not able to move. It was total carnage.

The Japanese don't do that sort of thing normally, so when they get let off the lead, they go mental. I was a bit of a mess myself, and I remember sitting in the foyer of the hotel, and then the next thing I remember was waking up in bed the next morning with no idea how I got there. I got up and went downstairs to see who was about, and the lady on reception was pointing at me and tutting. She really wasn't at all happy with me, and I had no clue why. I was told that I had puked in an ashtray in the foyer of the hotel, and just went to bed, leaving the contents of my stomach all over the place. Not my proudest moment. Kiyo, on the other hand, was really careful with that sort of carry-on. He knew when to stop.

A couple of days later, at Guadix, I had to reset and try to forget about the humiliation Kiyo had put on me at Almeria. That's the thing about being a racer: you have to be able to say to yourself, 'That's done', and move on like it had never happened. I thought to myself that it was all on him now. I was only going to get faster as I figured out the bike and tyres, and he had laid down the marker.

It started right there at that second part of the test at Guadix. I did a decent job as things started clicking into place. The track was more like a British circuit, whereas Almeria is more like a European GP circuit, with long corners that I wasn't really used to. By the time we left Guadix, Kiyo and I were very similar on lap times, and it was like Almeria had never happened. I had found a really good base setting for the bike, and it was starting to feel like mine.

When the first round of the season came at Silverstone, it was still March, so the all-new, highly anticipated Honda Fireblade would get its global debut at a grey, cold, damp airfield in Northamptonshire. The team said that the big boss, who was a real hard bastard, would be at Silverstone to witness the glorious debut of the bike, in person. Everyone was really scared of him, especially the Japanese guys, who said that he would sack you just as soon as look at you. So the boss came to Silverstone, and the whole garage was so under pressure that it was spookily quiet, like someone had died.

I got the message from Taddy that we really needed some good results, and it was all up to me to get them. The pressure was immense. Honda had invested an eyewatering amount of money into this project, and they expected results from the very start. That's the thing about being a factory rider: you've got the weight of expectation from a whole company on your shoulders, not just the guys in the garage.

Luckily, I had the best bike on the track at the time. The Suzuki would turn out to be our closest rival but it was a bit behind us, though that would be a situation that wouldn't last as the season went on. We also had the best tyres for Silverstone. Michelin had been racing and testing there, so they knew exactly what tyres to bring. I got pole position, and Kiyo was on the front row too. I was worried about the start of the race because I knew the clutches hadn't been sorted, and the bike was a bastard to launch.

I got a shit start because my clutch did the same thing it did at Almeria, but Kiyo got a good one and was first into the first corner. I got away OK in the end and was in something like 5th or 6th place. The track was damp in places after some rain, but I didn't panic about the slippery conditions and just got my head down. I passed everyone in front of me in the first couple of laps and went on to win the race. I think Kiyo finished 2nd or 3rd.

Pole position, fastest lap, and a win for the Fireblade in front of Honda's top brass. I was the golden boy in the team, and the relief was immense. If I'm honest, I can't remember race 2, other than I didn't win it; I think I was second. Getting race 1 done, and getting the win on debut, was such a big focus in the build-up that everything else that happened that weekend, including race 2, didn't really register. It was all about winning that first race and becoming the first person in the world to win on the new Honda Fireblade.

I won loads of races that year and got loads of pole positions and fastest laps, but I still missed out on the championship. John Reynolds and Suzuki took it by just twenty-nine points. To put it into perspective, third place in the championship was the other Suzuki rider Yukio Kagayama, and he was eighty-two points behind me, and Kiyo was 183 points behind me.

I got really close to the championship that year – the closest I ever would. That was the most 'factory' point of my career; Michelin had a whole truck full of tyres just for Kiyo and me, and the tyre bill for that year alone was over £300,000, and every bike that got written off was priceless. I was at the very top of my game and felt like I was in my absolute prime.

Honda paid me well in my first year, and we really should have won the championship. A few things might have stopped us – me choosing the wrong tyres at times, and some things Michelin did or didn't do, plus I picked up some injuries during the season. We all have our excuses, but the end result is what it is. Towards the end of the 2004 season, at the Donington round, Honda said they wanted me for 2005, but I'd already had loads of offers from other teams so I put my asking price up by loads to Honda.

I sat down with Neil Tuxworth and Honda UK's Mark Davies, who was really open-minded and really fair. I was saying that I wanted a six-figure salary, and they were saying not a chance. We were arguing in the back of the truck for over an hour and were £10,000 apart. Eventually I realised that I wasn't that bothered, because I knew I could go just two garages down from where I was sitting and get what I wanted, so I stuck to my guns. Honda said that they just couldn't pay it, so I suggested that if they really did want me to ride for them then we should just toss a coin. They went mental and said, 'We are Honda, and we don't work like that. We aren't flipping a coin'. Even so, I got a pound coin out and asked if they had any better ideas. They didn't, so we flipped the coin and I won, so they paid. To this day, I have no idea how they got that through the head office at Honda, but fair play to them, they honoured the deal.

With a new contract for 2005 all sorted, Honda took us to Japan to test the next year's bike at the Sugo racetrack. They had taken everything off our 2004 bike, and the 2005 bike was like a road bike when I got there. I couldn't believe it. They asked me what I wanted on my 2005 bike, and I said I wanted all the stuff that they had taken off the 2004 bike put back on.

We had got it just right by the end of the 2004 season, and it was a fully sorted race bike – we had even solved the clutch problems – but they said I couldn't have anything from the 2004 bike. It turned out that they had made some small updates to the 2005 road bike, so racing a 2004 bike wasn't on. The race bike had to look like the current road bike, and Honda wanted to go one step further and make the 2005 race bike look *exactly* like the road bike.

The 2005 race bike had a standard swing arm, whereas my 2004 race bike had a handmade bespoke one, which makes a massive difference to the way the bike handled. The 2005 bike had a different clutch, and all sorts of stuff, which meant that all my settings from 2004 meant nothing. I was back to square one again; that's just how it works. For example, when I tested it, the clutch didn't work properly, so instead of just using the clutch from my 2004 bike, they just kept working on solving the problem until it was sorted. Riding for a factory team is good, but it isn't everything, and you have to do it their way. Maybe it's an internal thing; I think they were just trying to get it really close to the road bike for image and pride. Who knows?

That trip to Japan to build the 2005 bike was amazing. Taddy took me to some places in Tokyo, and we drank a few sakes and ate some traditional Japanese food. It was the first time I ate cow's tongue, which was actually quite nice. I went to the factory every day, and I had to wear this HRC suit so that everyone looked the same. We would go for breakfast in a line, and everyone would eat together on this one big table at a certain time, and then it was back down to the race workshop.

Watching them working on the stuff was incredible; they are so meticulous and take so much pride in their work, even on the mundane tasks. Everyone really treated me so well, like royalty, which took a bit of getting used to, but that's the Japanese culture. Every hour or so, a buzzer would go off and everyone would stop what they were doing and start doing stretches and meditation. Taddy said that I had to do it too, otherwise it is disrespectful, so you have to get involved and start following what everyone is doing. Then the buzzer goes off again, and everyone goes back to work until the

147

next time the buzzer goes. The HRC workshop is a really special place, and sadly I've never been back since.

During that second year with HRC I did OK. I finished third in the championship, but I could sense a change was coming, and deep down I knew what it was. Kiyo was beating me more than I was beating him, and a Spanish guy called Gregorio Lavilla, who had been, amongst other things, a factory test rider for the Suzuki MotoGP team, was riding a full-factory Ducati that was miles ahead of our Hondas. He was beating everyone.

At about the third-from-last meeting, I went to Neil Tuxworth and asked him what the plan was for 2006, and he said everything was OK and not to worry. I was quite surprised, because I wasn't having the best of years and had just finished 6th or 7th at the previous meeting at Cadwell Park, which is no good for Honda. If you're not on the podium, it's a disaster. Winning is brilliant, 2nd is a bit of a defeat, 3rd is not cool, 6th or 7th is a problem, so I knew I was on dodgy ground.

The tyres that we were getting just didn't suit me at the time, and in the background there was a young lad who was making waves, called Karl Harris. He was riding really well on a standard Fireblade in another team, so I knew for sure that Honda would be looking at him. Sure enough, Neil came to me at the last race and told me that I hadn't got a ride for the next season. He said things had changed. I couldn't believe that Honda had done me again; it was like the end of 1998 all over. I was properly pissed off, not so much at losing the ride – I knew I wasn't getting the results – but at being told everything was OK when it wasn't. I told Neil what I thought, and I left.

Although I wasn't expecting it at the start, when I was at HRC Kiyo and I became really good mates. I've got one of his helmets from 2004, which he gave me. He races really hard but really fair, and he is a genuinely spot-on bloke. He didn't have much English, and I was really impressed by him when we used to have team briefings. They would last for hours as the team would go through everything, every nut and bolt, right through to the feel of the brakes and so on. Kiyo had to answer in English and sometimes he would struggle and answer in Japanese, but then he would get pulled up for it and be forced to repeat his answers in English. The only English guys in the room were Les, me and Neil – the rest were Japanese – but they all had to speak English for us.

Once, Kiyo and I were at a tyre test near Clermont Ferrand in France, where Michelin are based. It was one of the scariest things that I have done on a bike. Michelin just kept putting tyres in the bike and sending us out without telling us what they had fitted, getting us to do 5 laps, come in, new tyre, and go again, over and over. Every now and then they would test us with a tyre that they knew wouldn't work at all, just to see if we were trying hard enough. The next thing, I would be turning in to a 130mph corner, and the bike would just go straight onto the grass because there was no grip; it was terrifying.

In the afternoon, Kiyo and I had had enough, so while the blokes from Michelin were having their massive lunch, drinking their wine, and generally being French, Kiyo and me found this small building on the side of an old airfield and basically hid there all afternoon. That's where I found out that Kiyo smoked and liked a drink. Normally, he would go to the toilets and have a ciggie and would just take bottles of red wine back to his room to drink. He was really worried about the HRC bosses finding out, but once I discovered that side to him, we got on so much better.

Another time, we were testing at some French circuit in November. It was a pukka circuit with mountains all round it, but my god, it was so cold, and Kiyo was going round and round like a machine, and you could hear him spinning the rear tyre all over the place, and it was raining. It was so cold that you couldn't feel your fingers after a few laps, and ice would build up on the brake calipers and brake hoses. I was asking the team, what are we doing here? I was questioning the purpose of the test, you know, what's the point, what are we learning here, and generally trying to avoid having to do any more laps, and

149

there is Kiyo, going round lap after lap, flat out, while I just stopped in the garage.

He is simply an amazing rider with an incredible work ethic. The team would tell him to do twenty laps within a certain time, and he'd do them all within a couple of tenths of each other. He made me realise that there are a lot of people better than me.

On a good day, he was incredible, but when his head wasn't right, he was nowhere. I remember I had to tow him round at Croft just to try and get him qualified, and even then all he could manage was the last row of the grid. HRC were going to sack him, so they asked if I could help. Then two rounds later and he's breaking lap records and winning at a canter.

How he can turn a bike and spin up the rear is like no one I have ever seen. His tyre temperature was always 20 degrees cooler than mine because when you spin a tyre, there is less energy going through the carcass of the tyre, which is what generates the heat. By spinning the tyre so much, its outer surface disperses the energy and so the heat never reaches the carcass and therefore all the hot rubber on the surface gets smeared all over the track. I work the tyres differently because I'm not spinning them as much, so the heat gets into the carcass of the tyre and stays there, so my tyre temperatures would always be higher than his. We had massively different styles, and I tried his bike a few times, and he rode mine, and we both couldn't understand how each of us rode our bikes, but then he won the championships, and I didn't.

One good thing about getting dropped from the HRC BSB team was that I could race at the TT again. Even today, Honda don't let their BSB riders do any road racing. I've never been given a reason why; it's just one of those things. When I signed for them in 2004 I was told categorically that I wouldn't be able to do the TT and BSB. One good thing about getting dropped by HRC was that I could go back to the island ...

13

2006:
Hero to Zero

After Honda let me go at the end of 2005, pretty much all the teams in the paddock wanted me to ride for them. I was still capable of challenging for the title along with Gregorio Lavilla, who had a factory Ducati for 2006, and Kyio, who had kept his ride on the HRC Fireblade. Leon Haslam, Shane Byrne, Johnny Rea and Karl Harris were all breaking through as the next generation of riders, but I was still in demand.

One of the people who got in touch was Paul Bird. Paul has been around bike racing for years, and as well as helping riders individually he also was running his own race team, Paul Bird Motorsport (PBM). He still runs his team to this day, and he is a fairly big character with probably the biggest ego in the paddock. His team has a reputation for having the best of everything: the best trucks, the best hospitality and usually the best riders. So when he called me and said he was dropping the Ducatis that the team ran in 2005 and that he had Fireblades for 2006, I thought they wouldn't be too far off the HRC bikes that I had been riding for the previous two seasons, not least because of Paul's reputation for not being afraid to spend money.

I had a few offers from other teams, and Paul asked me what it would take for me to ride for him. To be honest, even though he was switching to Fireblades, and I knew that bike inside out, I didn't really want to ride for him. I'm not a big fan of the pressure that he puts on people in the team. You spend so much time with a team during a season of racing that it is really important to me that everyone gets on. What I do on the bike is so bloody dangerous that the last thing I want is an atmosphere in the team when I'm not on the bike. I am a people person and because at HRC the vast majority of people were Japanese, the culture that I'd got used to was very different to the typical Western culture in all the other teams in the paddock. At HRC, everyone treats each other with respect, and there isn't a single ego in the team, from the top to the bottom. The Japanese won't stand for it.

So, I made up a price that I was sure Paul wouldn't go for. It was more than what HRC had been paying me, so I was certain that he wouldn't come up with the money. I couldn't believe it when he said he would pay it. Now I had a problem and I was trying to come up with a way to get out of it without going back on what I'd said. If I say I'm going to do something, I'll do it.

So I said, 'Right, I want two cars', and he said, 'OK', although it is worth mentioning that I never actually got the two cars. Paul just kept saying yes to every single one of my stupid demands, so as a final shot at getting him to say no, I told him that I wanted him to get me a part as an extra on the TV series *Coronation Street*.

I thought he was taking the piss when he asked me to give him a couple of hours. About an hour later, Paul called me and said to be dressed in some plain clothes without any branding on them at 8 am the next morning. Turns out, Paul knows the actor Alan Halsall, who plays the part of Tyrone Dobbs in the show.

The next morning, Paul picked me up and we went to Alan's house, where we had a chat, and then he took us to the studio. We walked into the green room, which is only for the main actors and off-limits to extras, so straight away I pissed a few of the actors off – most notably Anne Kirkbride, who played Deirdre Barlow. Anne made a right song and dance about me hanging round the green room with her in it at the same time as her. We went round the set and had a look at it all, and we sat at the bar in the 'Rovers Return'. I was in heaven, being sat there with all the famous actors being filmed right in front of me. Then they said it was mine and Paul's turn, and they wanted us in the Rovers Return at a certain time.

When we got there, the film crew said they wanted us to stand by the hatch on the bar, walk round to the gambling machine and put some money in it, then play for a bit. After a few games, we had to go and sit on some stools by the fireplace next to the machine.

My big moment came, and I was standing there at the bar when the director said 'Action'. I didn't move, so basically they had to reset the whole scene, which takes ages and pisses off everyone involved in the scene, including all the crew. The director came up to me and explained that I had to go when they say 'Action'. I told him that I thought I could just wander over whenever I wanted; I didn't realise that every single movement is planned and scripted. So I said, 'Right OK, got it'.

The next time, as soon as the fella said 'Action', I set off and walked round the bar and started playing on the gambling machine. It was all going well until I won the bloody jackpot, so the machine started kicking off, with all these lights flashing and bells ringing. The director came piling into the scene, shouting, 'Cut, cut, cut', and he was fully pissed off. I didn't know why he was so stressed out, so someone explained to me that when you are an extra in a scene, you have got to be dead silent, and mime if you want to look like you're talking. The set has to be completely silent apart from the actors who are doing the scene.

By then, everyone in the room hated me so much because they had to reset the whole scene again and re-do it for a third time. This time I put the money in, didn't win, then sat on the chairs with Paul and started miming to each other. Paul started to snigger a bit, and I couldn't stop myself laughing, so in came the director again, shouting, 'Cut, cut, cut'. You can imagine just how much everyone was pissed off with me by now, especially the actors. We were just messing them all about so much. The whole thing was so unreal and, being a big *Coronation Street* fan, I was in awe of it all.

Eventually we got it done, and I told everyone I knew, so when the episode came out they were all watching. All that got left in the scene I'd filmed was my arm – they cut everything else out, which is probably no less than I deserve. I stole some beermats from the Rovers Return, pulled a pint, and they took pictures of it all, but I never got them. To top it all off, after that I had to ride for Paul that year.

To be fair to him, Paul did 90% of what he promised. The only thing was that the team didn't believe me on a lot of things that I knew would work on the bike. I finished the championship in 7th that year, and I know that the bike and I were both better than that. Their Fireblade had really wide yokes – which connect the whole front suspension and wheel to the frame of the bike. When I rode for Honda, the Fireblade turned really well, but I couldn't get the PBM Fireblade to turn anything like as well. The PBM Fireblade did have some better solutions to things like the throttle assembly compared to what we had at HRC. Phil Borley, who was the chief mechanic, came up with a very clever solution to the throttle assembly to stop the bike backing into corners, and it was brilliant.

PBM had in fact installed the whole front end of their 2004 Ducatis, so the bike now had wide yokes and it wouldn't turn. I tried to tell them that it wasn't turning for some reason and kept asking if I could try different things, including narrow yokes. They just said that I wasn't riding it properly. So Paul's promise that I would have free rein on what I wanted didn't really happen.

I eventually got my way at the last race at Brands Hatch and got just one front wheel and one set of narrower yokes to try. The bike was transformed; it was fantastic, it turned, gave feedback and felt totally different. I got a 3rd, which is a sort of OK result, but by the standard of results that I had been getting all season it felt like a win. Most of all, I felt like I was racing again, and I was well happy with proving that I was right all along about the Ducati yokes ruining the Fireblade's handling. To be fair, they used the Ducati stuff because it was really good-quality stuff which was left over from the previous season, but it wasn't a fit for the Fireblade.

This is what teams often do because they have budgets to stick to, and they get used to riders telling them shit just as an excuse for not being fast. I knew what I was talking about, coming from HRC, but when you've got a head mechanic working against you by telling Paul one thing while I'm telling him another, it is understandable that Paul would be loyal to his mechanic. Riders come and go, whereas mechanics tend not to. It was a shame, and I'm not being disrespectful to Paul's team, because they have been tremendously successful over the years, but that's what happened when I rode for them.

Now that I'm team manager, I will try and push our rider towards what the team has funding for, but if it comes to it I will give my rider what he wants, because I've been there. If he wants to turn the bike upside down, or tape a jam sandwich to the fuel tank, I'll do it – IF it makes him quicker. I understand that at PBM it would have been a big, expensive job to swap the whole front end of a race bike and that other things took priority in the budget.

It was at that last round at Brands Hatch that I was feeling some patter from the brakes and asked a mechanic to change the brake discs. He came back to me saying, 'Oh it's the end of the year, we will just use these old discs'. I couldn't believe it – I went mad at him and said to put some new discs on it. He didn't want to do it, but I stood over him and watched him do it. He never spoke to me again.

Mechanics like him, who think they know best, don't realise that a little bit of chatter from the brakes at 150mph going into Paddock Hill bend is absolutely terrifying and will hold me back from being 100% committed. If mechanics like him knew what it's like to have brake patter at 150mph, they would soon change the brake discs, but they think they know best.

Some people in racing miss the little details, like tyre pressure gauges. They will have one for years and never get it calibrated. The first thing I did when I joined a team was to ask when they last checked their tyre pressure gauge. Most of the time they can't remember when, and it pisses me off so much, because it is such a simple thing that can ruin a race weekend. There's no excuse for it. I make my mechanics calibrate their tyre pressure gauges at the start of every single race meeting. They hate me for it, but I've lost count of how many times they've come back and been surprised that they are out of calibration.

One of the teams I was with said they knew that their pressure gauge runs 2psi out, so I told them to throw it away, but they said they wouldn't. The rationale was that it was OK because they compensate for the difference. I went to the tool chest, found the pressure gauge and swung it around my head really hard, and flung it across the start/finish straight at Cadwell Park. It landed on the other side of the track and bits of it broke off.

The mechanic started having a moan at me, saying that it was his own pressure gauge, and that he had it for years. I told him that I didn't care, and that if I saw it back in the garage, I'd put a hammer through it. It only takes someone else who doesn't know that it is 2psi out to pick it up and use it, and then you're screwed. It's little things that teams miss, which why, with the team I run now, I do it right. Don't get me wrong: everyone makes mistakes and that's OK, but with us everything mechanical is double-checked. We've got two pressure gauges that both get calibrated first thing on Friday morning at every race meeting, to check one against the other, and so on.

Other simple things get missed, like the bike's ride height, which makes a huge difference to the way it handles. Mechanics will look at the datalogger and say that I have got 10mm of fork travel left, which I know, from riding it, that there isn't. So I'll ask if they've bottomed the forks out and taken them apart to see where they run to, and whether they've got all the references right for the datalogger. It's sad, but it doesn't surprise me anymore when they say that they haven't.

I've ridden for teams where it's taken me three meetings before it's occurred to me where to look, then have to go back through everything, thinking of all the setup stuff, and what I want the mechanics to do, then having to stand over them while they do what I want them to do, wasting a couple of meetings, and by then the season is over.

Even a factory team like Honda can still get it wrong, but they do loads and loads of testing and they work professionally to iron everything out before the first race. At HRC, we were putting carbon fibre rods under the yokes stanchions so we could try different flex in the chassis – that's how detailed we would go in testing. When we had handling problems with the Ducatis, we put lead in the wheel spindles, and you wouldn't believe the difference that it made to the feel of the bike.

In non-factory teams, some mechanics never believe the rider; they look at you like you're a total cock, so trying all that different stuff just isn't a priority when they're not prepared to work with you and trust you. I've fallen out with some very close friends over this, but we've made up straight after. I was riding a Ducati in 2010, and a lad called Jason Jones was my mechanic. I was saying to him that I couldn't go any quicker and that there was something wrong with the bike, but he wouldn't believe me. Eventually, after a lot of fall-outs, we found that there was something completely wrong with the bike. To be fair to him, it wasn't his fault either, but until then his default position was that I didn't know what I was on about.

It stems from the fact that there are riders – who I won't name – who will purposely make up all kinds of bullshit about the bike that's wrong, even undoing radiator caps to cause a fault. They'll do anything other than blame themselves. I've always been honest if I've ever not been at my best on the bike, I've apologised. If I'd started making up shit, I'd get caught out and I'd just be wasting everyone's time, including my own, anyway. I've always had the balls to stand up and admit it when I've messed up. The other side of that coin, though, is that I will also stand up and say if someone else in the team made mistakes or is bullshitting, and that it can't happen again.

In 1997, when I was on the V&M Honda, we were at Cadwell Park, and I went out of pits at the start of qualifying, and the engine just stopped, so I left it at the side of the track and ran back up the hill to the pits to get my spare bike. When I went out on my spare, the handlebar positions were all over the place, which is a really basic thing but makes a massive difference to how easy the bike is to ride.

I came straight back in and gave the mechanics a right bollocking; I had a proper tantrum. I spent so much time having a meltdown in the garage, screaming and shouting at everyone, that I dropped down the grid and ended up with a really shit qualifying position.

Later on, the team manager came and saw me and said, 'Right, Michael, you've got a bit of a problem. It's your mechanics'. I replied that the mechanics were shit and wasting everyone's time, and that I'd do it myself. He said I was going to have to, because they were all packing their tools up and going home. I went back to the garage and apologised to everyone for being a dick, and they apologised for the handlebars being wrong, and it was all OK, but it shows the pressure that everyone is under.

The thing is, in motorbike racing there are people who can ride anything. Shakey, for instance, can go stupidly fast on anything, so the demands put on the mechanics are much less. Unfortunately for me (and my mechanics), I'm one of those people who can feel 2mm of preload on a fork, or a click of rebound. I'm really sensitive to setup change. Sometimes I wish that I didn't have that feel, but in other ways it's good, because I think if you keep going with a setup that isn't right and you can't feel it then eventually it will throw you off.

To be a champion racer, it's best to be alone with a small group of people, and to be a natural rider who can ride around problems. What makes a good team is when everyone, including the bloke at the top, is competent. They don't have to be NASA scientists but if you tell them you want something doing, they must do it, no more, no less, no interpretation. They have to trust you, and you have to trust them.

When I stood in for Sylvain Guintoli at Suzuki in 2009, their electronics bloke wouldn't have it when I told him that the bike was running on into corners, no matter how many times I said it was. I knew it was doing it, and I couldn't ride it as fast as I knew I otherwise could. He just kept saying to me that Guintoli didn't complain, and I said that maybe he rides differently to me, maybe he holds the throttle differently to me, maybe he changes gear differently to me – but I knew that I did have a problem. Getting it through to him was impossible because his default was 'Well, Guintoli never said anything about that'.

Having the balls to stand up to mechanics or electronics guys is really difficult, and I regret not always having enough confidence in my early career. Then again, I was maybe too pushy at other times, but only because I knew what I wanted and would get frustrated.

Explaining exactly what is going on isn't easy. I took my daughter out in her car, and she said to me that there was something wrong with the gearbox. I said 'OK, Juliette that means nothing to anyone. What is it doing? Is it when you select a gear, or change gear?' and she just said, 'I dunno'. It made me chuckle, so I told her if I went back to my mechanics and said 'I dunno', I'd be crucified. She said, 'But I'm not a bloody bike racer!' – which is fair enough.

You've got to think all the time what you're feeling from the bike; you don't have to tell them what to do to sort it out, just what you're feeling, in detail. If the gear isn't going in, that's not enough; *how* is it not going in? Taylor Mackenzie coming into our team has been good for me, because I listen to him, and I'll question him, and I'll just make sure he has really thought about all the detail.

If he is talking about the suspension, I'll ask whether he thinks it's too hard on the front or too soft, at the top of the suspension stroke or at the bottom, and so on. It's good for him too, to have a team manager that is also a racer and who understands and won't doubt him. It's really important not to be afraid of saying what you think, because what you feel is always right; you've just got to be able to explain it.

I left PBM at the end of 2006. Paul and I didn't fall out, but he didn't think I was doing a good enough job, and I didn't think he was doing a good enough job. Looking back on it, it's a difficult one to say who was right and who was wrong, but the results weren't there, and Birdy doesn't stand for that.

PBM were looking at Johnny Rea for the 2007 season, so they took my bike to a race in Kirkistown in Northern Ireland for him to try. It was just an end-of-year exhibition race, and I had pretty much finished my contract with Paul Bird, other than racing in Macau later that year, so they gave my bike to Johnny to try as nothing more than a test. The little shit completely destroyed it, which I didn't know about until I turned up in Macau – and there it was, with the wide yokes and forks back in it again.

Steve Plater won the Macau GP that year and I finished 2nd. To be fair, I'm not sure that I would have beaten him, even if I had the proper yokes, forks and wheel in the bike, Steve was like a man possessed that year at Macau. If you wanted to beat Steve round Macau that year, you needed to be a very brave man. My bike was OK, but it wasn't anywhere near as good as it was with the narrow yokes.

I had seen Steve on the Yamaha during practice and thought he was going to be hard to beat, and of course he was on the orange juice all week and really behaving while we were all getting pissed. In the race, I had two tear-offs – thin sheets of clear plastic that are fixed to your visor with tape and a pair of small posts. There is a tab on their end so that when you're on a straight you can pull the tab and the whole tear-off comes off in your hand, and with it all the dead flies, meaning a clear view of things.

I had used both of my tear-offs by the second lap to clear my visor, not from the flies but from bits of paint from the walls. The barriers and walls in the twisty section were painted yellow, and I was sitting right behind Steve, who was leading. He was brushing the walls and barriers hard enough for bits of the yellow paint to come off, and it was all sticking to my visor. I'm sitting there, thinking that I'd never seen that before in all my years at Macau. Then through Mandarin Corner, which is a 4th gear corner, probably about 130–140mph, he hit his helmet on the wall on the inside. I thought, 'Mate, if you want it that bad, you can have it'.

He pulled a bit of a gap on me, and then I thought, you know what, I'll have another go, and I got back up to him. Then he came up to this backmarker and passed him really hard with his back wheel right up in the air while he was braking. He was 100% committed. I don't know how he stopped on, but he ended up gapping me on the last lap.

I think he would have been hard to beat either way. I'm pretty sure that if I had passed him then he would have just let the brakes off anyway. Steve is usually a fairly level-headed guy, and I don't know what came over him that year at Macau, but he wasn't afraid of putting himself in the barrier that day. Years later, he showed us pictures of that helmet with those marks on it.

I've hit the barrier in Macau once in the twisty section. Unlike Steve, who was doing it deliberately, lap after lap, it was totally my fault. It was a few years later and I was trying to catch Stuart Easton when he was on the Kawasaki and set the lap record that still stands today. Basically I tried too hard, and it bit me. I actually hit it with the back of my leathers, next to the hump between my shoulders. As I lean off

161

the bike I tend to twist my body in such a way that on this occasion the bit behind my shoulder made contact with the wall. I shat myself and let him go after that.

That was the end of the Paul Bird contract. I'd gone from thirteen podiums in BSB, a win at the North West 200 and a win at Macau in 2005, to nothing at all in 2006.

I was glad to see the back of the 2006 season, but I must say that now that we've both got a bit older Paul and I get on OK these days, and he is still running one of the best and most successful teams in the paddock.

14

PR, Money and Fame

There's no getting away from the fact that being a bike racer has some real perks, especially when you're at the sharp end of things. I've been lucky to travel the world, meet all kinds of people and earn a lot of money. The downside, for me at least, is that the people writing the cheques for that lifestyle want more than just for me to ride round in circles as fast as I possibly can. More often than not, they want me to do public appearances with fans, and PR stuff for them or their sponsors.

The problem is that I really don't like being the centre of attention, but if I know it will help people then I'll do it. Like local bike shops – one asked me to switch on the Christmas tree lights, and I did it for them. It was so difficult for me, but I know it would have really helped them out. I've been asked to do after-dinner speaking, and I'll always come up with an excuse not to. (To be fair, a lot of the times I am away anyway, but I'm always glad that I have a legitimate excuse.) I hate letting people down, but I really don't want to stand up in front of people and waffle. I don't mind so much if someone is asking the questions; I can get away with that.

I remember when Honda asked me to go on the TV quiz show *Question of Sport*, and that is my idea of hell. Honda was insisting that I had to do it, but I said no. They couldn't get their heads round the idea that I didn't want to go on prime-time TV. They kept saying it would be brilliant, but I repeated that there was no way on earth that I was going to do it. I know nothing about sport; all I know about is bike racing, in particular myself. I don't even know much about other bike racers. In fact, come to think of it, I don't really know much about my own career. Doing this book has made me realise that. Anything to do with football, golf, cricket, I know literally nothing. I told Honda that all that would happen is that I would embarrass them. Luckily they accepted this, and I didn't have to do it.

I'd take part in *Come Dine with Me*; I don't mind a bit of cooking or wine, so I reckon I'd be happy enough doing that. I'd also do *I'm a Celebrity ... Get Me Out of Here!* – in fact, I'd love to do that. I don't think I'd get bored. The challenge of not getting bored would fascinate me. I was watching it with my partner Faye recently (I know how to show a girl a good time), and I said to her that if I was in the jungle, I'd be causing so much shit just to try and not get bored. I would be nicking stuff in the night, then chuckling to myself and watching everyone else get confused the next day. I reckon I would be chucked out straight away. I'd nick food, swap knickers and generally cause mayhem. The contestants all get on too well now; it needs some devious bugger to mix things up. It's bollocks when they say they're going in to test themselves; they're all going in to win because the longer they stay in, the more they get paid. I heard that Carl Fogarty got paid really well to go in and landed a massive bonus because he won it.

Then there are the women. One of the things about racing is that you don't know if someone likes you for *who* you are or *what* you are, and that's something that I'm always wary of. Even though I met Faye through racing, she comes from a different world with a really big social scene. Like me, she wonders just how genuine the people she meets are. I think the fact that we feel the same way about people that we meet, and that we come from different worlds, means that it works well.

I remember going out with one girl, and I thought that I'd just be me, so I'd told her that I was a mechanic, which is sort of true. We went to this bar for our fourth date, and we were sat down having a drink when this bloke at the bar started looking at me. My date spotted the bloke looking at me and obviously had no clue why. I knew exactly why he was looking at me and just hoped he'd stay put. Eventually he came over and asked me for an autograph, which made my date start laughing. She asked the bloke why he wanted my autograph, and he said to me, 'Doesn't she know what you do?' So I said, 'Yeah, I'm a mechanic', which made him laugh. Then she chips in and said to the bloke, 'No, he really is a mechanic', which made his mate get his phone out and pull up a picture of me. After that, I had to tell her what I really did, and that I didn't generally like to talk about it. She was alright about it, but then she went back and told all her friends, and I thought, oh god, here we go. She was really nice, but it didn't work out between us.

I used to go out with Mick Boddice's daughter, Sue. Mick was a really successful sidecar racer at the TT and we were good mates, so his daughter was from a racing background like me. We were only young then, and I did lots of things wrong by her by being in the racing world and all the opportunity and temptation that seems to come the way of bike racers.

I think 100% that girls looked at me then because I was a bike racer – let's be honest, I'm no oil painting. I'd never get a job as a model, except maybe for shoes. I think racers give off a different vibe. I think the girls who go for racers generally like the danger, but I don't think they respect what we do; they just think you're mad. They must feel something you give off but it's hard to put your finger on what that thing is.

They like success too. It's all down to your results. If you're doing well, it's amazing how many people like you, not just women. One year everything is working for you and you're doing really well, and everyone is your friend ... then suddenly you're 10th and the same people just give a quick 'hello' and they're gone. I learned that quickly and it never upset me, because I had seen it happen to Dad. He was so popular with the crowds, spectators, fans, sponsors, and riders, then when he came back after being away for a year or so following his accident, no one spoke to him; he'd been forgotten. At the time it really upset me, but now I've been in it, I understand it.

I'll sometimes realise that someone's gone from the paddock, and I'll ask where they are, only to be told they retired or something for over a year ago, and I'll be shocked. As a racer, my life is so focused on what I'm doing that I don't register anything else that's going on outside of that.

You're in a bubble at races, and the older I've got, the more I just concentrate on my own thing. There could be World War Three going on outside the paddock, but I'm just constantly thinking about what needs to be done, and what's next in the schedule. I don't think about anything else. Everyone could clear off and I wouldn't notice, but I have to say that the people who I've meet in racing are really interesting – the fans, the people working in the paddock, and the celebrities. I've met people from all walks of life.

I met Bob Geldof years ago, at Brands Hatch. He was a really nice bloke. He came into the garage and hung around for a bit and was genuinely interested in the bikes, and the whole scene. He seemed to be quite excited to be there with the team and was really enjoying himself. I tell you what though: the attention us bike racers get is nothing in comparison to someone like him. It was constant for him: he literally couldn't move once he left the garage, which is probably why he hung around so much. You know, I remember so clearly seeing him doing the whole Band Aid/Live Aid thing when I was a kid. He was massive, and years later he's there in my garage, just talking to me like normal, which when all is said and done everyone is, of course.

I raced Simon Le Bon's Kawasaki ZXR400 for a few rounds, because he was a friend of Ray Stringer's. It was when I was riding the yellow McCullough Ducati 888. He came to a few meetings with his wife Yasmin; she was stunning. *Motorcycle News* wanted a picture of Simon, Yasmin and me, and Yasmin agreed, but you could see she wasn't happy about doing it. So they had us standing there, me with a jacket that is too big for me, and Yasmin is looking perfect – talk about beauty and the beast! I remember the snapper pushing his luck and trying to get her to pose, and she very quickly just said, 'No, just take the picture now, or not at all, that's it'. She was a really nice girl, really down-to-earth. I really liked her.

The Prodigy's frontman Keith Flint was another really down-to-earth person. He sponsored a team in the paddock and was around a lot, so I used to speak to him a fair bit. One day we got talking about concerts and music, so I told him a story about the only concert I'd ever been to, which was when I was at Renegade Ducati. Basically, the story went that the team owner Mark Griffiths bought all our team wear from the best places so we would look the same and really smart in the paddock. We looked the bollocks – everything matched from top to toe, and I still remember the jeans were Prada.

When we were racing at Oulton Park that year, Mark announced that he had a special treat for us all, to go and see Kylie Minogue in Manchester. The only condition was that everyone had to wear team gear except him on this night out, so you can imagine we were devastated because it was properly loud gear. We went into the concert and sat down like a bunch of matching idiots; I was so embarrassed. Afterwards, we went to a restaurant, and because Mark was a right show-off he sent a bottle of champagne to some girls on another table, and of course they came over and started asking what we did. I told them that we were a professional bowling team, which they thought was amazing. A little part of me died that night.

Keith looked at me in disgust as I finished the story and said he'd take me to a proper gig, so he took me to a Prodigy show in Bilbao. I was backstage, and it just blew my mind; it was unbelievable. I was shocked at how someone could change from being such a kind, gentle person backstage to a complete maniac the moment he set foot on the stage. He changed into a monster. It's hard to find the words to describe just how incredible he was.

He sorted everything for me – hotels, the lot. I went with him in his chauffeur-driven black car through all the crowds outside the venue. Inside the venue I couldn't see where the crowd ended; it was surreal.

When I heard the news that Keith had taken his own life, it stopped me in my tracks. It just didn't make any sense at all, and it still doesn't. Maybe there's something that changes in a person when they get to perform in front of hundreds of thousands of people, with every single one of them hanging on your every word and movement, and then have to go back to being 'normal'. Who knows? Obviously, he will be really missed by the music scene, but he was also a big part of our paddock, and he put a lot of time and money into it.

My dad knew Barry Sheene quite well, and he'd been round to our house a few times, so I only ever saw him when I was a kid and never really had much to do with him. He was at the North West 200 the year before he died, and he came up to me and said, 'Alright, Michael? How you doing?' I was struck by how the hell Barry Sheene knew me. He was asking me how Dad was, and we talked about him for a bit. Then he asked how my mum was too, by her name, Pauline. It must have been thirty years or more since he'd been at the house and I couldn't believe he'd not only remembered me, but also my mum's name. I got speaking to him and he was such a nice person. He must have been sick at that point and maybe didn't know it, but I could see how he got so far in life. He knew just how to make people feel good.

The Goodwood Festival of Speed is something I quite like going to. It's really relaxed and there are loads of really trick bikes and cars there to look at. Around about the time that he was just making it in Formula 1, Lewis Hamilton was there and was getting a lot of attention. I went on my own to ride some bikes up the hill and do some wheelies. When you get to the top, there is this holding area where everyone waits until the last car or bike gets to the top, then everyone goes back down. So we all pull up at the top and are hanging around, chatting and checking out the bikes and cars, and Lewis was there in his race car, doing some runs up the hill too. His car looked the nuts.

Anyway, I'd got an invitation to go to a dinner that night at Lord March's place, which is really exclusive. He's the main man there and organises the whole event, so getting an invite to the dinner is quite a scoop – there are probably only about twenty people who are invited each year. He's a real petrolhead, so he's not just all about the big-money cars and Formula 1.

I was at a table with his daughter Nimmy, and there's this bloke sitting next to me and – bear in mind that I know absolutely nothing about Formula 1 – I got introduced to him as Lewis Hamilton. He was a really good laugh, on the piss, telling jokes and funny stories, and generally good company, so eventually I said to him that it was nice to see a car driver not being a boring twat. I said, 'You lot are all so serious and up your arses and training all the time', and he looked at me a bit weird, at which point Nimmy said, 'That's not Lewis, that's his dad'. He had been introduced to me as Lewis Hamilton's dad, but all I'd heard was Lewis Hamilton. He was a really nice guy, and he told me how Lewis was really into his bikes and had followed me for years, which I'm not sure about; I think he was just being polite.

Making small talk with people is one thing I've never been good at. John McGuinness will stand there and talk to anyone for hour after hour about anything (as long as it's about himself). I don't know how he does it, and it's no disrespect to anyone, but the last thing I want to do is talk about motorbikes, or me. I like talking about normal things, nothing to do with racing. I've always found talking to strangers difficult, and I've always found myself shy when doing it. I question why anyone wants to talk to me – I'm not interesting, I don't feel special, I'm afraid people might think I'm boring. Then you get people like Steve Plater – he's brilliant and he sells himself every time he goes out.

I can't stand the pit lane walkabout on a race day; I'll do anything to get out of it, and I'll make up any story to avoid it. From the very first time someone asked me for an autograph, I've never liked doing them. I'm happy to do it if someone walks up to me and asks for one but standing there behind a table is torture for me. It really does feel like an hour out of my life that I'll never get back; it's hell for me. I just don't like being the centre of attention. Don't get me wrong: I'm very honoured to be someone that people want a picture with or autograph from, and I do think that it is a privilege. I don't stand there thinking, 'You knobs'; I do genuinely feel humbled. I'm very lucky and I know there are lots of people that want that attention and go out of their way to get it, but I'm not one of them.

I think it's also partly to do with being dyslexic. The prospect of someone asking me to write a message fills me with dread. At this point, you'd expect me to go on about how I really hated school because I couldn't really read or write, but actually I used to love going to school because I would cause chaos and wind everyone up. I used to be the thickest one at maths, for sure. I remember asking teachers if I could go to races with my dad, and they'd just say, 'Please, just go'. They were always happy for me not to be there. I never went back for my GCSE results; to this day I haven't got a clue what I got. I even missed some of the exams because I went to the TT with Dad, and even the school said that given my inevitable choice of career it wasn't worth me going in to take the exams anyway.

Give me something to do with my hands, no problem; but if I have to write my address, or someone else's name, I really struggle. Reading is really difficult too. I wasn't interested in getting it looked at because I really didn't see the benefit at the time, and the thing is, I need a reason to do something. If I don't see a benefit, I really struggle to stay focused on anything. My attention span is really short, so for example these days if I'm in a debrief with my crew chief Alec Tague, he really likes to take time over it and go through all the details as it's how his brain works, and it does my head in. Eventually I'll just tell him what to do, because I can't cope with how long he takes. I think it might be my dyslexia.

I've done some really cool PR things for employers and sponsors over the years, and I've done some really daft things that I wish I hadn't. When I was at HRC in 2004–2005, I was getting paid really well. Overall, between my salary and sponsors, I was making six figures, which is the sort of money that probably only the very top riders in BSB are getting now. At HRC I was only allowed a limited number of sponsors on my leathers. I had so many sponsors in those days that I was just making prices up to go on my helmet or one of the few spots I had available on my leathers. I was saying £5,000 for a sticker on my helmet, and they'd offer £2,500; I couldn't believe that they'd pay it. It was so easy up to 2006ish when I was doing well; I really couldn't go wrong.

Now it's nearly impossible. All the sponsors want their patches in the right place, right size, right colour – no one sees just how much goes into it. It takes months of work to get it right, and I usually start in November or December for the following season, which starts in March. You have got to make a living out of the sponsors, so I get my Shoei helmets and Alpinestars leathers, then earn my living by selling the space on them. Shoei have been good to me over the years, and I've had some amazing leather race suits from Kushitani, Dainese, Alpinestars, Furygan – and BKS were good at the time.

I've also worn some shit as well, and the *Simpsons* cartoon helmet is a good example. It was 2001, and I had a deal with FM Helmets. The manager, Dave Pinder, was a great guy, and I had some really good years with him and his helmets. I got paid crazy amounts of money just for wearing the *Simpsons* number – £20,000, to be exact, plus £5 per point, and £5 per helmet sold on royalties. It was such easy money and, as is always the way when you're on the crest of a wave, you really do think it will last forever. The *Simpsons* helmet happened around the turning point, when it was just starting to get harder to make money, so I would do more for it.

Dave said he wanted me to wear a special design for FM, but I was really keen on my dad's design because it stands out, and because it's me. Dave said that I couldn't have it if I wanted the money, so I caved in and agreed, but I didn't know what the special design was. Dave came to my house for a big reveal of the design, and he was so excited and happy. He stood on my doorstep, pulled the helmet out from behind his back, and he asked what I thought. I was actually speechless. So I said, 'Yeah, great, you'd better come in'.

So we stood in my kitchen and he put the helmet down on the work surface, and I thought, I hate it, and I've got to ride around all year with that on my head. It must have cost a fortune to get the rights to use the *Simpsons* images, and they paid me really well, so I wore it, but I couldn't wait to get it off. It just wasn't me at all.

FM were the biggest payers, and unsurprisingly the Scottish were all wearing them. I remember Simmo's helmet wouldn't fit him right, and he was getting really stressed out, thinking he had to make it fit so that he could get paid. I would see him squeezing it on, and it obviously didn't fit him, but that's how it was in those days; you just couldn't refuse money.

Another stupid thing I did for publicity was when *Motorcycle News* wanted me to do a photo, naked with my RC45. Back then, before the internet had really taken over printed media, *Motorcycle News* was massive, so it was a big deal to be featured in it. When I got to the location, they said pants off and everything, and I said no way. They said, 'It's OK, you're going to hold your crash helmet over your cock and balls' and I said, 'Not a fucking chance'. So they said, 'OK what we'll do is Photoshop your pants out', so I did the shoot and put it out of my mind. Then when it came out a few weeks later, the picture was a bloody double page; it was massive. It is by far one of the most embarrassing things I've ever done. So many people took the piss out of my five bellies.

The amount of time and money the big sponsors put into PR can be off the scale. In 2003, when I was at Red Bull Ducati, they closed the city centre in Manchester so that Sean Emmett, Leon Haslam and I could do some wheelies to cameras and a crowd. Everything was going just fine – Red Bull were over the moon, the crowd were loving it –and then Leon decided he wanted a go on one of our Superbikes.

At the time, he was our junior rider, competing in the Supersport class on a bike based on the smaller capacity 748 Ducati, so I think he was itching to try one of the Superbikes, and off he went. He popped a wheelie, but he didn't realise that the Superbike only had a thumb-operated rear brake. You use the rear brake to control the wheelie, and usually it is operated by the right foot, so he'd gone for the rear brake and there wasn't even a lever there. He flipped the bike right there in the middle of the street, in front of all the people from Red Bull, the team, the council, fans, everyone. To make it worse, the bike slid up a kerb and smashed into the bus shelter. The bike and bus shelter were destroyed.

At the other end of the scale, when Honda said to me that they had booked London City Airport and there was going to be a race between me, a Formula 1 car and a speedboat, I thought, ahh great, another weekend job of signing stuff and standing around. So I was moaning like hell about it and not that interested in it, but if Honda say you have to do it, you have to do it. Then I realised it was a TV programme that was getting filmed, so I thought it might be better than I thought initially.

They told me it was Jenson Button in the car and Steve Curtis (a legend in the speedboat world) in the boat, and that they wanted me to go and meet Jenson at Silverstone. I didn't really know much about the bloke or have an opinion on him, but I certainly had one after I met him for the first time. When I walked into the Honda F1 garage with all the film crew, he was walking towards us, and the fella from Honda stopped him to introduce us, and Jenson was really rude to the press guy from Honda, who was just doing his job. The press guy carried on, and said, 'This is Michael Rutter', and I held my hand out to him. He didn't shake it; he just looked me up and down, looking a bit confused. The Honda bloke explained that I was the other fella doing the London City Airport race with him, and Jenson just said, 'Oh my god, not that. Well, that'll be easy. We'll win that'. So I said, 'We'll see'. He was proper snobbish, rude and an all-round prick. He really got my back up.

So when the day came, I went to London City Airport, and the Honda F1 team were there, with dozens of people, and there was me and a couple of mechanics called Les Pearson and Chris Anderson, who all turned up in a white van, pulled the bike out, and were good to go. Once the boat people had arrived too, we all had a meeting to go over the plan. Honda said, 'Right, this is costing a fortune, so we're not going to mess about. We're going to do one race, and that's it. So there's not going to be any coming back with excuses and stuff, and wanting a rematch'. I was OK with that; it was just a bit of fun PR for Honda and a TV programme called *Fifth Gear*, so no big deal ... but I really did want to beat Jenson.

We couldn't start until 11 am, so they took us all into the airport lounge to sit down and have a coffee. Jenson had a private room all to himself with everything you could imagine. He was getting treated like royalty: he had waiters and all sorts, while the rest of us were rammed in a room like second-class citizens. That pissed me off even more. I'm sure if I was in his shoes I'd have said, 'Why doesn't every-one come in here – it's loads better in here'. I disliked him even more and was really determined to beat him, but I honestly didn't know how it was going to be.

I rode down to the runway, and I'd never been on a runway before, so I discovered that it's not smooth and in fact it's got deep cuts in the surface that run at right angles to the direction of travel, for maximum grip for the landing aeroplanes. It was a flag start, and I was next to the F1 car, while the boat would go alongside us in the Thames. When the boat crossed the line at full speed, we'd go. I was sat on the bike and I couldn't hear anything because the F1 car was revving its head off right next to me. Then the programme's presenter, Tiff Needell, dropped the flag to start the race, and I tried to launch the bike. It barely moved off the line and just did a massive wheelie more or less on the spot. I just about kept the front wheel down, but I did have to roll the throttle off loads before I could properly get going. I just got my head down and threw gears at it, and I bloody won! I turned around and the F1 car came flying past me way after I crossed the line.

I rode back up to the start line, doing some wheelies for the cameras, and Jenson was going mad, shouting and screaming that he wanted a re-run. I started straight back at him and said that there'd be no re-run, that he lost, and those were the rules. The F1 lot started coming out with all this stuff about the F1 car on the grippy surface needing less traction control.

Basically, there was so much grip on the surface that it screwed up the car's electronics, so his car took ages to get going. Poor old Jenson kept whining like a baby, saying that it wasn't fair, so I started winding him up saying that I won fair and square as per the rules, and that I was refusing to do another race. Eventually he got his own way, and Honda said I had to do it again, so off we went again.

For the second race I got off the line perfectly, and went into the lead, and thought I've done it again, then the F1 car came past me like I was going backwards. My bike was wheelying so I was losing some speed, but I think the aerodynamics of an F1 car make a massive difference once it gets moving. He annihilated me. In the end, they had him down as winning it, but he didn't; I did, based on the original rules.

John McGuinness told me another story about Jenson Button. Honda wanted John back for an awards thing, and Jenson was flying into Heathrow on the same plane as John. Obviously, Jenson was in first class, and John was in economy. When they got off the plane, someone escorted them through arrivals together, and – bear in mind that they were going to the same do, in the same place – a car pulled up outside the airport for Jenson, and it had got his suit hanging up inside it ready, and he gets in the car, shuts the door and drives off. John had to get a taxi.

It shows just how worlds-apart car and bike racing are, although to be fair that sort of detail was probably in Jenson's terms rather than Honda showing favouritism. If I was Jenson, I'd have gone, 'Do you want a lift?', but John reckons Jenson never said a word. Out of all the famous people I've met, he's definitely the worst.

15

2008: North West 200 Ducati

2008 was a really good year for me. Nick carried on with the Kawasakis, and I got a few offers from other teams. One of them was from a fella called Alistair Kennedy, a businessman from Ireland who used to sponsor me with a hotel during the North West 200, and we'd got to know each other and got on well.

Alistair really wanted to run a race team and decided that he would go into it like Mark Griffiths did with Renegade Racing: in a big way. Alistair bought everything needed to run a single-bike team for a whole season. He chose to brand the bike as 'NW200', simply because he loved the place and the race, and his wife Adele is really into bike racing too. He was already one of the event sponsors, so having 'Alistair Kennedy' written on the side of the bike as well made no sense to him, and because he was good mates with the promoters, he chose to use the team to promote the event for them.

The Ducati 1098 had just come out, and Alistair bought me a pair of the 'F08' spec ones. The 'F' spec Ducatis are full-blown factory-built, race-spec versions of the road bike that they are based on. As well as being made with the best components and materials, the engines are tuned and ready to race. They don't come with any road gear, like headlights and so on.

The 1098 replaced the outgoing 999, and it took advantage of a new rule that allowed TWIN-CYLINDER engines to be up to 1200cc, so the F08 race bike had an 1198cc engine and was THE bike to have. I didn't really care about the rule changes, because oh my god, they were just beautiful when they turned up, and they were both just for me.

I was really looking forward to the season for lots of reasons, not least because of the North West 200 branding on the bike and being able to support an event that has been so good to me and Dad over the years. It's a race that's been a big part of my life for as long as I can remember. I never got to go to the North West 200 with Dad because I was still at school when the race took place. I think the teachers were more than happy to let me out of school for a few weeks for the TT to give them a break, but a couple of weeks in May too was probably a bit much.

It's a brilliant race meeting, set in a spectacular location. The track is an 8.97-mile triangular lap in Northern Ireland that links Portstewart, Coleraine and Portrush. In a car on a normal day it might take fifteen minutes to get round, but on closed roads on a race bike it takes just over four minutes. There are a few really long straights that even with the addition of chicanes in recent years still see the superbikes reach speeds well over 200mph.

I was the first person to break the 200mph barrier in 2004 on my HRC Honda Fireblade. I found out later that not only was I the first person to break 200mph there, but I was also the first person to break 200mph on a superbike, anywhere in the world. Honda had also done it with their Grand Prix bike in 1993 at Hockenheim in Germany, which was a properly quick track. It was a really big moment in bike racing that everyone was talking about. It just didn't seem possible then that a

eve Hislop rescuing me from the angry fans at Knock-ll after I knocked him off on the last lap.

Shane "Shakey" Byrne. Never a dull moment.

The crowds at BSB in 2002 were brilliant.

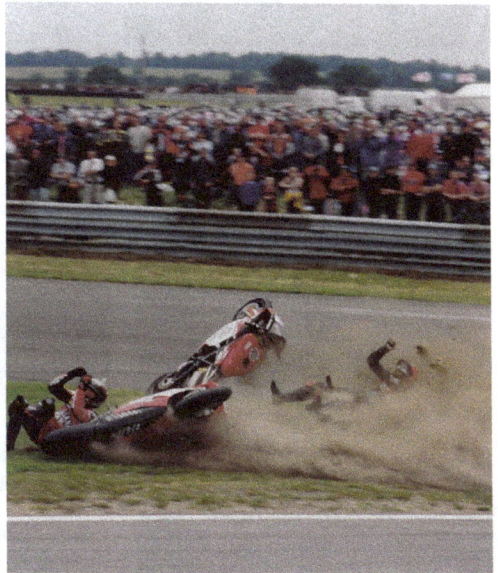
The moment that probably cost me the title in 2002, and a sore neck even today. Thanks, Shakey.

Sean Emmett. Maddest teammate of them all.

Tady Okada.

The HRC culture in the garage. All business.

The win that I simply had to get. The pressure was immense. This is relief more than joy.

Winner's trophy after my first race with HRC, and first win for the new Fireblade anywhere in the world.

Two hand-built factory HRC Fireblades with my race number on. The peak of my career.

ove the fact that people want an autograph from me, but I really don't like being the centre of attention.

Johnny Rea when he was my teammate. Luckily he didn't take any advice from me.

on't care what the TV programme broadcast. I won that race fair d square.

205 IN 2005

After I became the first person to go over 200mph on a superbike in 2004, there was some hype that I might manage 205mph the following year.

Kiyo was another seriously quick teammate.

My TT comeback in 2007.

2009 TT press launch. I'm still wearing my Yamaha leathers. I quit the team a few weeks later, and entered privately on a Bathams sponsored Suzuki.

The first deal I did with Bathams for the 2009 TT, I painted the bike yellow, the same colour as their delivery van.

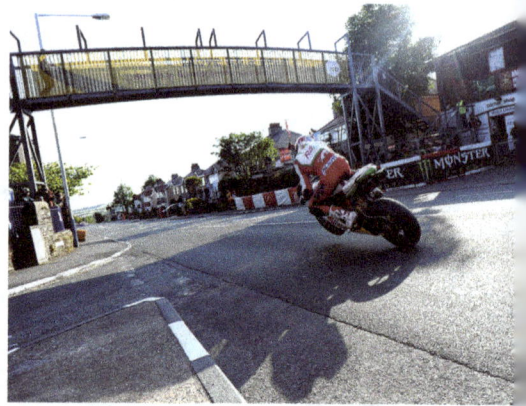

At the top of Bray Hill on a Ducati in 2011 that didn't really want to be there. Still the fastest ever lap by a Ducati at the TT.

Win number 7 at Macau.

John McGuinness has a corner named after him at the TT. I've got a whole street named after me at Macau, or at least that's what I like to think.

y 8th win at Macau in 2012 was delayed so much
at the streetlights were on by the end of the race.

Macau GP in one picture.

Me and John McGuinness at the Suzuka 8 Hours race for
Honda TT Legends in 2013. He had only just started
talking to me again after I beat him in the TT Zero by 1.7
seconds.

nda TT Legends team launch in 2013. An appropriate
me for the team, given the teammates I had.

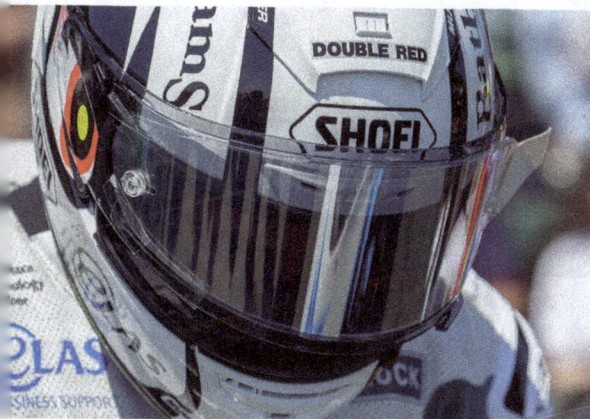

Riding for Mugen means I had to drop my
usual red/white helmet design, which was
Dad's design. His mechanic, called Roy
Johnson, came up with it as way to help
Dad to stand out. There's no other meaning
or significance to the red/white colour
combination.

Winning my second piston-powered TT after 19 years. I took a little bit of extra time to take in the view from the top of the podium.

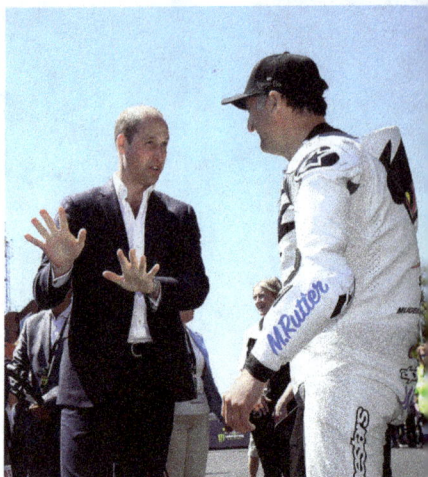

Meeting Prince William before the start of the 2018 TT Zero race. I accidentally swore at him twice.

There really isn't anywhere else like the TT.

A £10,000 cheque in one hand, and a distraught John McGuiness in the other. It doesn't get much better.

Winning is still winning. It feels good whether it's electric or petrol power.

One of the closest misses I've had at the TT was when the carbon fibre seat unit on my Mugen broke. It's one of the risks of racing a prototype bike.

Just coz.

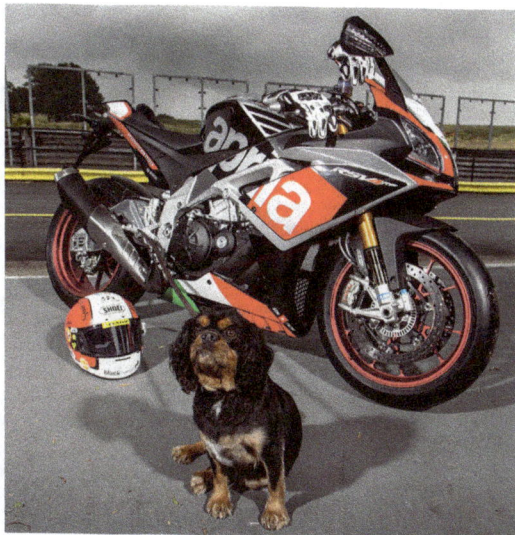

Desmo, my dog. He went everywhere with me.

Testing road bikes for *Performance Bikes* magazine.

Fulfilling a lifelong ambition. I did just about manage to keep my breakfast down!

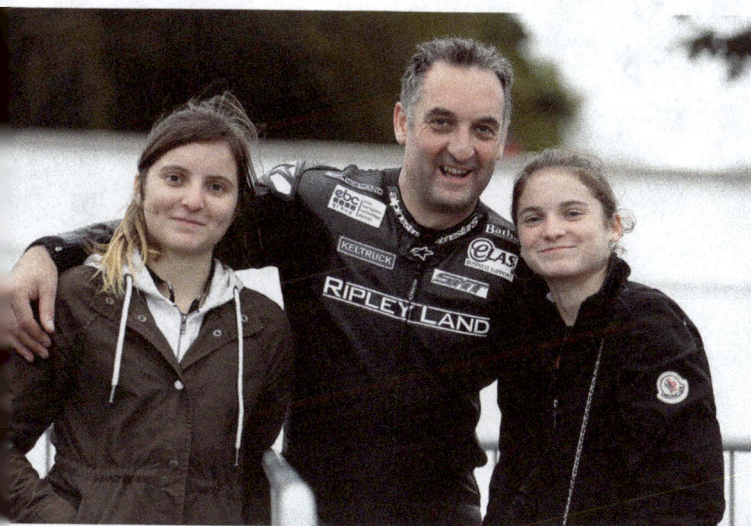

Juliette & Cecilia have been part of the race paddock since they were born, just like me.

What can you say? Flat out at the TT on a MotoGP bike.

race bike could top 200mph, and then, 11 years later, I'd done it on a modified road bike, on a road course.

I can still picture it vividly, and according to the bike's datalogger I actually went quicker in practice, but they didn't have anyone operating the speed trap in practice, so it didn't count. It was an evening practice, so it was probably about 8 pm and the conditions were absolutely perfect. I was on my own, going towards Station Corner, and my Fireblade had some trick Michelin tyres, which were really grippy in a straight line. That might seem like an odd thing to say, but tyres today don't have to last because they are designed to cope with spinning all the time, which means they'll actually spin in a straight line, which costs you outright drive. Back then, the tyres had to last, so they dug in harder and got more power down to the road.

I was going down that straight and it was just dusk. The air must have been perfect – you know, the temperature, moisture, wind, density, everything, it was like a supersonic boom. It was so weird; all the lines on the road joined up and the bike was revving flat out in top gear, I thought it must have been easily doing over 200mph. The datalogger actually said 210mph on the wheel speed sensors, which confirmed what I already knew at the time – that it was easily the fastest I'd ever gone in my life.

Something changes with aerodynamics at that speed; it's so hard to push it through that 200mph. Everything felt light; it just wasn't normal; the pressure difference was massive. I was being sucked down onto the tank. I couldn't believe it. I was watching the rev counter, buried right into the red, thinking, wow, this is bloody quick, in top gear, and I just stayed tucked right under the screen for as long as I dared. At the end of the straight, I lifted my body before I braked, and my torso was like a big sail as the windblast nearly sucked me off the bike, and I remember getting a big shock at just how strong the force was. I learned pretty quickly that if I'm braking from very high speed, I need to shut the throttle and start braking a split second before sitting up, instead of doing all three at the same time as usual.

The aerodynamic pressure on the front of the bike at that sort of speed is so great that just shutting the throttle is like hitting the brakes.

It was like nothing I'd ever felt before. I knew it was special. I got a massive hit of adrenaline when I got back to the pits. I just kept saying over and over, 'That was unbelievable'. I was lost for words. Then, in the race, when it happened officially, I knew I must have managed it because the crowd all the way round the circuit were waving their programmes at me, which I figured meant that the circuit commentator must have told everyone that I'd done 200mph. The road-racing fans will wave their programmes to the race leader on the last lap as a mark of respect, but I'd never seen as many programmes waved at me as I did on that lap. It really was the most incredible feeling. A really special day, that was.

No one can ever take those sorts of milestones or race wins away. Just after I win a race I think, right that's done, that's out of the way, and move on to the next thing. But as I get older, those sorts of achievements start to mean something more. The 200mph thing was great on the night because it was a big talking point, but then the next day, for me, it was gone. Now when I look back it's amazing what I have managed to do, a bit like growing up with Dad winning the North West 200 nine times.

At the time, his achievements didn't really register with me. I didn't really become aware of my dad's status and achievements until I went to the NW200 with him, and I was blown away. He was like a god; everyone knew him. I'd say 90% of the people who followed Dad then followed me after, so I had a fan base in Ireland from the word go. He was the main man at the race for years, but that counted for absolutely nothing when I raced there for the first time in 1992.

I thought, 'What the hell am I doing?' and I didn't sleep well for about a week before because I didn't know what to expect. I'd never been in a road race before, and I felt a lot of pressure because Dad had done so well there and was held in such high regard. I just didn't know what to expect. It was weird.

Dad and I went in the van with my Honda RS250 and stayed at the York Inn. Dad always stopped there as it was run by the same people who used to own the Sea Splash Hotel, where he used to stay when he raced there. The owners moved to the York Inn at some point, so Dad moved with them. They sponsored me by giving us a room for our stay, and I was treated like royalty, which was great. I was Tony Rutter's son, so I was automatically a god in some people's eyes. I'd already worked out by then that Dad was a big deal, but it was my first time going to Northern Ireland with him, to see it first-hand.

We were in the same hotel as the Honda team, so Steve Hislop and Phil McCallen were there with all the Honda mechanics. If I hadn't already felt the pressure of being Tony Rutter's son, I would have then, as I also knew there were people staying at the same hotel as us who would be keeping an eye on how I got on, just because of the name.

There was a bar/restaurant area under the rooms, and I'd always heard that the Irish liked a drink, but I never believed it until I saw it there with my own eyes. They were there night and day. When I got up really early for practice the same locals were still in the exact same spot that I'd seen them in the night before, and still drinking. The locals are the nicest people you could ever possibly meet and are so generous and welcoming. I've always been made to feel at home there. They love their road racing and are really up on the history of the sport, so anyone who has anything to do with it is treated like family.

My first time on a closed road on a race bike was an evening practice, and so I had all day to think about it. Phil McCallen took all the newcomers out on a bus tour and did a sort of track guide. I couldn't understand a word he was saying, so none of it went in. Eventually, the time came, so I just went out onto the course and tried to remember which way it went. The speed and whole sensation of riding so fast on a public road that's been closed was a massive shock to me, but I enjoyed it so much, which is why I've kept going back. It was so different to anything I had experienced up to that point.

It was so fast, and the walls and everyday stuff on the roadside was so close that the overwhelming feeling I had was being absolutely scared shitless of dying. I wasn't the slightest bit bothered by the fact that I didn't know which way the track went. I was just thinking that it was properly dangerous, but I carried on and stayed out on the bike because I knew that was the only way to learn the track, but I couldn't stop thinking I could die doing it.

I knew already that I could die doing it because I'd heard of so many people who died doing it while I was growing up. Then the racer inside came out of me, and when I came into the pits to look at the lap times, my first thought was that I was going too slow. In an instant I went from thinking I could die to wanting to go quicker, and that is the exact moment when I became a road racer. Then you start racing with people, and that's it: death goes to the back of your mind.

The main reason why I go back now is because the North West 200 is so special, so unique and so fast. I'm lucky enough to have raced on the old circuit layout that was even faster than the current one. Now there are three chicanes to slow you down, where before there wasn't anything. It was unbelievable coming down towards Metropole: I would have been flat out for two miles, sometimes three or four abreast, and slipstreaming at 190mph+. It was amazing.

It makes the hairs on the back of my neck stand up when I think about how fast today's bikes would be if they still ran the race on the old layout. Even though they now have the chicanes, you still get well over 200mph. The chicanes also split the groups up into smaller ones now, so you don't get as much of the big groups, all just inches apart, hammering along at 200mph.

That closeness on the straights to get a slipstream can sometimes get a bit too close. During a 600cc race back when Guy Martin was starting to come up and earn a name for himself, he came past me into one of the really fast corners at Mather's Cross when I was just tipping into it. He came up the inside of me into a space that just wasn't there and rammed into me when we were both flat out in top gear. I know what it's like: you pick up a slipstream from someone, and build up a bit of momentum until you come up to the back of their bike and all you want to do is not waste that momentum and just pass the bike in front of you. Basically, he misjudged his closing speed on me and the gap between me and the grass on the inside of the corner.

On the next straight, I picked up his slipstream and pulled alongside him, and I just kicked his bike on the fairing because I was so angry at what he did. The race got red-flagged for someone crashing, so we pulled up on the grid to wait for the restart and, fair play to him, he came straight over to me, apologised and said he was out of order. Obviously, I wasn't going to let him off the hook – I was still pissed off about it – so I said to him, 'Yeah you were'. But fair play to him, he came up and faced up to it. He knew that he could have killed us both.

Guy really should have won a TT. In a lot of ways he's been a bit like me, where that just on the day, he hasn't been as good as that person who did win, simple as that. You know, I think he has been really unlucky not to win one at all, because he has been up there for a few years, and he has had loads of 2nd places. There is so much luck needed at the TT, and it's never quite found him. It's a shame for him because at the time, racers probably didn't want him to win because they were jealous of how famous he became away from bike racing, for being a bike racer.

He is massive now, but I've always had a lot of time for Guy, mostly for the way he handled himself after he messed up in that 600cc race with me. There was a phase where everyone in the paddock was quite anti-Guy, but I think it was mostly down to the fact he was seemingly getting paid so much money and had got himself such a huge fan base without really trying. A lot of people in the paddock were just envious, which is a shame, and I really do genuinely wish he had won one, because I think he really does deserve one. On the flip side, you could say he has been incredibly lucky when you consider the crashes he has got away with.

Speaking of luck, when Stuart Easton had a massive accident at the North West 200 in 2011, and made a mess of his pelvis, he thanked me, bizarrely, afterwards for saving his life. We had been out at the Anchor Bar the night before and got pissed on Guinness. The Anchor Bar is amazing – we've always gone there, and it's like a time warp, where it's not unusual for it to be light when you come out. That night, there was John McGuinness, Stuart, a few others and me, all absolutely on it. It was a great night out with a few mates that basically escalated into a massive session.

We had the whole of the next day to sober up because practice wasn't until the evening. When the session came, Stuart had this huge crash and smashed his pelvis to pieces, as well as his femur and some other stuff. He was in a really bad way, but to this day he reckons that the only thing that saved him was drinking so much Guinness. His insides got split open during the crash, but because he had so much Guinness with us the night before, he'd woken up that morning and cleared himself out empty. If he'd not had such a massive shit that morning, he genuinely could have been in real trouble due to the damage he did to his bowel and other organs in the accident.

What a place though, and the crowds and people in Ireland are so enthusiastic, like nowhere else in the world. I genuinely love the place. I remember crashing my Ducati while in the lead in 2002, and by the time the bike got back to us after the race, all the stickers had been pulled off it to be kept as souvenirs. The thing that makes that particularly amazing was that they were underneath a layer of lacquer, so they were basically impossible to peel off.

I can go to the pub over there, and although everyone will say hello, and although I don't normally like a load of attention, over there, they're really good with it. You get the odd one or two pissed up people that can be annoying, but 99% of them will go, 'Alright, Michael?' and that's it. They'll let you have a drink and do your own thing.

I guess maybe the younger road-racing fans don't realise what my dad did or who he was, but I don't class myself as famous or young anymore. I can walk anywhere now, and I don't get grief. In 2002, when I raced there with Renegade Ducati, it was crazy, but then it faded and calmed down. I didn't think the attention that I got would come back, but then when I was at HRC it did. I couldn't move. Now I just laugh at the people that are being hunted down for a selfie, and I can walk down the back of the garages and no one recognises me or is interested in me. They're all looking into the garages for the current big names, like Peter Hickman, Dean Harrison and Michael Dunlop, which makes me smile because once upon a time that was me.

I've never felt like I'm carrying my dad's legacy on. I think having the Rutter name helped at the beginning of my racing career in Ireland, probably more than it did in England. In Ireland, I've never stopped being Tony Rutter's son; some people still even call me Tony. I don't feel like I ever stepped out from his shadow, not that I particularly want to. I'm really proud of what he achieved and how he did it, so I've always been happy to stay in his shadow. The North West 200 is still his gig, as far as I'm concerned.

Back in BSB, we had the North West 200 all over the sides of the bikes, a massive hospitality setup, and all the trappings of a big team. I had some good results with some podiums and a win. I finished 6th in the championship behind Shane Byrne, who won his second BSB championship that year. Leon Haslam, Cal Crutchlow, Tom Sykes and Leon Camier were the others who finished in front of me. Look at them all now; they have all gone on to achieve amazing things. Looking back now, that was a really strong field in 2008.

The bikes were really different to anything else I'd ever ridden. Electronic rider aids were coming on strong around then and were becoming an ever increasing part of setting the bike up, and grasping how to ride it. I remember the electronics bloke alone cost £45,000 for the year, and what was frustrating for me was that I could only go as quick as the bloke with the computer could let me.

It was really the first bike I raced that had pukka electronics, and really you had to be flat out when you got to the apex of the corner, so as soon as you got your knee on the floor, that's it, you've got to open the throttle full. Having ridden bikes for so long without them, and instinctively feeding in the throttle based on how much grip I can feel, it was hard for me to just whack the throttle open fully in the middle of the corner and let the electronics do the rest.

I got used to it, but I wasn't getting the very best out of it like the younger lads; they were all quicker at adapting to it than me. Sometimes it wouldn't work, and the bike would slip, slide and launch me out of the saddle, and sometimes it would be amazing. Once we all got our heads round it, it was such a clever system, and then I had to figure out how to set the bike up for it as well, to cope with the way it could accelerate at full lean.

I remember being at Mallory Park, and the traction control was really annoying me while going round the long, fast right-hander called Gerard's Bend, so I thought I'd turn it off – and holy shit, that was a big mistake. I did about three laps, and I was knackered because the bike pulled so hard. Eventually, and inevitably, the rear lost traction, came round on me and threw me off in a big way, so you basically couldn't use it without the traction control. It was part of the bike.

I missed the TT in 2008 because Alistair didn't want to do it, and we didn't have enough time to get ready to do it right. I'd been offered rides at the TT, but I always like riding the TT with the same bike and team as on the short circuits.

We did win at the North West 200, when I just pipped Guy Martin and John McGuinness to the post. I can't imagine not winning the race that we had spent the entire season promoting! We also entered the Macau GP, where I qualified on pole position and finished 2nd to Stuart Easton.

Towards the end of the year, the financial crash started to happen, and Alistair was feeling the pinch because he was in the building trade. For a brand-new team in its first year, it was too much to take on and we had so much to learn about all of it. We also had John

Laverty on the cheaper version of the bike, which could be raced in the superstock class. It was basically the production bike rather than the 'F' spec version like mine, so the team were trying to accommodate him too.

The combination of the recession starting to bite and the sheer cost of that season meant that Alistair needed to put the brakes on.

16

2009: Going to the Pub

At the end of 2008 I was one year into a two-year deal that I'd done with Alistair Kennedy, and he called me up and said that he wanted me to retire from racing and run the team for the second year of my contract. I was shocked. I mean, I was still only thirty-six and felt still well and truly in my prime, still with plenty of years left in me.

There have been plenty of times during my career when I've thought, 'Why do it?', but it's something that I get so much pleasure from, even though I know how dangerous it is. I never get very close to any of the riders; the one or two that I did get close to in my early years aren't here anymore. I try to do my own thing and keep a bit of distance between me and other riders, so that if it does happen then it's not such a big blow. You know, I'll speak to them and be nice, but not get too close because you have to be able to move on. There are the ones who choose to walk away, and I really admire them for it; then you get the stupid ones, like me, who carry on ... but the thing is, I just can't see it as a choice now, let alone back then. I don't know anything else.

When I was starting out, I always thought that when I got to thirty years old I'd finish. Everyone around me said that once you get to thirty, that's it. Then I got to forty, and I thought that really should be it now, but the feeling that racing gave me at forty, and even today, is the same as when I started. At the time of writing this book, I'm forty-seven and I've been racing for thirty years, and I have no clue where the time has gone.

I don't think I have slowed down speed-wise. Obviously, I have got more careful and less fit, which has slowed me up. One or two laps is fine, but the days of lap after lap after lap at lap-record pace are gone. I know that I think about the risks a bit more than I used to. I think the big difference is if I'm about to overtake someone, as a youngster I would just do it, but now if I pause for even just a split second to think about it, it's too late.

Other than those vague birthday milestones, which seemed very distant at the time, I've never put a time or date on when I want to finish. I could turn up at the first round this year and go, right, that's it. I won't make a big deal of it; I'll just stop. In the meantime, I still do it, simply because I love it. I haven't yet found anything that can beat the feeling of sitting on a race bike going down that pit lane to go out on track and race. To this day I still think how lucky I am to still be doing it at this age, and enjoying it.

So, back in 2008 I said to Alistair that I wasn't ready to stop, and I wasn't even remotely interested in running a team, so I said, thanks a lot, thanks for your help, you go your way, and I'll go my way. Alistair was OK about it and understood; he actually put some money into Rob McElnea's team, just to get me a ride on the Yamaha, which, to be honest, I didn't want him to do. I have known Rob for years, and I've got no problem with him, but I've never really liked the way he often won't pay riders.

I got speaking to Rob about riding the Cadbury's Boost Yamaha years ago. He said I could ride for the team for no money, and of course I was always looking for money. It's only right that the rider should be paid by the team. I always said I'd rather ride for someone else who will pay me. It's easy to look back now and say I should have taken the Boost Yamaha ride, but at the time, when you've got a mortgage and kids, you have to earn money as well.

My parents weren't well off enough to support me, and we didn't have any big sponsors, so I felt that I always needed to get a salary from the team. If I could go back and tell my younger self one piece of advice, I'd tell me to get a manager. I think I would have listened to one too. I needed someone who saw it from the outside and could take a longer-term point of view when I was too close to it. I needed someone who could basically help me make better choices.

Then there is training and exercise; I just hated it and still do. It's the worst thing in the world for me. I have got no interest in it what-soever, but a manager would have kicked me up the arse and made me take it more seriously. Nowadays, I get teammates who are running and cycling, because they have to, in order to be super fit, but back then you could get away with it.

Rob's team for 2009 was me, Graham Gowland and Chris Walker, and I tell you this: a three-man team never works. Ever. On top of that, it was a brand-new bike from Yamaha. The 1000cc YZF-R1 got a complete redesign in 2009, with the big news that its engine was getting the same crossplane crankshaft that Yamaha adopted in their MotoGP bikes. It's seriously clever stuff, and they still use it today in their MotoGP bike and Superbikes. In short, the crank pins on the crankshaft are offset by 90 degrees so that the pistons all rise and fall independently of each other, unlike in a conventional engine, where they rise and fall in pairs. Without getting too boring and technical, the effect is a smoother power delivery that in theory improves grip and tyre life. There was a real buzz about the bike because of all the MotoGP hype that came with it, but I didn't like riding it.

The engine was really clever, and I could see a lot of potential in it, but the chassis was really stiff. The team had braced the frames in all different places; it just didn't feel right at all, and I was actually scared

190

on it. I just didn't like it. We got to the North West 200, and when I was going down the straight at the best part of 200mph it was that stiff that the bike would shake so hard that my feet got thrown off the foot pegs like a rag doll. I was at 200mph and not able to fully control the bike.

The only good R1 in 2009 was the one that the Yamaha factory was racing in World Superbikes with an American rider called Ben Spies. He was winning races for fun on it in World Superbikes and eventually won the world championship. We tried to copy it, but it just wasn't the same. There's only so much you can do. If you need new frames or yokes, you don't have the time to test and develop that sort of change mid-season.

After the season the team found that the frame was braced too much in the wrong places; they would have been better off if they'd just left the frame as standard, but they welded bits of metal to the yokes and headstock, which makes a massive difference to feel. However, if you do it in the wrong places or too much, it can ruin a bike's handling.

I couldn't get away from the thought that there was no way I could do the TT on that R1. I really couldn't bring myself to do it, so, for the first and only time in my entire career, I quit a team mid-season.

I was surprised at how easy it was to do, considering that I always stuck with a team despite having wanted to quit mid-season plenty of times before. It is a measure of how evil that Yamaha was. I was barely able to ride it at the North West 200, which is a billiard table compared to the TT course, and I knew that I'd be in deep shit on it at the TT. It could have hurt me badly; it just wasn't right at all. I really felt I'd rather not do anything and just wait around for something to come up, someone to fall off or get sacked. So I called Alistair and said, 'I'm sorry, I'm out. I can't carry on with this'.

I had absolutely nothing, and really no idea if I'd race again that season. Little did I know that this set of really negative circumstances – which had led to me being out of a ride mid-season with no prospect of a ride and my reputation damaged – would lead to the start of my relationship with Batham's Ales, which would turn out to be arguably the defining moment in my racing career.

I wish I could tell you that this turn of events was a result of a brilliant bit of prospecting by me, or fantastic market research that I'd done, but in fact all that happened was that I went to the pub with Dad. We went to the New Inn in Wordsley, which is near where I live and is my dad's favourite pub. Significantly, as it would turn out, it's also a pub owned by Batham's brewery.

We were sat at the bar, having a beer and telling the landlord all about me quitting the team and having to miss the TT. He said that I should go and speak to Matt and Tim Batham to see if they were interested in sponsoring me. They are sixth-generation brewers at Batham's Ales, which is over 140 years old, and the brewery is behind one of their other pubs, the Vine Inn in Brierley Hill.

It is such a brilliant pub and brewery that's been there for generations. Along with the beer itself, the Vine and the brewery are a proper piece of Black Country history and have barely changed in 140 years. Now they have twelve pubs in the area, but the Vine is the original, and well worth a visit if you're ever in the area.

I've always liked the quote from William Shakespeare on its frontage, which reads: 'Blessings of your heart. You brew good ale.' I even had it painted it onto some of my crash helmets in the past. I'd grown up drinking the stuff, but I'd never once thought to approach them for any kind of sponsorship. It was just the place that brewed the beer that I always drank, and that my dad always drank.

So I went to the Vine and asked if Matt and Tim were in, and if they could spare me a few minutes. I had never met them before but I got shown into the boardroom where I officially met with them for the first time. I told them about what had happened, and that I had nothing for the TT, which was only a couple of weeks away. I asked them straight out if they were interested in helping me out. I told them how much money I'd need to run a bike at the TT, and they both looked at each other and said, 'Yeah OK'.

I couldn't believe it. I was so used to sponsors dithering and messing me about and wanting to negotiate and have the last word, but Matt and Tim were really easy to deal with, straight down the line. They are regular guys like me: Black Country born-and-bred bikers and, as it turned out, fans of my dad and me. They were on board immediately and just told me to do whatever I needed to do in order to get to the TT.

I bought a Suzuki GSXR1000R because one of my old mechanics, Les Pearson, was working at Crescent Suzuki in Bournemouth. They were the people who ran the Suzuki BSB team at the time, so going to them was the easiest and fastest way to get a quick bike built and set up – which they did in just two weeks. With the bike built, I got a loan of the little Batham's delivery van, loaded the bike and a pop-up awning into it, and drove to the TT. Jason Jones, my mechanic from the year before, came to help out, and Stuart Easton came along to help too. It was like starting all over again, which, looking back, I suppose it was. We did that TT properly old-school: out the back of a van, with a couple of mates helping out as a favour.

There is a story about why the bike was painted in such a shitty yellow. I asked Matt and Tim what colour scheme they wanted, and they weren't really bothered, and to just do it 'sort of like Batham's'. I went back to my car, not really sure what they meant by that, and right there outside the brewery, I saw a van and thought to myself, 'Ahh no, their vans must be the same shitty Vauxhall yellow colour as this one'.

I couldn't figure out how I was going to make that colour look OK on the bike, but I really wanted to be loyal to Batham's – after all, they had totally dug me out of the shit – so I painted the bike yellow, and I put a massive Batham's sticker on the side of it. It was the best I could do with the time available.

About six months later, Matt and Tim asked me why I painted the bike that horrible yellow, and I said that I had seen one of their vans at the brewery and copied the colour for the bike. I couldn't believe it when they said that it wasn't their colour; it was just the standard colour of the Vauxhall vans that they used to deliver the beer. That's the story behind why that bike was such a horrible colour with just one sticker.

It was probably by far the worst colour bike that I've ever raced, and the punchline is that the whole time I was cursing having to ride such a horrible-looking bike but consoling myself that it would make Matt and Tim happy, they were wondering why on earth I would paint my race bike such a shit colour.

The whole thing was all so last-minute, and the bike looked like a piece of shit, so it was inevitable that we would have problems. A bearing in the gearbox broke in practice, so we had to get that all rebuilt over on the island.

Stuart Easton was one of my pit crew, and his jobs during the pitstop were to take the fuel cap off, pass me some water, polish the screen on the bike, and clean my visor. Basically, Stuart panicked really badly, which I didn't think he would, and managed to get everything he was supposed to do wrong. When I arrived in the pit, he sprayed polish all over the screen first instead of taking the fuel cap off, which meant Jason couldn't refuel. Then Stuart eventually took the fuel cap off and started cleaning my visor, but I had to shout 'water' for him to give me some water first.

Once the bike was refuelled, I shot off down Bray Hill, and Stuart had left all the polish on the bike's screen, so the thick layer of polish on the screen just flew off, all over my visor, and I couldn't see a thing. Worst pit stop ever.

Everything about the 2009 TT was on a wing and a prayer, and to this day I don't know how but I finished 7th in the Senior TT, which was simply amazing considering how last-minute it all was. There are people who will prepare all year for the TT and spend a fortune only to come away with nothing.

Only a couple of weeks before finishing in the top ten of the hardest motorcycle race on the planet, I was sitting in a pub with my dad, moaning about having nothing for the TT, or the rest of the season. It just goes to show how fortunes can change really quickly in bike racing. Anyway, we just got through it, but that was the start of my partnership with Batham's. Matt and Tim had got a taste of it and enjoyed it.

We sold that yellow Suzuki to Chris Walker, and the first thing he did was to paint it all up in black. He used it for himself at the end of the year because he'd also fallen out with the team. It's funny, but that bike was the one that I used when I quit the Yamaha team, and then later Chris did too.

So I got back from the TT and basically rode anything I could in BSB, just to keep at it. Crescent Suzuki were the first to call. Their rider Sylvain Guintoli had joined the team from MotoGP and was Suzuki's big name. He broke his leg really badly at Donington Park, which was just before the TT. Maybe they called because I'd done really well at the TT, or maybe I'd have got the call anyway – I don't know. Either way, I got to ride the bike at Thruxton.

It was in the back of my mind that the last time I'd raced in BSB, I didn't even get in to the top fifteen to score any points and had caused a bit of a stir by walking out on a team under a cloud, so I was obviously keen to prove my point: that it was the Yamaha, and not me, that had underperformed.

To the outside world, me quitting a Yamaha ride must have looked mad. Leon Camier was riding one in BSB too for a team sponsored by Airwaves chewing gum, and they had the same full-factory bikes that Ben Spies was on when winning in World Superbikes. Leon was taking the piss in BSB on his, and eventually won nineteen of the twenty-six races that the championship had that year. Rumour was that the team he was riding for (GSE) had a budget of £1.3 million.

Leon was so dominant that he had the title wrapped up with four races to go, which was a nightmare for the BSB organisers and promoters. After that season, the BSB organisers introduced the 'Showdown' points system, which basically means it is impossible for a rider to win the title until the last round. It guarantees a big finale to the season, which keeps people interested and coming to the races. The system is still used to this day, which goes to show how racing that's dominated by one person is bad for business. It's quite a controversial system because there are some riders who under the old system would have been champions but under the new system aren't. I'm not one of them, so I don't really care.

The Suzuki had a 'blipper' system, fairly new technology at the time that lets you downshift gears without using the clutch. There is a sensor in the gearshift that remotely 'blips' the throttle when it gets actuated. It's clever stuff that's common nowadays, and it really makes a big difference during braking and corner entry. The team had a crazy foreign electronics bloke that was looking after all the bikes' electronics, and for the life of me I don't know how Sylvain rode that thing; it was awful.

For instance, I'd be braking and turning into a corner when the bike would accelerate all on its own, just when I was wanting it to slow down. I'd tell this electronics guy what was going on, and he would say it wasn't, because it didn't show on his computer. I started to get really pissed off with the guy because he just was not listening to me, nor even slightly interested in any of my feedback, only what was on his laptop. I started saying that I didn't care what it showed on his computer, and that the bike was accelerating into a corner. He never believed me, because his computer didn't match my feedback.

I should have kept my mouth shut because I wanted to keep the ride, and this is one of the few things that I regret. I just kept saying that their blipper was wrong, and that their computers, which they were depending on so much, were also wrong. I just knew it wasn't right. I think the main crew chief Les Pearson, who built my TT bike, believed me, but the electronics bloke wasn't having it. It was a one-rider team, so there's no other rider there to back you up.

Anyway, I got a pair of 5th places at Thruxton, which was a decent result considering no one could get close to the two Airwaves Yamahas. I was still with the team at the Knockhill round, which was my third meeting with them, and the bloody thing accelerated while I was braking for the hairpin and dumped me on my arse. I went down really slow, but that was the last time I rode the Suzuki. The team had got a lad called Tommy Hill lined up to ride it, so I was back out in the wilderness again, hoping that he didn't do better than me on it. Tommy did well on it, with a best of fourth place, but, luckily for me, didn't make me look stupid. Not only that, but they did eventually find a glitch in the electronics that was opening the throttles exactly as I said it was.

After the Suzuki, I got a one-off ride for SMT Honda at the very next round at Mallory Park, which I actually got paid for. Their rider, Jason O'Halloran, had got injured, so in I went. The bike was pretty good and I really like Mallory Park, so it was a fairly straightforward race weekend. I turned up, rode the bike and finished 4th and 6th in the two races, well in front of Tommy. Job done.

Then I rode a Kawasaki ZX-10R for Nick Morgan, which was a lot better than the one I rode in 2007. It was just for one meeting, standing in for Simon Andrews. It was a three-race weekend, and I got the exact same results as their regular rider, and my teammate for the weekend, Julien Da Costa. He got a 10th, 11th and a DNF, and I got an 11th, DNF and a 10th. That's about where the bike was, to be fair; Simon's results on it were generally in the bottom half of the top ten.

I was fairly satisfied that I'd done enough on the Suzuki, Honda and Kawasaki to at least clear up the fact that my results on the R1 at the start of the season weren't me being 'past it'. I'd come back from the TT and raced at five back-to-back BSB rounds on three different bikes, but then the phone stopped ringing. I'd benefited from a brilliant run of 'bad luck for some riders but good luck for me', and now the tables had turned against me. There weren't any spare seats; no one needed a stand-in rider.

After missing a couple of rounds, Alistair still had the NW200 Ducatis from 2008 sitting in a garage somewhere, so we decided to get them out and dust them off for the last two rounds at Silverstone and

Oulton Park. I didn't have a computer, which you basically can't run the Ducatis without, so I got hold of 'Desmo Dave', who used to work for the GSE team when they had factory Ducatis before they switched to Yamahas. He knew loads about Ducati engines and the electronics, so we muddled through and got on with it. It took a while to get the bike running right after retiring in the first race at Silverstone, but eventually we did get it there or thereabouts, and got an 8th place finish, all out the back of a van.

I rode every manufacturer's bike that was raced in 2009, except for an MV Agusta that someone was racing that year in BSB. I finished off the season by riding a Kawasaki at Macau for Nick Morgan's team and finished in 6th place, which I was reasonably happy with. Stuart Easton won the race, just a few months after being a helper at the TT for me and making a mess of my pit stop, which I think shows how unique and special the bike racing community is.

That's one of the reasons in particular why I still love road racing. it's still quite old-school, and you can let your hair down a bit, have a beer, and everyone really does help each other out. Don't get me wrong: it's bloody serious when it's time to go racing, but it's a totally different atmosphere to BSB. Road racers don't take themselves nearly as seriously as the BSB riders.

It was quite an interesting year, and I didn't do too bad on any of the bikes I rode, apart from the Yamaha. Walker and Gowland got some good results on it eventually, but I never regretted leaving the team, and I still don't to this day. I left because I was genuinely afraid the bike was going to hurt me, so much so that I was prepared to miss the rest of the season, including the TT.

As it turned out, my decision to quit Yamaha at the start of the 2009 season would ultimately set me up with Batham's. I didn't realise it, but a whole new chapter of my career had begun.

17
2010 & 2011: Last Chances

The 2010 and 2011 seasons were the beginning of the end of a few eras, my own included. The organisers of BSB had already brought in a single-tyre rule in 2008 as a way to reduce the cost of racing, and in 2010 they introduced a specification that let teams enter into what they called an 'Evo' class, which didn't allow all the (very expensive) trick rider aids.

Traction control, anti-wheelie, launch control and engine braking had all become essential if you wanted to be at the front, and all became central to the performance of a race bike and part of its overall architecture. Manufacturers and teams were throwing massive amounts of resource and time at the electronics as there were big gains to be made by having the better kit and better brains on the job.

The 'Evo' class had no rider aids, and all the teams that competed in it were given identical ECUs for their engine management. I'd say about half the grid was made up of 'Evo' riders and the other half made up of those of us still using full-blooded superbikes with all the bells and whistles. There were definitely loads more bikes on the grid which proved almost immediately that there was something to be said for the idea. Above all else, the organisers want full grids, so you'd have to be blind to not see that it would be only a matter of time before all the expensive riders' aids would get banned in British Superbikes.

2011 would be the final year of full-on, no-expense-spared, factory-prepared race bikes in BSB. From 2012 BSB took the brave decision to put itself out of step with a lot of other superbike series, including World Superbikes, and ban all electronic rider aids. For the absolute purist, it was a terrible thing. To some, BSB had become sanitised and manipulated in the name of entertainment; to others, it was a simple choice that accepted that the global financial crisis of 2007–8 had made big sponsors, and even manufacturers, reluctant to keep writing big cheques like they had before in the name of corporate one-upman-ship, and adapt to the less affluent new world.

I joined the Riders Motorcycles team in 2010 to ride a Ducati 1198, like the one I rode in 2008. Riders are Ducati dealers in Bristol owned by Phil Jessop. His son Martin was up-and-coming, and Phil wanted him on a decent bike alongside someone who could help teach Martin a bit. It was a good arrangement, and a good way for me to get on a really good bike for a couple of seasons.

I didn't have many offers, because if you just look at the results 2009 was a pretty shit year – plus I was starting to get old. I was being sponsored by Batham's then, so that brought something to the team, but the fact they also wanted me because of what I could teach Martin made me realise for the first time that, almost without notic-ing, I'd become the oldest bloke in the paddock, and had moved into the final phase of a racer's lifecycle. We go from 'up-and-coming', to 'contender', then finally 'experienced warhorse', before finally retiring.

Looking back, from 2007 onwards my career was on a downward curve; it had peaked between 2002 and 2006, when all the top teams wanted me to ride for them and I'd had the best of everything. HRC in 2004/05 especially spoiled me because it was perfect, as in I didn't have to worry about a thing and literally everything was taken care of for me, every single detail. All they wanted me to do was get on the bike and race it as quick as I could, and that's all; nothing else. Being a racer was so simple then, except for the travelling and pressure of expectation. Every other season after that was all about finding sponsors to get me into the right team instead of me calling the shots and them coming after me.

I wasn't bitter at all, or even sad. If anyone had said to me, even in 2007, 'That's it, you're done racing', I'd have been completely satisfied. The cycle happens to everyone who's ever raced, and I'd seen it happened to Dad. He went from four-times world champion to more or less nobody in an incredibly short space of time.

It doesn't last forever; it can't. We are all just passing through. Even the greatest racers of all time start to become old news. Just look at Rossi – there's always someone coming up behind. I'm realistic and realise that I can't go on forever, nobody can, but at the time of writing this book I've just got back from the 2019 TT races, where I finished in the top 7 of every race I entered, lapped at over 130mph, beaten John McGuinness in the TT Zero and broke my own lap record, so I'm not done just yet!

In 2010 I was thirty-eight years old, which is ancient by today's standards. I don't think there's anyone on the BSB grid that's thirty-eight today, let alone winning BSB races, making it to the Showdown and finishing 5th in the standings. However, it was getting physically harder, especially in Superbikes, to be able to compete with the younger, fitter lads, who all take training far more seriously than I ever did. 2010 was the season when I won my last BSB race – two to be exact – and 2012 was my last BSB podium. Those two years were really my last run at the title.

Having Martin in the team in 2010 did mean that I only had one bike for the season, but it was OK. The bike was brilliant then, but the Ducati wasn't going to last beyond 2012, when the ban on electronic rider aids in BSB came in. More than any of the other bikes on the grid at the time, the Ducatis were built around having rider aids, and without them they were virtually un-rideable.

We took it to the North West 200, and basically it blew up in practice week, so I had to race the team's superstock bike in the superbike races instead. A superstock spec bike is in a much lower state of tune than a superbike; in fact, it's not tuned at all. In simple terms, it is basically a standard road bike with all the stuff like headlights and road bodywork taken off. You can upgrade the suspension, exhaust and tune the fuel injection, but that's about it; you can't even upgrade the tyres for race slicks. A superbike will have a modified chassis, a bespoke swing arm, and you can tune the engine extensively.

The superstock bike that Riders had brought with them was the then brand-new BMW S1000RR. As a road bike it had significantly moved the game on in terms of engine output and chassis setup – and it was the first production road bike to have adjustable traction control. It was a major step forward for road bikes by BMW and it took the other manufacturers years to catch up and offer the same level of spec and power in a standard road bike; some still haven't. It instantly became the go-to bike for the superstock class, and Riders were no different, so instead of just riding the BMW in the superstock race, I raced it in the superbike race too after the Ducati blew up. It turned out that both the BMW and superstock racing would feature a lot in my career, right up to the present day.

The other significant event that happened at the North West 200 that year was that Steve Plater, who was riding for Honda Racing in the HM Plant colours, had a big accident. He knocked himself about a bit and he was bloody lucky to get away with it. It was only a few weeks to the TT, and there was no way Steve was going to be fit in time, so Honda asked me if I would ride for them, and since Riders didn't want to do the TT it was an easy decision.

I ended up racing the HM Plant bike in the superstock race, and raced the same bike but in Batham's/SMT colours for the superbike and Senior races. Robin Croft at SMT sponsored me for those races, so all I had to do was swap the fairings for Batham's/SMT ones, or HM Plant ones, depending on what race or practice session I was in. It was quite good using the exact same bike for all the races because I got really dialled into it and ended up doing quite well on it. I got a 5th in the Senior, and an 8th and 9th in the Superbike and superstock races, which I was pleased with, considering what was going on at the front.

It was the 2010 TT where Ian Hutchinson won five races in the same week, Conor Cummins had his horror crash at the Veranda corners (and flew off the edge of the mountainside, all caught on camera by a helicopter), and Guy Martin had his massive fireball crash in the Senior race at Ballagarey. Guys crash happened on the fifth-gear corner quite close to the start of the lap, and he'd just refuelled, so his bike was brimming with 24 litres of race fuel. He lost control of his bike, and it burst into flames, and there was this massive fireball; it was absolutely incredible.

I was behind Guy on the road when it happened, so I was the first one through it all. The heat off it was incredible, and then I saw him lying in the road, motionless. To be fair, I wasn't surprised, because it was such a fast place to crash, never mind the fireball that followed. I really thought he was dead, but at the TT you have to switch off to it and get going again. I nearly made two mistakes myself further down the road because I wasn't really concentrating, just wondering whether Guy was dead. By the time I'd got to Handley's Corner a few miles later, they stopped the race, which I was really happy about because I'd become a bit of a danger to myself. Guy was fine, and no doubt his crash helped with the promotion of the film *TT3D: Closer to the Edge*, which they were filming that year.

I watched the film and thought it was OK, but the main thing is that it raised the profile of the TT, which is always a good thing. Guy Martin featured quite a lot in it, and even though I can't tell what he says half the time I can tell that he's really passionate about whatever it is he's going on about, and fans love him for it. It's a

203

shame he packed in bike racing, because he was good for our sport. Every sport needs a maverick like him, someone who just stands out and appeals to create interest.

The Conor Cummins crash is simply mind-blowing when you see it; it's hard to believe that he survived, let alone made a really good comeback to the TT. I know he struggled to come back and found it difficult in a lot of ways, but fair play to him, it's not slowed him down; he's bloody hard to beat round the TT, and gets on the podium here and there too. He was pushing Guy and Hutchy for the race win when it happened. He broke five vertebrae in his back and had a couple of 10-inch rods put in to hold his spine together, and one of his arms needed loads of screws and plates. I don't think anyone would have blamed him if he just left it all and spent his days in the coffee shop that he owns in his hometown of Ramsey on the Isle of Man.

Ian Hutchinson's five wins in the same week that year was really special too. No one in the history of the TT had ever won five races in the same week before, no one has since, and I'm not sure anyone will either. it was a clean sweep of all the solo events, so for someone to win six they'll have to repeat the seemingly impossible once-in-a-century achievement AND a sidecar or electric TT too. I believe that his record will stand forever.

There are some absolute giants of the sport who never got close to what Ian managed in 2010. The previous record of four was held by Phil McCallen, so the likes of Joey Dunlop, David Jefferies, McGuinness, Hislop, Hailwood, Agostini never got close to that in one week. I mean, Robert Dunlop got five TT wins in his whole career, and Hutchy did that in just one week.

It's impossible to overstate just how incredible his clean sweep was, but it all changed a few weeks later for him in a race at Silverstone, where he got tangled up in a crash. He made a right mess of his leg and he's never been quite the same since. Mind you, he did win three in a week in 2016!

Those three accidents are perfect reminders of just how quickly and easily things can change in our sport. One minute you're on the crest of a wave, and the world is at your feet – then boom! You're on your arse and back to reality with a massive kick in the balls, just like the end of the 2010 and 2011 seasons for me.

I had a really good run at the BSB title in both seasons with Riders Ducati. I qualified for the 'shoot-out' in 2010, by being in the top six with three rounds left. I was actually in 4th place in the championship at that point, but then the wheels came off my challenge with four non-finishes in the last seven races. It was game over for 2010, but I did win the race at Silverstone, which would turn out to be the last BSB race I would ever win, and I ended the championship in 5th, which was my best finish since I raced for HRC in 2005.

In 2011, it was a similar story. I was only five points outside the 'shoot-out', and Kyio was in the sixth and final place in the championship, and he was on a shocking run of form, which carried on to Cadwell Park. I would have easily overhauled him and got into the 'shoot-out' if Josh Brookes hadn't punted me off the track going into Hall Bends. I was actually leading the race, and I thought no one would pass me through Hall Bends because no one ever overtakes there. I've raced at Cadwell Park for decades and never seen anyone get passed there.

I had been leading for about five laps and had been trying like hell on the parts of the track where you can overtake, but kept it smooth and safe to get through that section clean with no mistakes. The next thing, there's a black Suzuki wedged up the inside of me, and I had nowhere to go, so I had to lift my bike up and go straight onto the grass, and down I went. I hit the ground so hard that I thought I was going to die – which sounds really dramatic, but I had actually broken a couple of ribs and couldn't breathe. They stopped the race and stretchered me off, and that was the end of that. I tried racing the next day but it was too painful. Brookes just got disqualified from the race.

In 2011, Shane Byrne was back from his spell in World Superbikes and would go on to dominate BSB for a long time. He was riding the HM

Plant Honda that year, but he had raced the Ducati 1198 in 2008 for the GSE team when they were full-factory. I could never get mine to go as fast as theirs; we tried all sorts, like making lead bricks to go under the seat (and not small amounts; I'm talking about a 3Kg lump of lead), and we tried little bits under the bottom yoke to try and get it to turn better. To be fair, it wasn't unusual to do stuff like that; I've always been one for experimenting with weight distribution and that sort of thing. I've sawn bits of frames out on the inside and put metal tape over it to see if the tape rips. Sometimes the tape would tear because there's so much flex happening in the chassis. To this day, I'll still put some lead in the wheel spindles to see what the effect is. It's never-ending; the bike is never right. Even when I would win a race, I would always come in and go, do you know what, let's add a few more clicks of that, try a different spring, or whatever. I'm always looking to make it a bit better because I know that it can always be better. You never stop trying to get an advantage.

However, a lot of why I was struggling to match Shakey and the others that year was down to my riding style not really working with the rider aids. My riding style was holding me back because I use a lot of lean angle instead of standing the bike up as early as possible after the corner apex and basically avoiding the traction control intervention. The new generation of mega powerful bikes with electronics need to be ridden slower at the corner apex by braking earlier and harder to a slower speed, then turned, stood upright as early as possible and fired out of the corner. I'd spent nearly twenty years riding bikes that had much less power, so I'd brake later and softer to carry more speed through the apex of the corner and maintain momentum. The effect of this on a bike with traction control is because I stay on the side of the tyre for longer, I am also on the traction control for longer.

My riding style is less of a problem at the TT, which is characterised by being more fast and flowing, with relatively few 'short circuit' style corners, which is to say long, or slow. The TT is fast point-to-point stuff. I was expecting the Ducati to be fantastic, but it was evil. It just weaved its way all the way round, and all the way down the long sixth-gear straight at Cronk-y-Voddy. It was terrifying.

We had oil issues too, with it blowing oil into the catch tank, which would then set alarms off on the dash because of low oil pressure. It just wasn't built for going round the TT; the sump was too low for some of the big bumps and compressions. The last thing you want is for the sump of the engine to smash into the road; that can escalate really fast into something nasty. We had to lift the sump up by raising the ride height of the whole bike, which worked OK, but generally it wasn't really suited to the TT. Saying that, I did a 126mph lap on it, which to this day is still the fastest lap of the TT course by a Ducati.

Martin had some good results, even though at the time, and I think he'd admit it himself now, he thought he already knew it all. We had a few disagreements about bits and pieces, but overall it went well. It was a two-year deal, and for 2011 we branded ourselves as Rapid Solicitors. They were an accident claims company and had wanted to help a young lad called Mike Booth, so we added a super-stock bike to the team for him. He lasted about five meetings because he had a lot of crashes and did a lot of damage. Unfortunately, there are no prisoners in racing, and if you're not getting results and are smashing up bikes then it's not going to last. Riders ended up having to put a stop to it. It was a really big, well-funded team, but the repair bill was massive.

It was a great couple of seasons on the Ducati, and with the Riders Motorcycles guys, which we rounded off by taking the 1098 to Macau at the end of the season. I remember seeing Stuart Easton there on a factory-built Kawasaki ZX-10R for the Paul Bird team and thinking he could be a problem, but I felt like I was on it, and my Ducati was really well suited to Macau. I thought Easton wasn't going to beat me, but he just disappeared out of sight. I finished second, and today I still take comfort from the fact that in order to beat me that day he had to set a lap record that was so fast that it has stood for nine years and counting.

Even though my riding style (and hairstyle) were becoming dated, I was still a contender during the 2011 BSB season, which ended up being a classic. The championship went down to the last corner of the last lap of the last race between Tommy Hill and John Hopkins. You couldn't not get excited about it; there was drama and tension to the very end.

I was the highest placed Ducati in both the 2010 and 2011 championships, in 5th and 8th position, but the new breed of bikes from Yamaha, Suzuki, Kawasaki and BMW were emerging as more competitive, and certainly less expensive to run, than the Ducati. Plus, the BSB rules were going to take the electronics away, and there was no chance that Ducati was going to work without them as it was built around the electronics. It was time to look for something else.

18
TT Zero

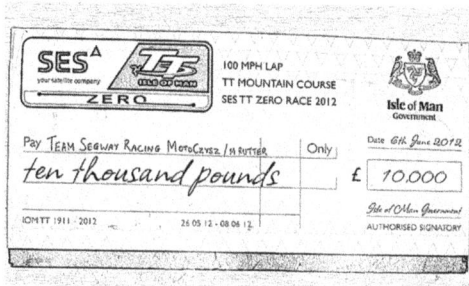

Strictly speaking, 2009 was the first year that electric bikes raced at the TT. It was called the TTXGP and it was put together by a group of people who got together with the Isle of Man government. I was busy focusing on getting my career going again in 2009 with the last-minute rescue deal that I'd just done with Batham's brewery, so the whole electric bike thing pretty much passed me by. I didn't know it at the time, but the rise in interest of electric vehicles, especially from manufacturers, would mean that the 'TT Zero' race format, re-launched in 2010, would play a big part of my TT career. After 2009, the people who had run the TTXGP race and the TT organisers and Isle of Man government couldn't agree on how to move it on, so the government took over the class and added it to the other classes as a full-blown TT – the TT Zero.

MotoCzysz won the 2010 race, and soon after I got a call out of the blue from them. They asked if I was interested in riding the bike in 2011, which I was, mainly because the Isle of Man government had put up a prize of £10,000 to the first person to lap the TT course at over 100mph on an electric bike. An American lad called Mark Miller had won the single-lap race in 2010 at 96.82mph and he was relatively new to the TT, so without any disrespect to Mark I figured if he could

209

manage nearly 97mph then I should be able to get close to 100mph. I knew a fella called Wayne Mitchell who used to race with my dad years ago, and he was working at Segway, who were looking to promote their brand. Segway make a product by the same name – those electric-powered two-wheel things that you stand on and ride around on, which I can't really see the point of – but anyway, Wayne got them to sponsor us in 2011, so I put my name down to race the MotoCzysz electric bike.

MotoCzysz was the brainchild of a bloke called Michael Czysz. It's an American company that designed and built race bikes, and Michael was a bit of a visionary. He saw the move towards electric vehicles was going to happen at some point, so was getting involved with that whole scene. He was really into racing and was an ex-professional racer himself, so he was all over the whole idea of using the TT as a showcase for his technology. Every now and then you come across people like him, who really 'get' what it's like to race, and who are really switched on and ahead of the game with technology and design. Sadly he died of cancer in 2016, and the sport is a poorer place without him.

So when the 2011 TT came around, I went to have a look at the bike, and it was so trick: there was carbon everywhere and it had oval forks, which I'd never seen before. There were really trick details all over the bike, it was beautiful, but it was also basically a bomb on wheels. Everything was made so light on it, but the batteries weigh a ton, so all in all it weighed 260Kg, which is 100Kg heavier than my superbike, so when people assume that because it's an electric bike and not yet lapping as fast as the petrol-powered bikes that they're easy to ride, they bloody well aren't. The extra weight takes much more effort to get to turn and hold a line. For my first lap on it, the plan was just to go out and get some data. The electric bikes go out at the end of the evening practice session, just before they re-open the roads, so before I went to do my practice sessions with the other teams that I was riding for that year, I went to see MotoCzysz about an hour before, to see if I could have a bounce on the suspension to see how it felt. I pushed on the handlebars to bounce the forks, and one of them snapped off in my hand, and Michael said, 'Oh, that's not good'. I couldn't believe what had just happened and replied, 'No, it fucking isn't. Are you for real?' Then, with a totally straight face, Michael said to me that it would be OK, that he would glue it back on with some fancy aerospace glue that he had. He said that it should really be given forty-eight hours to set, but we only had a couple. You can imagine that I wasn't very keen on riding it that evening.

I got back in after finishing practice on the 600 and Superbike, and I was dreading the electric bike. I said to Michael that I had decided not to ride it that evening because I was worried about the handlebar, but he was such a clever bloke, and so persuasive, that somehow he talked me round. He said to just ride round and get some data for the team, and to be careful. So, for my first-ever lap of the TT course on an electric bike, I held onto the top yoke instead of the handlebar that had been glued, all the way down Bray Hill on this 260Kg battery on wheels, and rode the rest of the lap mostly one-handed. I would only hold the handlebar in places where I didn't really need to turn the bike, but everywhere else, where you have to push or pull on the handlebars, I would let go of the glued handlebar because I was so scared of it coming off in my hand. Looking back, it was madness!

The bike was just amazing but it was horrendous on brakes because there wasn't any longitudinal flex from the oval forks. The forks were so solid and the bike was so heavy that when I braked hard on it the frame of the bike was bearing more cornering forces that it usually would if there was some flex in the forks. If I hit a white line in the road while braking hard, it could send the bike 3 or 4 feet one way or the other. It was really scary, but it was only because the forks had been designed to be even more aerodynamic than the usual tube design, which they probably were, but what they gained in being more aerodynamic than tubular forks they more than lost in braking performance.

The electronics were fantastic and a real eye-opener for me. I didn't know what to expect really; I suppose there was probably a bit of me that thought because it was an electric bike that it would be simple and crude. I was wrong. Michael said I could change the engine braking, which also is linked to the way it recovers energy for the batteries, so during the next practice lap I decided to have a fiddle with the dial on the dash that Michael told me adjusts the engine braking. The next time I shut off, the rear wheel locked solid because it had so much engine braking available. I did shit myself a bit and put the dial back where it was before I started messing with it.

The bike was a feat of engineering, especially considering how small the company was. During the race, the bike overheated a bit, and there were a few small issues, but luckily I won the race with a 99.604mph lap. It was the first electric bike TT that I entered and I won it, so my win tally for the TT doubled to two. But more than the win, I was only 0.396mph away from a £10,000 bonus. Barring any freak occurrence, it was obvious that the 100mph barrier was going to be broken in 2012 and someone was going to get that ten grand, and I wanted to be in the mix for it. I was going to have to go back again in 2012, and my old mate John McGuinness fancied a bit of it too.

I started road racing well before John, and in the early part of our road racing careers I was faster than him, but I was on slightly better machinery, and I'd been riding superbikes for longer than him, which helped. John has done bloody well, and he did the right thing by sticking with the TT when I stopped. He has made a lot of money and a massive name for himself. He's so passionate and knowledgeable about the TT and his whole life is about those two weeks. When I came back in 2007, he was the man to beat, and since then I haven't had many chances to beat him again at the TT – until the 2012 TT Zero ...

I stuck with MotoCzysz for 2012. It made sense. We had all learned a lot the year before and I really liked Michael. We had a brilliant bike for 2012 that I was certain would deliver a 100mph lap. It was McGuinness's first year on the Mugen, and they weren't messing about. People often mistakenly believe Mugen to be owned by Honda, but it isn't. Mugen was set up in the seventies by Hirotoshi

Honda, who is the son of Honda's founder, Soichiro Honda. Mugen is an independent company that makes go-faster stuff for Honda cars and race teams, so they really know their stuff.

Mugen also have the 'Shinden' project as part of the business, which is dedicated to developing an electric bike. Basically, there's a team of engineers working all year round on just the one bike, and just one race – the TT. It really matters to them because it was the TT that Soichiro Honda chose to go racing at in the sixties as an unheard-of upstart from Japan, and by doing so, he put Honda on the map. So, you see, the TT has a really special place in the hearts and minds of the Honda family, and this has a lot to do with why Mugen take the TT so seriously.

Mugen turned up to the 2012 TT with a load of mechanics and had the flashiest bike I'd ever seen. It was really something else. McGuinness was going to make me earn that £10,000, and to be fair, looking at the setup and sheer number of engineers that were there, I don't blame him for thinking he had a chance at it. However, I did think he was going to struggle to beat me, purely because we had more knowledge. McGuinness had been taking the piss out of the electric bikes, but with the prize money on offer, he suddenly got competitive on the Mugen. I kept my mouth shut.

In the end, it was fairly straightforward, and I beat John by twenty seconds and won the £10,000. I got this big presentation cheque made out for £10,000 and a posh TT watch for winning the race and breaking the 100mph barrier. That night, I wedged the cheque on his motorhome windscreen for him to see while he was in there. All three of us on the podium actually went over 100mph, but my lap was the quickest.

For 2013, John and Mugen would come back with lessons learned from their first race at the TT the year before, hell-bent on revenge, especially John.

During practice week, I had put a bit of tape over the dashboard of my MotoCzysz, where the battery life indicator was, and the team had worked out in practice how much power to use by certain points on the lap. I'd picked six places on the course and used a pencil to mark the different areas where I could use different power. We worked it all out. We were pretty sure that we knew what I needed to have and where on the course. On the Mugen, you just ride it flat out and it works everything out for you and decides on how much power you can have. Our approach couldn't have been more different. I was going to save some power for the last bit of the lap and make up time over the Mountain.

For the race, John started behind me, and I was sure that he was going to catch me, simply because he is brilliant round the TT. He said that he caught sight of me on the Mountain, which means that because we started ten seconds apart then he could be fairly certain that he was actually leading on corrected time. If you can see the person that you started behind, you know you're actually ahead. I reckoned that if I saved as much power as I could on the first part of the lap for the climb up the Mountain then I'd have a chance. It was really complicated; I was trying to do everything else as well – ride the bike, check my pit boards and try to work out where I was on the course relative to where my marks were on the dash-board. It was hard because I constantly wanted to use a bit more power here and gain a bit there, and I just thought, 'Michael, just keep to the plan'. At the Mountain, John reckons I just opened the bike up and dropped him, and he couldn't do anything about it, but actually I was just sticking to the plan.

I crossed the finish line, and all the commentators were saying that McGuinness had won it. The Mugen team were delirious, and all celebrating and cheering. Then John finished and his time came up to reveal that actually I had won it by just 1.7sec. I couldn't believe it – my lap speed was 109.67mph, and John's was 109.52mph. John was not at all happy I went to shake his hand, and his exact words were 'You're a fucking bastard. You were sandbagging all week'. God's honest truth is that I wasn't; I was really trying all week and working out my plan for the race. I did have a lot more power left by the time he caught me, so while his Mugen started limiting his power, I started using my extra power that I had saved for the Mountain.

John was absolutely gutted, but I thought he was joking, and when we were on the podium, he was still saying to me 'This isn't a proper race, this is a fucking joke'. I was just laughing at him, saying that he shouldn't have eaten so many pies. I didn't realise he really took it to heart; he thought he'd won it, and when I started realising that losing the race had upset him so much, I really started winding him up. To this day, if you see him in the post-race interview, you can see he's wounded, and his face is proper angry.

The best bit was that I was riding for Honda then too in the Honda 'Legends' team, so John was getting the piss taken out of him by me, Neil Tuxworth and Michael Dunlop. We all just kept bringing it up every time we were with him for the rest of the TT and the other races we did that year. He didn't speak to me until the end of the year, when we were on a flight to Suzuka. I was at the back of the plane, having a gin and tonic at the bar and feeling pretty bored when John came up to me and apologised for being a dick.

It was at the 2018 TT Zero race that I met Prince William. I think he is the most famous person I've ever met. Wow, what a really lovely bloke he is. I was racing for Mugen that year after a late phone call after McGuinness, who was originally due to ride it, had a massive crash at the North West 200 a few weeks before. I hadn't planned to do the TT Zero in 2018, but then suddenly, there I was, meeting Prince William.

I was really nervous about the race because we'd had a load of problems with the bike in practice. At the bottom of Barregarrow, which is probably one of the biggest bumps on the whole lap the carbon seat unit which is also attached to the rear suspension broke. It is really fast there, and the corner is at the bottom of a really steep hill that would see the bike's suspension compress a lot if the road simply flattened out. Instead, the road drops away from under you, and the bike actually goes really light, to the point of actually leaving the ground. You come back into contact with the tarmac just as it starts to rise again, so the overall effect of compression is dramatic. In the Senior race earlier that week, James Hillier, who rides for Kawasaki, damaged the bottom of his engine there, and all of its oil emptied all over the road. I was next along, hit the oil and had a massive moment. I was bloody lucky to get away with that one. Mugen had said to me that McGuinness had gone 20mph quicker than me through there, and I should be able to take it a lot quicker, so I took it flat out, and it broke. The whole of the rear subframe that I was sitting on just broke with the force of that bump, so I was basically sitting on my seat, which was sitting on the back tyre, while I was trying to get the bike stopped. Barregarrow bit me twice in 2018, and I was really lucky both times.

For the race, I was worried all night before – but this time about the seat, though Mugen had air-freighted a stronger one in from Japan for the race. I was more nervous about anything else that might break, because every time you go out on a bike like that, you're going faster and asking more from it. It's the most nervous I've ever been on a start line during the build-up. I was starting number 1, and I had Lee Johnston on the other Mugen behind me. Lee is a tiny fella who weighs nothing, so he was a genuine threat. The pressure was all on me because I had won every TT Zero that I had entered, as in I was four from four, so I was the one everyone, especially Lee, was aiming for. As I'm walking up to the grid, Prince William was stood there with my bike, and all the people that are usually milling about on the grid had been pushed right back out of the way.

I got introduced to him, and he asked me if I was looking forward to the race. I said to him, 'No, I'm absolutely shitting myself'. He started laughing and asked why, so I told him about all the problems we'd had in practice, and he said 'OK, well good luck. I hope to see you on the podium'. He was so good; when I was speaking to him I could tell that he really does know about bikes. I asked him if he still had the Ducati that I heard he had a while ago, and he said that he did. He was asking what the Mugen was like to ride, and I started going into it. He really got it and started asking quite specific questions, such as what's it like turning into a corner, how does it behave, and the sort of questions only someone who rides a lot and is interested would ask. I told him about the engine braking characteristics, and that I could turn it up or down, and he was blown away. I was telling him about the feel of it, and he was asking proper questions and definitely not just doing polite pleasantries. I'm sure he must be really good at doing pleasantries, but he really did know what was going on, and about the tech behind it. He was really in to the Mugen, and the whole TT; he's obviously an enthusiast, and a really nice bloke too. You could sit down with him in a pub for a few pints and have a really good night. Within minutes the conversation was so normal that I had totally forgotten he is the future King of England.

Eventually he pointed out that the race was due to start, and I had genuinely forgotten about that because he was so interesting, and I blurted out, 'Oh shit, OK', and he said, 'Look, good luck', and off he went. That was twice I'd sworn at him in the space of ten minutes. He had spent so long with me that he didn't have the time to talk to the rest of the riders before the race like he was supposed to do, but to be fair to him, after the race he went to see all the TT Zero competitors in the paddock.

The next time I saw him was on the podium, and he said to me, 'I told you you'd do it', which was a fantastic thing to say. It meant he really was listening to me and understood how worried I was before the race. He gave me my winner's trophy, and I told him that he should probably get off the podium before he got soaked with champagne, and the last thing he said to me was 'Right-o, I'll get going in that case', and down the steps he went. As he was walking away from the podium, I was watching him and his security when they played the national anthem. Prince William stopped and stood to attention, but his security blokes kept walking. Eventually they clocked that they had abandoned him and stopped too, until the anthem was finished.

After I won the 2018 race, I had a 100% winning record in the TT Zero, I had been the first person to break the 100mph barrier, and in the

2018 race I set a new lap record of 121.8mph on the Mugen. The bikes are getting faster and faster now, but there is still a shortage of teams taking part. Saying that, I can see it gaining popularity with manufacturers now that electric vehicles are becoming more popular.

Mugen contacted me for 2019, and they said that McGuinness was doing the TT Zero with them, and was I up for it? I said, yeah no problem at all but that I wanted the exact same treatment as John; I wanted it to be fair. Even though I'm sure the crowd would probably prefer John to win it in his comeback year following his accident, I had a perfect record of four wins from four starts at that point, which I wanted to try and maintain.

I said that I wanted there to be one or more spaces between our starting positions, so if I went at 1, I wanted him to go at 3, or vice versa, which they agreed to. When I got the entry list, it said that I was going at number 1 and that John was going at number 2. I said, that's not fair and not what was agreed, as he would have an advantage by starting just ten seconds behind me on the road. If you set off ten seconds behind someone at the TT, you'll definitely catch sight of them at Braddan Bridge, and that gives you some extra – it gives you a target to chase. Starting twenty seconds behind virtually guarantees that doesn't happen. Mugen said it was done, so that was it, but somehow, even though I had accepted that John was going to start at number two, when it came to the race, he was number three.

Practice was terrible due to the weather with sessions getting cancelled almost every day, so track time was limited. I managed to get out for the first session, but John missed it because he stayed out for an extra lap on his Norton and broke down. I'd got an early advantage, but for the second session it was me who got stuck out on the Mountain when my Kawasaki broke down, so I missed my lap, and John got his. While I was stranded out on the Mountain I thought, what can I do to try and annoy John, so I stood in the road and flicked the Vs at him when he went past. I got the marshal to take a photo of it and posted it on social media. It got a massive response, which goes to show that you can win a race or have loads of followers on social media, but people love that stuff.

We only had one lap of practice each before the race, so there was still a bit of guesswork during the race as we were still trying to work out braking markers and stuff. I set off from the start so much harder than I have ever done before. I was in such a hurry that out of Quarterbridge and Braddan Bridge the rear tyre span up. I usually like to give the tyres a chance to get up to temperature, so I was asking a lot from the rear tyre that early in the lap. Then I hit a white line through the two fast lefts going into Kirk Michael village, and lost the front end, which was also a first. Luckily, the front tyre regained grip and I got away with it. I was pushing so hard that I thought, if he beats me, fair play to him.

I knew John was struggling, he wasn't having the greatest week, and in contrast I was having a good week. He also hadn't been there for a couple of years, and I know how hard it is to come back. I knew I had a chance to beat John in the race, which doesn't happen often, so I took it by setting another lap record of 121.909mph to break my own previous lap record. It was TT win number seven, which equals Dad's win tally at the TT and maintained my record of five wins and five lap records from five starts in the class.

In some ways, electric bikes are no different to petrol-powered bikes. Acceleration off the line isn't that exciting initially, but when you get to the top of Bray Hill and it's picked up speed, the acceleration is much more familiar, like a 1000cc bike. The only noise that you can really hear is the chain, tyres and, at high speed, the wind. You can also hear the crowd cheering as you go by, which is really strange at first but is actually really cool. Birds in the road don't hear you coming, which is weird, because they normally do and have flown away before you get to them.

The first time you really know that you're on something different is when you shut the throttle for Quarterbridge and you don't down-shift or use the clutch. There is no gear lever or clutch lever, and your foot and hand just instinctively want to do something, so when the levers that your foot or fingers are looking for aren't there, it really distracts you and confuses your senses. Also, when you get back on the throttle, you have no idea where you are in the rev range. You get so used to hearing the sound of the engine and being able to anticipate the engine's response to throttle input depending on the pitch that the engine is at. For example, at Ramsey hairpin I didn't think it would spin the rear tyre because I had no rpm reference, but then it did spin up, and with none of the usual engine sounds you get when a rear tyre spins up. The other thing about the motor is that it doesn't feel like it has as much engine braking as my BMWs, but the hydraulic brake setup is first-class.

The chassis on the Mugen is very good. They have packaged the weight so well that it tricks you into thinking it's something that it isn't. You have to remind yourself all the time that it's actually a pretty heavy bike, and that's probably what holds me back in a few places. I know it's really heavy, but it doesn't feel it at all; you know it's an illusion, so you do wonder what is happening that you can't see or feel.

It's properly fast and when all is said and done, my peak speed of 167mph on it is still 167mph ...

19
2013: Honda Legends World Endurance

On paper, 2013 had all the ingredients for a good season. I joined a team called Quay Garage Racing, which was owned by Ian Wollacott, who had been in the paddock for years and was actually the first one to get Tyco sponsorship, which nowadays is associated with the main BMW team. Tyco are a security company based in Ireland, and when Ian got them to sponsor him for the 2011 season, he was able to buy the ex-Honda Racing Fireblades, the black HM Plant ones.

He had a knack of signing up-and-coming riders like Peter Hickman and Tommy Bridewell, who both scored the team's first BSB podiums in 2011, but Tyco moved their money to another team called "TAS" in 2012 and left Ian in the lurch. He stopped a few years ago, and I haven't seen or heard much of him since.

Ian never really found a sponsor to replace Tyco for 2012 or 2013, so when I joined, and brought some Batham's money with me, the team got entered as Batham's IWR Honda, but the top and bottom of it was that we didn't have anything like enough money to run the bikes. They were OK, and I don't want to be too down on the team because I know exactly what it's like now that I'm running a race team myself, but if you've got just one mechanic working on the bikes in the week, it's inevitable that things are going to get missed. It's not enough resource to be properly on top of every last detail, and in BSB, if you aren't then you're nowhere.

For the first three meetings, the sensor that measured the suspension travel was 10mm out, which is massive and basically means if you treat whatever the datalogger tells you as gospel and it's out by that much, you'll be looking for answers to problems that don't exist. Then we found out a few meetings later that the ride height on the rear shock was machined 10mm out, so all the ride heights that we thought were OK were actually miles out. We got really lost on the bike setup, and by the time we worked it out we were three or four meetings in, and the season was already over by then. You've got to be up there scoring points from round one, not using round one, two and three working out why the bike isn't handling. It was another example of me saying one thing and mechanics saying another. It didn't go that well, to be honest.

Speaking of pissing mechanics off, one of the things I used to do when I joined a new team was make them watch the 1980 film *Silver Dream Racer*. I still show it to people now, and pretty often they threaten to punch my lights out if I show them again because they think it's that bad – but I think it's the best film ever.

Silver Dream Racer was my bible, and I used to run from where I lived in Crestwood, risking my life by running up the rail tracks and across the fields, to a video shop in Pensnet, to rent *Silver Dream Racer*. I rented that video more times than the rest of the UK put together. I loved it. Roger Marshall was in it as a double for David Essex, who was playing the main character, and apparently I was there when they did a bit of filming for it at Silverstone. I would only have been about

2013: HONDA LEGENDS WORLD ENDURANCE

six years old at the time, so I can't really remember, but Dad said he'd taken me that year. Dad wasn't an extra or anything like that, but you do see him a bit at the beginning, in actual race footage. To this day, I'd love to meet David Essex. Two completely different endings were filmed, and both were released. I always play the nice ending.

When I join a new team, I'll make them watch *Silver Dream Racer*. I'll put it on and then close the doors so they can't get out. Some of them come back saying that it's brilliant and can't believe they've never seen it; then there are those who have threatened to kill me. Over the years, more people have enjoyed it than have wanted to kill me.

A good mate of mine called John Barton got really aggressive when I showed it to him. John is a pretty handy TT racer and still actually races at the TT, as well as now working with Milky Quayle as a rider liaison officer for the newcomers at the TT. He and Milky do a fantastic job of bringing in the TT novices and steering them through their first TT safely. John and I have been good mates for years, and a while ago he said he'd never seen *Silver Dream Racer*, which surprised me because he's much older than me. He said he never watched it because he'd heard it was shit, so I made him watch it. John is usually a fairly chilled-out, normal guy, but after the film he said if I ever show him it again he would punch my lights out. I took it personally; it hurt ...

In 2013, I signed with Honda to be part of their 'TT Legends' team, alongside John McGuinness. The team was Honda's official endurance and road racing team and was a big setup. John had been with Honda for years already and at the time was adamant that he would be with Honda for his whole career. He split with Honda four years later, in 2017.

As I said earlier in the book, Honda always say you've got a job for life, but I told John at the time that he was dreaming if he thought he'd be at Honda forever, and that no one has a job for life. I'd had that same promise made to me by them, and twice they'd taken it from me. They are very convincing and you really do believe it. They make you feel part of the family, but everybody has got their shelf life. That's why when any of the young riders ask me for advice I'll always say get out of it what you can from the manufacturers while you can, because you're only there if you're doing the job. As soon as you're not, they'll drop you for someone who is lapping quicker than you. That's how racing is.

If John had stuck at BSB, he would have been at least as good as me, probably better, but he is a lazy bastard – that's his problem. Don't get me wrong, I'm lazy, but he's the next level. That said, the good thing about him is that he rides bikes all the time; he mainly rides enduro bikes, which keeps him bike-fit, but the bottom line is that he's got no willpower to eat healthy. He will eat shit all the time; anything that's bad for you, he'll eat. I'm sure he'd say the same about me.

I think John started racing after me – he certainly did at the TT, because he told me recently that he remembers spectating when I was making my debut on the Medd Honda in 1994. John and I have never really fallen out, but I have to say that whenever I beat John it really does make me smile a bit extra, and I know he feels the same when he beats me. I think it's because we've been knocking about for so long and, like me, he's still there now. There aren't many people that I'm still racing against today who I raced against at the beginning. We've been really lucky to have such long careers.

Obviously, his career has panned out differently to mine, but our friendship is like a marriage: we've had our ups and downs, and obviously he's the rich part of the marriage. If John ever needed anything, or vice versa, we'd always help each other out.

He is massive now, and it's easy to see why. He absolutely loves the TT and he's been so successful at it. You don't just fluke 23 TT wins; I mean, I know how hard it is to win one TT, so to win twenty-three is simply extraordinary, and he deserves all the trappings that come with that.

When you get a factory ride, you pump your chest out and think you're the boy, and John was the same when he got his factory ride –

he snubbed all of us – but we're all guilty of it when we get a good ride, or even a factory ride. He's really tight, and I know everyone thinks I'm tight but I'm the first one to the bar, unlike him, he hasn't ever even been to the bar. He doesn't know where the bar is.

I remember winding him up about it once. We were at a show, for Feridax, who import Shoei helmets into the UK, and I was on at him to get some money out, saying that he never buys a drink. He got a £50 note out and he ate it in front of me and the bar staff and said, 'That's how bothered about money I am'. He'd rather eat a £50 note than buy a round of drinks. The woman behind the bar had never even seen a £50 note.

John and I had some really good times over the years, and there are always other people who come and go that we will knock around with, like recently there would be Ian Hutchinson, Gary Johnson, Lee Johnston, Peter Hickman and James Hillier. Before, it was people like Stuart Easton, Steve Thompson, Jim Moodie, Ian Simpson, Iain Duffus and Dave Heal that John and I would hang around with. It is always the same kind of people in the circle where when there's something going on, it's usually one of the people in the group that's involved.

The circle has changed over the years as riders have come and gone, but John and I are still at it. It's the racing that we all have in common. Even though we are all different people and at different stages of our careers and we all approach our racing differently, inevitably we all get along because fundamentally we are all wired up a bit wrong. I've seen things go on with other riders that I can't even mention, otherwise I'll get in a lot of trouble, but what I can say is that it's been hilarious.

The first test for the Honda Legends team was at a Dunlop test track in the South of France, and John went out first on this endurance-spec Fireblade, and when he came back in, he said to me, 'Michael, the bike is shit. It doesn't turn, it doesn't stop, it doesn't do anything right'. I replied that it couldn't be that bad, but when it was my turn to ride it,

I found out he was right. My god, he was right. It didn't turn quickly at all, and I crashed and broke my leg.

I got back to the garage, determined that I was fine, and Glen Richards, who was the other rider in the team, was telling me that even he could see that I'd broken my leg. I said to Neil Tuxworth that I'd be OK by the afternoon, and I went to lie on a mattress on the floor in the back of the garage. I was lying there and my leg was swelling up really badly, so the team stepped in and took me to hospital. I got the French doctors to put a temporary plaster cast on it so I could fly home, because I didn't want them operating on me. They really didn't want to let me out so soon, but I was determined to get back home. I discharged myself once they put the cast on and I went to the airport. Walking through the terminal was absolute torture.

When I got back, I went to the hospital in Telford, which everyone said not to do because they'd have my leg off. I asked the doctor what needed doing and said that I'd get it operated on somewhere else. He asked me why I would do that, so I just said that I didn't trust anyone there, and that I needed to go racing in the next month. That seemed to fire him up, so he said to me that he would sort my leg and get me ready for the first race. He was fantastic, and true to his word. He pinned it and screwed it all back together and got me sorted. Fair play to him, a month later I was at the first round of the World Endurance Championship, the iconic 'Bol d'Or' at Magny-Cours, back in France.

Michael Dunlop and Simon Andrews were also at the Bol D'Or, and obviously I wasn't exactly fit after breaking my leg, so I was the slowest rider throughout practice, and the Bol D'Or is a twenty-four-hour race, so it's physically one of the hardest races, especially at the pace that the front-runners are riding. There's nothing held back; everyone is flat out for the whole twenty-four hours.

The team decided that as well as being the slowest rider, I was also probably going to get slower as the race went on, so they decided to just use Simon and Michael and John for the race. I was pretty gutted but I understood. The team said not to worry and just to have the weekend off, so I went and got really pissed.

I woke up the next morning on race day, and Honda said they needed me to ride for the French Honda team because one of their riders had bottled it and walked off. I had never even seen the bike, let alone ridden it. One of their other riders started the race, so the very first time I rode the bike was when I rode down pit lane for my first stint, with a massive hangover.

Later on, one of the other riders crashed heavily when we were in 3rd position, and I thought, thank god for that – I don't have to do any more. The next thing, there are loads of French mechanics throwing spanners at it, and straightening it; I thought there was no way that they would get it repaired. Then there was a tap on my shoulder, and I was told to get my helmet on. Moments later, I pulled out of the pits, and that was the second time I'd ever ridden the bike.

It was dark, drizzling, the bike had new slick tyres fitted, and I'd never raced at night before. The first time I went down the straight, the side panel ripped clean off the bike. It was horrendous, but I kept going. You can't stop, no matter what, when you're on track. You don't come back into the pits unless it's the end of your stint. Unbelievably, the UK Honda Legends team didn't finish, and the team I rode for finished in 8th position after completing 784 laps.

The ABS system on that Honda was useless, but Honda insisted on us racing with it on the bike, which I assume was so they could market the ABS system on their road bikes being as the same as ours. During practice at the Suzuka 8 Hours race when I was braking for the last chicane, there were about six riders in front of me. The ABS system kicked in as soon as I pulled the brake lever, and the bike just wouldn't stop, so I ploughed through all these riders who were stopping at the normal rate. I didn't knock any off, thank god, but they scattered all over the place, wondering what the hell had just happened, and all blaming everyone but me.

I got away with it completely, but to make sure I decided to head straight from the escape road, across the track and into what I thought was the pit lane. I thought I'd be able to disappear completely before they all worked out that it was me who was out of control. What I didn't realise was that there are two pit lane entrances at Suzuka, and I'd gone down the wrong one. When I got back to the garage, Neil Tuxworth was there waiting for me, and he said that race control had been onto him and told him to send me up to see them for using the wrong pit entrance.

Apparently, they were properly pissed off, so I was preparing for a proper bollocking. I got to the room and there were long faces all around, so I got in first and started straightaway with a load of old shit about how I used the wrong entrance because it was nearest to where I was in the gravel trap, and I didn't want to spread any more gravel on the circuit than absolutely necessarily. They all looked at each other and then thanked me. I couldn't believe it; I'd totally got away with it on the track, and in the officials' office. I'd been properly jammy.

For the next session, I didn't want the ABS on, so I got Jules, my mechanic, to take the fuse out, but the Japanese mechanics were always there, looking at everything Jules did to the bike. The plan was to take the fuse out, me jump on it and go before the Japanese could do anything. We timed it perfectly, and the Japanese went mad while I was going down the pit lane. It was worth it though, because I went so much faster in that session than any of the others. We had to put it back in for the race though – it's Honda, and it's the way it's got to be.

In the race, during my stint on track, it was so hot and humid. Imagine being in a sauna with your leathers on; it was horrible, and the bike wasn't handling – it didn't turn and it didn't brake. I thought it was getting worse, and then I realised that it had a puncture, so I decided to pit early because I was losing so much time.

The thing is, there is always someone on the pit wall, and if you want to come in, you've got to tell whoever is on the pit wall that you want to come in so they can get all the mechanics ready for you. I could see that Tuxworth was asleep on the pit wall, and I was thinking that I only had about ten laps left on my stint, so I thought, I ain't putting up with this anymore, and just pulled into the pits. No one was ready, so when I got to the garage they asked why I had pulled in. I told them that I had a puncture, the bike just didn't work, and blamed Tuxworth as the reason they didn't know I was coming in.

I don't know how many times Dad did Suzuka, but I went with him as a kid once, and spent ages going round and round this go-kart track that they've got there at the circuit. It must have been about 1980/81, and his teammate was George Fogarty, Carl's dad. Dad and George used to knock about with each other a lot, but I never really had much to do with Carl; he's a bit older than me.

I always thought he was arrogant, but I've always respected him massively as a racer; it's impossible not to. I used to ask James Whitham, who's one of Carl's good friends, what he was like and James always said he's great once you get to know him, but I could never see that. I just didn't like him.

After Carl had retired, I got speaking to him at the North West 200, just after he had been in the jungle filming *I'm a Celebrity ... Get Me Out of Here!* I had bet on him to be the first one out, believing that no way would anyone like him. I said to him, 'Do know what? I never liked you until I watched *Celebrity*', to which he said, 'It's funny you should say that. A lot of people say the same thing'.

We got on really well and met again at a Motorcycle Show somewhere with his wife Michaela, and spent hours and hours talking about his dad George, his mum and my dad, he was great. Michaela has always been really nice. But Carl, to me, is a changed man. It's weird how you can change your opinion of someone once you get to know them.

I did the Suzuka 8 Hours race just the once, and it was such a brilliant experience. It's such an incredible track to ride on; it's just fantastic, really fast and very challenging to get right. That was the same race that Kevin Schwantz was also racing in for Suzuki. He wasn't making a comeback as such, just doing a bit of racing for fun, I suppose. Having said that, he was right at the sharp end throughout the whole event. He still had the magic that earned him a Grand Prix world championship in the nineties.

I never realised he even knew me, but in the build-up to the start of the race I was sitting on a chair on the grid because I had been nominated to start the race for the team, which was quite a big deal. So, I was sat there while all the circus was happening around me, and there was press, mechanics, VIPs, celebrities and all sorts going on, when, out of nowhere, Kevin came over to me and said, 'Alright, Michael? How's it all going?' I was shocked and, if I'm honest, a little bit star-struck.

I had met him briefly at Macau when they did a past winners thing the year before, but that's all, and there he was, stopping at my grid slot to have a chat with me. We had a really good chat for ages about the bike that started it all for him in 1985, a Suzuki GSXR-750, and how he would love to find it and get it back. It was Dad's bike that Kevin used in the Transatlantic series over in the UK, a sort of America vs. UK series that was a big deal at the time. Dad had not long had his crash, and his race bike, the GSXR, was Motorcycle Mart's, so with Dad out of action they lent it to Kevin. He was a complete nobody before the first race he did in Europe on Dad's bike, and then he blitzed everyone. The rest of Kevin's career is history.

He has always been my hero, so as well as him remembering me, and then having a good chat with him at Suzuka about Dad, it was really special because I also got to race against him there too. He was so incredibly fast; it was unbelievable for an old boy. It was amazing to sit behind him and watch because I had watched all the races of him on his Pepsi Suzuki in GPs. I was together with him on the track for about five or six laps and was able to watch him. He just leans off, gets the power on and gets the bike sat up.

His style hasn't changed; it was just like watching the races back when I was a teenager. Every now and then I'll catch up with him at Goodwood and it always feels really special to spend time with him. He is just as mad as he ever was. He is really genuine; there are no sides to him. What a rider, what a legend, but best of all, he is a really good laugh.

Michael Dunlop was one of the other riders in the team, and he was so fast back then. He should have stuck to racing on short circuits, because he'd have been phenomenal in BSB. I'm not sure he would have won it, but he would definitely be a contender. I've won something like twenty-eight or twenty-nine BSB races, which is brilliant, and they all really do mean something, but when you win a TT it's like nothing else, so I get why he has focused more on the roads and in particular the TT. It's in his blood, and he probably knows that he'd never get the same high at BSB as he does at the TT. I think I'm just one of the few racers that do a bit of everything. They're all just races to me, and when one meeting is finished, you simply go on to the next, whatever that is. Short or road or whatever.

I remember realising just how popular John was with Honda at the time, when they asked me to go to Castle Combe to test something – I can't remember why exactly, but John couldn't do it. All three of the teams Fireblades were there – mine, Michael's and John's – and I had to try different things on mine and Michael's bikes.

At the end of the day they asked if I wanted to go out on John's bike, and there was a joke about how no one rides John's bike except John, so I wasn't going to pass up the opportunity. If my bike was, let's say, the average, Michael's was below average (to be honest, it felt like a wreck), and John's bike was a factory bike – it was perfect. I know he's still got to ride it, and it's not all down to the bike, but his bike was on another level. I'm not saying that I would have beaten him if I'd had his bike, because round the TT John is head and shoulders above most of them out there, and at the time he was by far the best.

It does show you that if you're doing the job, Honda will give you the very best, which is right and how it should be. I didn't begrudge it.

You think there can't be that much difference, but there is. Halfway through practice at the TT, I was helping the mechanics to replace my engine for a fresh one. They said to me to go to the truck and get a new engine and, totally by chance, the first engine I pulled out had 'John McGuinness' written across it, and they said, 'No, not that one'. I said that I thought they were all the same, but they said that the engine was for John, that it was built just right, everything matched and assembled to perfection. I'd had that treatment at HRC in 04/05, getting the best of everything that Honda had, way better than what other Honda riders were getting. I'm just making a point that it's not all as equal as it looks sometimes.

In BSB, Ian was expecting big results, but there were massive established teams with budgets far, far bigger than ours who struggle to get the sort of results he was looking for. We did the best we could with what we had, but Ian's expectations were far too high, and the Honda was getting a bit dated by then.

My season in BSB ended with 10 DNFs and a best result of fifth for me. It was miserable and, looking back now, probably the beginning of the end for me in the superbike class. I only raced superbikes in BSB for one more season, and while the Honda Legends thing was pretty average results-wise it was a fantastic experience that I do look back on fondly.

20
Classic TT

The Classic TT has become one of my favourite races of the season, and I really look forward to it as much as I look forward to the TT itself, but for different reasons. The atmosphere at the Classic TT is completely different to the TT; it's much more relaxed, like a festival rather than a race meeting. It's definitely more fun and a lot less intense, because the bikes are the stars of the show.

There are all sorts of bikes from all sorts of eras, and everyone really gets into the spirit of the event. It takes place alongside the Manx GP, usually in late August, and in many ways has saved the Manx GP. I suppose the best way to describe the Manx GP is that it's the TT but for amateurs or, to be specific, people deemed not to be experts. It's the stepping stone for people who want to do the TT; they can go and race on the same course and not have to worry about big-budget factory bikes tearing round the course at the same time with fully committed professionals riding them at average lap speeds up to 135mph.

The Manx GP has never really quite had the same level of interest as the TT, but it must be said that the likes of Hislop, Fogarty, McCallen and other greats all came to the TT via the Manx GP. It has always been, and still is totally relevant, and is a brilliant way for newcomers to serve their TT apprenticeship before lining up along with guys like Dean Harrison, Michael Dunlop and Peter Hickman.

In 2013 Paul Phillips and his team had the idea of adding the Classic TT to run alongside the Manx GP, to boost visitors to the island and the general profile of the Manx GP. Getting a lot of the current and recent TT star riders back to race old classic bikes appeals to two sets of people – TT fans and classic bike enthusiasts – all of whom then get to watch the Manx GP too. It's a proper festival of motorcycling, with something for everyone.

The Classic TT was a brilliant idea, but I never really had any thoughts about doing it until I got asked to ride Cameron Donald's bike in 2014, a 500 Matchless for Ripley Land Racing. Cameron had a crash so wasn't able to ride, which proved to be really lucky for me. I went along not really sure what to expect, but I ended up enjoying it so much because it was low-pressure, with a much bigger emphasis on fun.

I'm sure that long after I've stopped doing the TT, I'll keep doing the Classic TT as long as they'll have me. When I got there, the bloke who owns the bike said to me to go as quick as I could and just enjoy myself, I couldn't believe how easy-going he was, and how excited he was about his bike being put round the toughest racetrack in the world. I think I lapped the quickest on a single-cylinder bike in the history of the TT races at that time. I've been every year since then, with the same team, same bikes and same people. I've been lucky.

In 2017, a fella called Jan de Vos from a racing team called Red Fox Grinta got in touch to see if I wanted to race their Ducati,and I thought we could paint it in the same colours as my Dad's F1 race bike. The bike was brilliant: it had a 1200cc air-cooled Ducati engine but apart from that it was for all the world just like Dad's F1 bike. I went for the complete look and got Alpinestars to make a replica suit just like Dad's, right down to having 'Tony Rutter' on the back. I also had his 'TR' logo on my crash helmet to complete the look.

I raced it in the Senior race, which is basically really trick, and in some cases really highly tuned, Suzuki XR69s and Kawasaki ZXR750s, so my air-cooled Ducati was a bit like taking a knife to a gun fight, but it really did look amazing. I finished 13th on it. I did win the Junior Classic that year too, but more importantly it was just a brilliant couple of weeks and great to be able to do such a nice tribute to Dad, especially as his health wasn't great then and he couldn't make it to the race.

The Classic TT also gives you the chance to ride different bikes. The year before I did Dad's tribute Ducati, I raced a really trick Yamaha FJ1200 in the Senior race and finished in second place behind Michael Dunlop. The bike was phenomenal: it had a really trick chassis made by Harris, and the engine was so fast. Roger Winfield, who owns it, gets me to ride it in the Phillip Island Classic too each year, and each time I ride it I'm blown away by just how much torque it has, and how nice it is to ride.

Saying that, it is a bit scary because you don't know when the pistons are going to come flying out of the cases. One time, the engine blew up so hard that it blew my foot off the foot peg. I was probably doing about 160mph just after Ballaugh in fifth gear when it happened. I don't think I've ever been on a bike when the engine has blown up so violently. When I eventually got it stopped, I parked it up, and because I had seen a few mates just before it blew, I thought I'd walk back up the road to see them. As I was walking back, probably the best part of half a mile, I was picking bits of the engine case up all the way. It had literally chopped the engine in half.

In some ways the Classic is more dangerous than the TT because there are so many old bikes out there that are what they are – low-tech and unreliable. I remember following a Manx Norton that was pissing so much oil out that I had to keep my head below my screen to keep the oil off my helmets visor. I pulled alongside the rider and tapped him on the shoulder to let him know, but he just shook his head at me, so on the next straight I did it again but this time slapped him on the back and pointed to his engine. He got the message and pulled over, but oh my god, there was oil everywhere; my bike looked like someone had literally emptied a whole can of oil all over it afterwards.

In other ways, because you're travelling at much slower speeds, you could argue that it's a bit safer, although there was one time when I thought it was the end for me. During the 2017 Senior race, my neighbour Robin 'Bastard' Wheldon was watching at Gorse Lea, which is just before Ballacraine, with my daughters Juliette and Cecilia, and as I went past I thought to myself that I'd better not crash there ... so instead I crashed at Ballacraine.

I tipped into the corner and the front of the bike just went from under me because I hadn't realised that the front tyre had picked up a puncture. As soon as I felt it start to tuck, I opened the throttle as wide as I could to transfer some weight to the back of the bike and try to pick the front end up, but it kept on ploughing and ploughing towards the bush on the inside of the corner at the apex. I couldn't duck any lower on the bike, and eventually I hit my head on the banking on the inside of the corner and got knocked off the bike. It seemed to take forever to have the crash, and I could just see the banking on the inside coming at me. I knew that it would be my head that took the hit, and that was the thing that really made me think I was in big trouble, hitting my head. In the end, I got away with it.

My approach to the whole event is much more relaxed – not just compared to the TT but also most other races. It's nice to be on the podium, but for me it's really just about having a bit of fun. A lot of people say it's a bit of fun for them, but believe me, they're pushing; admittedly not as hard as they might at the TT, but they're still pushing bloody hard, especially for the age of the bikes. I did a 125.7mph lap on the Yamaha, which is about what I would do on my first few laps of practice at the TT on my BMW superbike, so some of the machinery out there is pretty full-on. The Paton is the best bike, and it is really well set up, so obviously McGuinness rides that so he can just clear off and win.

2018 was the fourth year that I rode the Ripley Land Racing 500 Matchless, and every year up until then I had problems with it. The first year, I was leading, and it blew up on the Mountain mile; I was stuck up there for ages before I got it back to the paddock. The second year, it blew up again, and the third year was when I had the puncture and crashed at Ballacraine. So, for 2018 I decided that somehow I had to finish; even if I had to carry the bike round, I had to get it to the finish line.

I started the race, and somewhere during the second lap the gear lever snapped and fell off. Normally on bikes from that era the gear shift is on the right side, but the boys at Ripley Land Racing had come up with a system of linkages and levers so that the gear shift was on the left-hand side of my bike, where I'm used to it being and where it is on modern bikes. After it happened, I kept going all the way to Ramsey because I thought at least there would be some people there who might have some spares and tools that I could use to try and fix the bike.

I pulled up in Parliament Square, and there were loads of people, all wondering what was going on as I got off the bike and started going round everyone asking for a gear lever. A marshal tried to help by making a gearshift out of the linkages that were still on the bike, but nothing fitted, so I decided to have a look round all the old classic bikes that were parked up there. I must have looked a sight, just running up and down the rows of classic bikes in my full race leathers.

Eventually, I started asking people if they could help, and I went up to some bloke and asked if he knew who owned a bike that seemed to have a gear shift that would fit. He said he didn't know whose it was but that I could use his if I wanted. I took a look at it, and it wasn't any good because it was the wrong size spline. I went back to the bike that had something that looked like it might work and got some tools from a marshal and tried taking the gear lever off it. The bloody thing just wouldn't come off with the tools that I'd borrowed from the marshal, so just as I was about to resort to using a hammer and screwdriver to get this gear lever off the bike, another bloke came up to me and asked what I was looking for, so I told him and he shot off on his mountain bike to the nearest bike shop. I never thought I'd see him again. I was certain he'd never find what I needed.

There were hundreds of people all hanging around, watching me basically trying to commit a crime in broad daylight, nicking a gear lever off a parked bike with a hammer and screwdriver. I suddenly saw sense and realised the madness of what I was trying to do, but in my defense I was desperate. I decided to give up; I'd been all round the car park and for the life of me I couldn't find a lever that would fit. It was time to concede defeat. And then, just as I was making my way back to my bike, the bloke who shot off on his mountain bike came running up to me with a kick-start lever, which is nothing like a gear lever, and he asked me if I thought it would do. He said it was the only thing the shop had with a spline that matched the spline on the shaft it had to go on. Suddenly I saw a glimmer of hope, and I said to the bloke that I'd make it work.

I took apart what was left of the gearshift assembly and re-assembled it all on the right-hand side of the engine, where it originally would have been on the bike, with this kick-starter as the gear lever. When they guys adapted the bike to move the gearshift to the left-hand side, they also had to move the rear brake from the left-hand side to the right hand side, so the whole layout was the same as a modern bike, so I was going to have the rear brake and gear lever (which was actually a kick-starter) both on the right-hand side of the bike.

I couldn't get the kick-starter to go on the shaft because it was a slightly smaller diameter, so I levered the clamp open as wide as I could with the screwdriver and hammered it onto the shaft. Then I couldn't get the pinch bolt on to it to secure it because I had levered the clamp open so much. A marshal was standing over me and just said what I knew in the pit of my stomach – that the kick-starter wasn't going to stay on without a pinch bolt.

I'd come this far and wasn't going to throw in the towel, so I said to the marshal that the lever would hold, and I hammered the hell out of it a bit more, and off I went. It was so weird; with the gear shift and brake on the same side, you have to use a lot of back brake on those old classic bikes because the front brakes are really shit, and the rear brake is loads better. As it happened, on the plus side, it was now in a race shift pattern (push down to change up a gear, and pull up to change down a gear), so I thought that was alright. I didn't have to try and deal with a gear shift pattern that was the wrong way round for me, as well as the lever being on the wrong side of the bike.

I thought, that's it, we're on it. I finished the lap and started the third lap, thinking to myself that it just had to last for one more lap, and it was all going OK until I got to the Mountain mile again: I went to change down a gear, and there was nothing there – the kick-starter had gone. I couldn't believe it. So I rode the rest of the lap in top gear and retired, I was gutted.

A few months later, in November, I was at the bike show at the NEC and this bloke came up to me and said he had something belonging to me. He said that he was watching the race, and when I went past him I was followed by the 'ting ting ting' sound of the gearshift/kick-start bouncing down the road. He said that it came to a stop right next to him and he'd kept hold of it until he tracked me down. He was such a lovely bloke, and he insisted on giving it back to me, which pretty much sums up the difference between a classic event and a modern one.

The Classic TT really is a great race to be part of. It's a bit like the Goodwood Revival, which is a bit of fun too, but there's a lot more going on at the Classic TT. I really do think it's breathed some life back in to the Manx GP too. I love the variety of bikes that I get to race during the festival, and while I've picked up a couple of wins and second-place finishes at it over the years I can honestly say, hand on heart, that's not why I go.

Bottom line is that I love racing bikes, and I've been around race bikes my whole life, growing up with Dad racing. I love all sorts of bikes, and I love riding them. New, old, fast, slow, sports bikes, touring bikes, naked bikes – I really don't mind as long as it's got two wheels and an engine. Racing has to be enjoyable, otherwise what's the point?

I suppose I'm fairly lucky that I get a kick out of hammering down the Sulby Straight on my superbike at 200mph as well as rattling round on a 50bhp Matchless G50 from the fifties. Some racers just want the crazy yee-hah stuff and aren't interested in the other side of it, the nostalgic side.

Michael Dunlop really likes the Classic TT too. If you haven't seen it, look up when he rode a 1957 Gilera there in 2017. He went for the full look to compliment the bike, with a big beard, pudding-bowl crash helmet and goggles, and he push-started the bike too. There are a lot of current TT stars who wouldn't ride at all, let alone go that far, but I suppose that's what makes the world go round. I'm just glad that I'm not one of them; I love it.

21
Macau

I'm not going to lie: I first went to race in the Macau Grand Prix for the free holiday. What can I say, I'm just like every other racer that has been and ever will be, or at least I was at that point in my career. Fundamentally, bike racers are weak and shallow; we'll do anything to ride a bike. That's why most don't make any money during their time as bike racers; they just can't say no to free stuff, or a trick bike to ride. It's a vicious circle.

Back then I had no expectations or idea of just how Macau would become part of my career and more recently my personal life. I will have literally just finished my 25th Macau Grand Prix a few days before this book goes on sale, so at the time of writing I don't know if I'll have added to my record-breaking nineteen podiums or eight wins there, but I do know that Madame Tussauds in Macau will have added a waxwork model of me to the Macau Grand Prix Legends display, alongside Ron Haslam, Michael Schumacher and Sebastian Vettel, so something went right for me between my first visit there and today.

Macau and I just clicked, and as well as having loads of success on the track over the years I just absolutely love going there to race and spend time somewhere that's so different to home. I even met my partner, Faye, there years ago.

It's a mad place, like nowhere else I've ever been to. It's on the south coast of China and used to be a Portuguese colony until 1999, when it was returned to China, in the same way Hong Kong was returned by the United Kingdom in 1997. Both Hong Kong and Macau are now part of China, but both are able to govern themselves. It's built mostly on land reclaimed from the sea, so it's only twelve square miles. The Isle of Man, which is small, is twenty times bigger than Macau in area, but Macau has a population nearly ten times larger than that of the Isle of Man, making it the most densely populated region on the planet with 55,000 people living on every square mile of land.

Despite being not much bigger than my hometown of Bridgnorth, Macau has the eightieth largest economy in the world, almost entirely as a result of the gambling industry. Virtually the entire region has laws that ban gambling except for Macau, so pretty much anyone in neighbouring China or Hong Kong who wants to gamble has to go to Macau.

The gambling industry in Macau absolutely dwarfs that of Las Vegas, which is often considered to be the gambling capital of the world. In fact, the gambling industry in Macau is seven times bigger than that of Las Vegas. Las Vegas is for stag parties and wannabes; Macau is where the real high rollers go. It's eye-watering just how much money gets left behind in Macau by wealthy gamblers from China and Hong Kong, as well as tourists.

When you think about the wealth, the size of the place, the density of the population, the gambling culture and, more recently, the opening of Western casinos, you've got a recipe for an anything-goes kind of place. It's hardly a huge stretch of the imagination to understand why someone thought closing the roads and having a race round a 3.8-mile lap, with either Armco, brick walls or the South China Sea as run-off areas, would be a good idea. It started as a car race in the mid-fifties, and the motorbikes were added as a support race in the late sixties. These days, the car race is still a big deal and very much the main event. It's the final round of the World Touring Car Cup, and there's a

242

Formula 3 race there too, which the likes of Lewis Hamilton, Michael Schumacher, Mika Hakkinen and Sebastian Vettel have all won on their way to Formula 1.

A fella called Mike Trimby raced in Macau years ago, and when he stopped he set up IRTA. The Macau Grand Prix organisers asked him to help them with the bike race, and Mike knew what he was doing. He knew what bike racers are like, so he offered the riders a free holiday in Thailand after the race in Macau. He sold it to us as an end-of-year bash that wasn't important, but it ended up being important for me, even though I've never had start money for it.

Macau has always been a bit of a party at the end of the year and has always been a bit chaotic. It's never dull. There's always a gang of us from road racing and short circuit racing that go. We aren't that different when it comes down to it; we all like a freebie. So I used to go there, ride round as quick as I could, enjoy myself, then go for a week in Thailand to let off some steam at the end of the season.

The week in Thailand was much more than a post-Macau race holiday: it was a blow-out after a whole season's racing, which used to be just as mad as the race week. Obviously it's changed today – Mike isn't involved any more, there's no Thailand trip – but there is still no money in it; the only money I've ever made from Macau is from my sponsors. The prize money is around £2,500 if you win, which is better than a kick in the teeth but it's nothing compared to how much it costs to do the race. It barely covers the cost of the tyre bill, and I'll never retire on it, but the race and place are very different to anything else that I do, and I really enjoy doing it. I have been lucky to have sponsors that like it too.

My first Macau was a bit of an anticlimax. If I didn't have bad luck then I wouldn't have had any luck. I'd gone there with John Hackett on my McCullough Ducati in 1994 which blew up on the first lap of practice, so any thoughts I might have had of making a big debut went up in smoke, with the rest of the engine. But it wasn't all doom and gloom: we had a really good few laughs, and more often than not I'd be on the wrong end of some of the standard classic pranks.

After a night out, in the hotel lift the guys used to get out of the lift upon arriving at their floor, then reach back in and press all the buttons so that the lift stopped on every level. I was on the fiftieth floor so would have to spend the next twenty minutes just standing in the lift as it stopped on every floor. The bastards kept doing it to me all the time in Macau, and every time I wouldn't realise what they were up to until it was too late.

One time after the race, we were staying at a hotel in Hong Kong and this time I was staying on the lower floor, so I thought I'd get the bastards back. My big moment arrived, and I could barely contain myself; as I stepped out of the lift I went, 'See ya, then, lads', and pressed all the buttons. They were going mad, and as the doors closed all I could hear was 'You wanker!' from inside the lift. I was so pleased with myself that I was chuckling out loud as I zig-zagged along the corridor to the room that I was sharing with John. He had gone to bed early and said that he would leave the door open a bit for me; eventually I got to the room and opened the door that was left ajar.

I was really drunk and busting for a piss, so I went straight to the toilet, switched all the lights on and had one, while leaning against the wall because I was so drunk. By that point I was feeling a bit rough, so I thought I'd better get some sleep. So I got into bed – and straight away realised that there was someone already in it. I thought it must have been John, so in my drunken state I was trying to figure out what to do ... when suddenly I realised there was a Chinese bloke in the bed there next to me!

I'd walked into the room, closed the door, pissed all over this Chinese bloke's toilet seat and got into bed with him. I was so confused, and I sat there looking round the room, trying to work out what the hell was happening, when it finally dawned on me that I was in the wrong room. I shot out the room and looked at what floor I was on to confirm my theory.

I'd got off the lift one floor before I was supposed to. I was so focused on pressing all the buttons in the lift that I'd not really checked it was my floor. But how unlucky is that? The same room on a different floor, also with the door left open? It summed up my first Macau Grand Prix. I eventually found my room and woke John up and said, 'You won't believe what's happened to me'. He didn't.

It's almost impossible to go to Macau without drinking; it's a common theme there. I've always gone to try and enjoy myself, and maybe it's held me back a bit, but, for me at least, the Macau GP is really about enjoying the place and the end of season school's-out atmosphere.

On one occasion, it chucked it down with rain on the Friday night, so Saturday got cancelled, and they said Sunday was also looking like a wash-out. That was it; we were done, and as far as I was concerned that was the season finished right there and then. I was on holiday, so John McGuinness and I went out for some drinks, and for some reason we were drinking champagne all night, and I hate champagne.

The next morning, you've never seen such glorious sunshine, and a bone-dry racetrack. I thought 'Aah, shit'; I had the mother and father of all hangovers and I knew that they would run the race. I was in a terrible state, but at least the race wasn't starting until about 1 pm, so I did have some time to recover. Even so, I remember being so dehydrated that after just the warm-up lap, I pulled up to the line at the start of the race and my tongue had stuck to the roof of my mouth. It was a fifteen-lap race, and to this day I don't know how, but I won. Granted, I had a trick Ducati that year, and clearly some luck, but considering I was in such a state after just the warm-up lap, it's a miracle I finished the race at all, let alone won it.

Sticking to the subject of drinking in Macau, on one occasion we got out there the week before the race and spent the time setting up and doing promotional stuff. On the first night, we were on the beers until something stupid like 6 am. Then, out of nowhere, the organisers showed up at the hotel and said there was a charity go-kart thing at 9 am that we all had to go to. As you can imagine, we were all hanging, and no one was at all bothered about going, but we all had to do it; it was part of the contract.

We got taken to the go-kart track in a minibus, and when we got there we all sat at the table as our hangovers started to kick in hard. Stuart Easton, Mark Miller and Gary Johnson were by far in the worst state. In contrast, the car racers all showed up immaculate, fully fresh and perfectly presented. The people running the go-kart place gave us some posh blue overalls, showed us round the karts, which were brand-new, then asked if we wanted a drink of coffee or coke. I couldn't believe it when Gary Johnson asked for a beer, and I was more surprised when the bloke said no problem and asked him what beer he wanted. Just to be sure, we asked them if we could drink booze and race the karts. I couldn't believe it when they said yeah, no problem, and showed us the bar right there at the go-kart track.

At 10 am we were all back on the beer again, except this time with go-karts, and the event was due to go on till 4 pm. You can imagine what happened next. We were drinking cocktails, shorts, beer, you name it, and spent six hours just messing about in the karts. It wouldn't happen anywhere else in the world. Everyone was so drunk that there were people driving the wrong way round the track. The karts were just coming apart all over the place; it was carnage.

Mark Miller fell asleep on the grid for one of the races; he was sat in his kart, unconscious. Even the bloke with the flag was running across the track, trying to dodge karts. There were karts flying through the air and all sorts; it was so dangerous and at the same time it was like a cartoon. How no one got seriously hurt I'll never know, although when Mark Miller went to sit down on the minibus back to the hotel he missed the seat completely and broke his finger. Needless to say, by the end the karts were all destroyed. The car guys, who had obviously treated it much more seriously than us, were disgusted. That event has never happened since. Years later, I found out that the kart track was owned by Faye's family.

Every year, the organisers always got us to do some sort of car racers vs. bike racers thing. We really hate each other, but after the go-karts episode I think they hate us more. Once we played football against them and just battered them for the whole game. We had a few big people in our team like Simon Beck, which helped on the pitch but also after the game.

We were able to lift up the car drivers' people carrier and put blocks under it, just enough to get the wheels off the floor, so when they went to pull away they were all sat in it, clueless as to why it wouldn't move. The best bit was that once they figured it out they couldn't do anything about it because they're all really small and weak.

Macau is all about extremes, and if at one end of the scale you've got wacky races and pranks on the car racers, at the other end of the scale you can get thrown by something unexpected and quite deep. While I was on the grid before a race one year, this German TV reporter came up to me and asked if I was easily offended. I said I wasn't, and asked what it was that he wanted to ask me, so he came out with the question of whether I believed in god, which threw me completely.

Usually on the grid, I get the same questions about what the plan is for the race, if I'm happy with the setup of the bike, who do I think will be my main rivals and all that sort of normal stuff. I asked him where he was going with the question, because when I get a random question like that then I'm automatically suspicious of it being a piss-take.

The reporter said he just wanted to know what people like me think about religion, faith and god, given what we do for a living. I thought it was a fair question from him; he seemed genuine enough, and to be honest, in all my years of racing I'd never been asked the question, or even really thought about it, so I had a think, and said, 'Probably not, no'. He said 'probably'? and pressed me for a yes or no, so I said, 'OK, I'll say no, then'. He asked why I didn't believe in god, so I gave him my rationale – along the lines of how can God let good people go, but not people that have done really bad things – and he seemed happy enough with that.

Then he moved on to asking other questions about ghosts and stuff – totally random stuff, nothing to do with racing. It turned out that he presents the German equivalent of *Most Haunted*, and I was instantly more interested in what stories he had than vice versa, so we got talking about haunted castles and things like that while sat on the grid, a few minutes before the race is due to start. I asked him if he had ever seen anything, and he said he hadn't but that he had felt things, and been properly shit-scared in some places. I got one of my sponsors over to join in the conversation, because I knew he was into ghosts and that sort of stuff, and then to my surprise he gets his phone out and starts showing us pictures of ghosts, including what looked like a boy being hanged. It really messed with my head moments before the race, but it's another example of the sort of random, mad stuff that only seems to happen in Macau.

A more predictable line of questioning that you get at Macau, or on the subject of Macau, is how it compares to the other road races that I do, like the North West 200, and obviously the TT. The short answer is that it doesn't; everything about it is totally unique, and even how we get the bikes there and back is like nowhere else. They get airfreighted out in special containers but come back to the UK on a boat, so they spend weeks at sea. We have to literally cover them from front to back with grease and penetrating oil like WD40 to stop them rotting at sea, with the salt in the sea air. It takes ages to clean them when they get back because as well as being filthy after the race, every single component is covered in some sort of protection against the elements at sea. It's a full nut-and-bolt strip and clean.

The course itself is short compared to the TT and North West 200, and I would describe it as a street circuit rather than a road circuit. It's entirely surrounded by high-rise buildings, so there's a really unique – and slightly claustrophobic – sense of being enclosed. The buildings make the bike sound different too. I can hear the sound of my own bike, and anyone else's who is nearby, bouncing off the buildings, which you don't get at the TT or North West. There is also the humidity and heat to deal with at Macau, which adds to the unique nature of the challenge, as well as the feeling that I'm a long, long way from home.

I wouldn't say that the Macau Grand Prix is any more, or less, dangerous than any other road race; it's just different. The TT is long and really fast, but for the most part I'm racing on my own there, against a clock. The North West 200 is a much easier course to ride, but it's a mass start, so I'm racing really close to other riders, slip-streaming and competing for track position at 200mph. At the time of writing, the Macau lap record, set by Stuart Easton in 2010, is an average of 95mph, the North West 200 is 123mph by Michael Dunlop, and the TT lap record is 135mph by Peter Hickman, so Macau is a relatively slow lap. However, the whole lap is lined entirely with Armco barriers that are taller than me in places, and brick walls, so there is zero run-off anywhere.

The bottom line is that every race at every racetrack I ever entered during my whole career has been dangerous. I've seen lads die on the start line at a regular racetrack like Cadwell Park without even moving. It may seem strange, but I don't differentiate between any of the road races and any of the short circuits as being more or less dangerous than another. There will certainly be bike racers who will see one track as more dangerous than another, but, rightly or wrongly, I just don't. They're all just strips of tarmac, and each one is unique and has its own unique challenges and dangers. Macau is no different, except that it actually is.

22

2014–2019: Old Dog, New Tricks

|stuck with the IWR team for 2014, and they swapped the Hondas
|for the BMW S1000RR, which had all the ingredients to be a good
race bike, but the harsh reality was that the team just didn't have
the budget for getting the right expertise that you needed then
(and now) to manage the electronics on the latest generation of
sports bikes.

The bottom line is that there is only so much power that you can put
down through a tyre, and with everyone on the same control tyre the
racing is very close and the margins are tiny. You need the very best
person on electronics to make the difference, otherwise you'd be
nowhere. Nowadays there are plenty of people who are good with the
electronics, but in 2014, when it was relatively new, there weren't
many. It's a different generation of electronics now to the type back in
the Ducati days of 2010, but the fact is that electronic rider aids had

crept back into the picture again, and in 2014 the team just didn't have the know-how.

The sheer cost of running a competitive superbike then and now is so big that it's the single reason why I switched to the superstock class two years later in 2016 when I set up my own team. To run a superbike I'd need a big team bursting with electronics expertise, which would in turn need huge funds, and I knew I couldn't do it. With superstock it's much simpler and financially easier to run a bike and be competitive.

In short, the 2014 BSB season was a bit of a non-event for me, but the North West 200 and TT were a different matter. All the limitations of the bike don't really apply to a track that's as unique as the TT course and the North West 200. I finished second in both the superstock races, missing out on the win in both by 0.5 seconds – to Alistair Seeley in the first race and Michael Dunlop in the second race. There was also a couple of fourth places in the Superbike races, so I was really looking forward to the TT. The BMW seemed much more suited to road racing than short circuits.

At the TT, the bike was really strong and I came away with a 6th in the superstock race, a 5th in the Superbike race and a 9th in the Senior, which I was really happy with. More than that, though, I'd lapped the course faster than I ever had before, and I did my first lap at an average speed of over 130mph. Everyone was going at it really hard that year, and at that time only a few people had broken the magic 130mph lap, so to be in the mix felt great, especially as everything in the BSB championship had been so mediocre for me.

I started the 2015 season without a full-time ride for the short circuits – for the first time in twenty-two years. However, I did get a call from a bloke that I used to race against in Macau called Rico Penzkofer, who had by then set up his own race team. Penz13 are a German team that run BMWs, and he asked me if I'd be up for riding at the TT, North West 200 and Macau. He also asked if I'd fancy racing in a road race at a place called Frohburg in Germany, and so began a few seasons of doing new and different things that I didn't really see coming. I also got a call from an Italian bike manufacturer called Paton asking me to ride their twin-cylinder bike in the Lightweight TT, and since it didn't clash with any of the races that Penz13 wanted me to ride in, I said yes. It would prove to be a decision that would lead to something very special for me, but not for another year.

The North West 200 and TT were really good that year, but the race at Frohburg was brilliant. There was a few of us from the UK who went, including Lee Johnston and Gary Johnson, and it was proper old-school back-to-basics racing. The circuit was really remote, so it was like riding through someone's village then out the other side, racing round T-junctions. It was also really fast in some places, so we were passing each other a lot. It was new to me and something I hadn't done before, and to be honest, it had been a while since I'd done some-thing different. It was exciting and a lot of fun.

Lee Johnston and I decided to really mess with Gary Johnson's head at Frohburg. The thing is, as well as being the biggest prankster in the paddock himself, Gary always wants to change everything all the time on his bikes; he's always fiddling and really picky. I knew that the bike he was riding there had been in a crash the week before, so I kept saying to him that when I'd been following him, I thought his bike didn't look right, and that I was sure that it looked a bit bent, and Lee would do the same. Then we'd go back to the motorhome and watch Gary through the window as he went back to his bike, and he'd be getting his mechanics to change everything on it, after every session. He went round and round in circles with that bike, looking for a problem that wasn't there until his head went completely. There wasn't anything wrong with the bike, but by the time the race came he was certain that his bike was bent and just couldn't bring himself to ride it flat out.

I got a couple of podiums that year, and even though I had my own race team the following year, I went back with Penz13 and won all three superbike races. I'd definitely love to go back, and one day I think I probably will.

There was another race that I did with Penz13 in 2017 – the Imatra road race in Finland. I'd always wanted to race at Imatra because of an iconic photo of Barry Sheene racing there in 1978, at the Grand Prix of Finland. In the photo, he's wheelying across some railway lines on his Texaco Suzuki, and I absolutely loved that picture and thought it was so cool. There hadn't been any racing at Imatra since 1986, but it had started back up in 2016, so when the chance came the following year, I couldn't pass it up.

I had never raced at a circuit like Imatra. It was quite special, especially the start/finish straight, which is spectacular because it is really narrow and lined with trees. It was also flat out, something like 180mph with either crowds of people right next to you, or trees. The track is a lot like the North West 200, in as much as it's got some properly fast straights and some slower fiddly bits too, but the setting is different. It's basically in some woods, whereas the North West 200 is on the coast. The crowds were massive, and the people were lovely, so it's without a doubt another place that I'd love to go back to.

I've been asked to go back to loads of different places like Frohburg and Imatra since I did them, but it's just having the time to do it, especially now I'm running my own team. For sure, if someone told me that there was a bike ready, and all I had to do was turn up, I'd do it – especially in Germany, where the beer and sausages are too good not to go again anyway! Stuff like the Pikes Peak Hill Climb or a land speed record would also get me going. I'm all up for trying new things, but I do have my limits.

About five or six years ago, Dad asked me to do a land speed record thing for a friend of his who'd decided to build a motorbike with a Chinook helicopter engine. I said not a chance, that it had to be the most dangerous thing in the world, but Dad was on at me for ages to do it, trying to tell me that it would help me. After a few weeks I asked him if *he* would do it, and he said not a chance!

I'd love to do a land speed record attempt somewhere iconic like Bonneville Salt Flats in Utah, USA. I watched a film called *The Fastest Indian*, starring Anthony Hopkins. It's a true story about a fella called

Burt Munro who built his own bike and took it to Bonneville to break a record. I thought it was brilliant. It's probably what made me have the first thought about going to Bonneville, but I wouldn't want to go with something that's got a Chinook helicopter engine. Something modern, high-tech and really fast would be good.

Another thing that I didn't see coming was when I started testing bikes for *Performance Bikes* magazine in 2014. I never really wanted anything to do with media, but a mate who works for the magazine talked me in to helping him by datalogging and giving feedback on road bikes. Surprisingly, I've ended up really enjoying it, and trying loads of new bikes that I otherwise would never have ridden. Some have surprised me, and some have disappointed me.

To be fair, I do get the best bits of road testing: I'll show up, ride the bikes, log the data and they write down my thoughts. I'll also do a bit of van driving with them if we're going abroad, but I do now appreciate how much time and effort goes into those tests, which I didn't before. There's so much to organise, and a lot of standing around waiting for stuff that you never think of when you see the finished magazine.

Jeremy McWilliams loves all that testing and evaluating stuff too, but it's fair to say that he approaches it very differently from the way I do. He's still very intense and ultra-competitive at everything. At the Phillip Island classic race in 2019, we were out playing pool with Glen Richards and one of the press guys from Australia. I was on Jeremy's team, and without him knowing, I told the others that we should play for £20 a frame and keep doing "double or quits" until the pot got really big – then I'd start deliberately playing badly, and lose the game to try and wind Jeremy up.

Poor old Jezza, he just couldn't cope when I started playing really badly and doing really daft things like scuffing the cue ball. He was so overwhelmed with rage that he was actually rolling round on the floor, close to tears. He is quite possibly the most competitive person that I know, and he will not stop until he's satisfied that he is done, and that he is the best.

When I ride the press bikes, I don't hold back, and nor do the other testers. More often than not, we'll arrive at the same assessment and verdict for the bikes, but apparently the readers like to see a 'pro' like me giving a verdict from time to time. It's a really good laugh, and I really do enjoy it, because there's very little pressure on my part. I don't have to worry about any deadlines or do any of the planning. Not many people get given keys to all those new bikes, and because I love motorbikes the value of this opportunity isn't lost on me. I hope I can keep doing it, but I know time eventually runs out for everyone.

As well as motorbikes, the other thing I love is aeroplanes; they're another big part of my life. I always had it in my little brain that if I wasn't a bike racer, I'd like to be a fighter pilot. I was fascinated by the World War Two era in particular. I used to reckon that if I were around during World War Two, I'd definitely have put myself forward to be a Spitfire pilot. I really liked the idea of it ... until I got the chance to do it.

A couple of years ago, Faye gave me an experience gift which allowed me to have a flight in the back of a Spitfire, which was a genuinely life-long dream of mine. When the day finally arrived, I was taken through all the safety stuff, and they made me watch a video all about it. I was thinking to myself that I wouldn't be scared of any of it, and that the instructor probably didn't know what I did for a living. So I watched it, and thought nothing of it, then put the flight suit on and met the pilot. He said he was going to video me while I showed him what I had to do if I needed to get out of the aircraft. The video was their evidence that I had taken in the information in the briefing video.

The procedure for getting out of the cockpit in an emergency was the same as when the original pilots had to do it: pull the screen back, undo something, pull the seat up, open the door and a load of other stuff that I'd decided was all too complicated. I told him that if the plane was going down, I would stay put and enjoy the last few moments of my life in the cockpit of a Spitfire and that I was OK with that, as there aren't many better ways to go. I got told off, and he had to show me it all again.

Then they started up the Merlin engine, and my jaw hit the floor – it was so impressive. The pilot taxied over to the runway and took off really smoothly. It was a beautiful day, and we went out over the white cliffs of Dover. It was literally perfect in every way.

The plane felt so small, like I could reach out and touch both wing tips. I felt really vulnerable and couldn't stop wondering how the hell young lads went to war in something so small and flimsy. The pilot let me fly it for a bit, and then he went out to sea, turned around, and came back towards the white cliffs, and did a really slow, smooth roll. Now, I'm not into rollercoasters and stuff like that, because I get sick really easily, but when he did the roll I never felt a thing.

He asked me if I was OK, and I said yes, so he went back round and did it again, this time with a good bit more G-force. He dipped the nose, and then whacked the stick back full, and this time I could hear the engine working much harder, and I'll always remember that the engine smelt like a classic bike. The combination of the extra G-force and smell of the engine nearly made me puke, but I hung on.

Then we flew over to Brands Hatch, and he asked if I wanted him to do a lap, so I said OK. He must have really been going for a quick lap time, because the G-force felt really strong as he was chucking the plane about. I had to tell him to stop because I couldn't cope and was about to heave my guts up. He landed, and after all the years of thinking I could be a fighter pilot, I realised a few things. It was bloody dangerous because there was no protection from being shot at, and while I'm sure that I would have got used to the sick feeling it really put me off. My already massive respect for the people that flew the Spitfire and other planes like it in World War Two went through the roof. Bloody heroes, every last one of them.

One of my sponsors, Sean Eagle, let me fly his plane to the North West 200 once. I flew it pretty much the whole way there and all but landed it, but Sean took it down the last 5 metres or so. After the race, I got so drunk that on the way back I fell asleep, so I didn't get involved with any flying. As Sean was coming in to land, I woke up and said I didn't think it sounded right, and he said it hadn't for about the last half an hour. Then just as the engine coughed, James Whitham cut in front of us and landed, so we had to wait a little longer before we could land. We both jumped out to take a look at the engine, and the thing was covered in oil. Some of the bolts that held the cylinder head on had snapped, and the engine was literally falling apart. We couldn't have been more than a few minutes away from the engine just dying.

One of Sean's mates got Dad a ride in the plane for his sixtieth birthday, and I said to the bloke not to go too mad with Dad in the back. The pilot just took off and straight away went vertical through the clouds. The next time I saw him was about a mile away behind me, upside down all along the runway, doing loads of stunts. Poor Dad; when he got out, he was covered in sick and was as white as a sheet. It did make me laugh though.

I did a couple of rounds for the Gearlink Kawasaki team in 2015 to help them out, and I was still getting the odd call from superbike teams for one-off rides here and there. I was happy to help and was sometimes able to go in and point them in a direction by passing on some of the knowledge that I'd accumulated over the years, but it was then that I really started thinking about running my own race team.

I realised that you can moan all you like about how people run their team, or what they spend their money on, but they're doing it the way they think is right, and I just started thinking that I wanted to start doing it the way I thought was right.

Batham's racing started in 2016 with me and Alec Tague. Alec was a mechanic who I'd seen about in the paddock for years, and he was working for Robin Croft at SMT Racing at the time. Robin was keen to do mostly just road racing, and Batham's wanted to do the short circuit stuff too, so basically we used Robin's workshop and truck, and he put a bit of money in, then Batham's put the rest of the money in. It was a really good deal for everyone.

I didn't really know Alec at the time, and as I've said before plenty of times in this book, it's very important for me to have a mechanic that

257

I trust, and who trusts me. I had actually asked a fella called Warren Beardsley if he would work on my bike in Macau at the end of 2015 because I had worked with him on the HM Plant Honda at the TT in 2010 and got on really well with him. I really rated the standard of his work, but he couldn't come to Macau that year, so the only other person that I knew, and who had a good reputation, was Alec. We got on really well, so it went from there, and he's been in my garage ever since at every single race.

At Batham's Racing, we can do whatever we want, and use any bike. It's great to have the freedom and flexibility, but to step up to the next level we'd need to get a manufacturer on board, and the problem with getting a manufacturer on board is that everything gets bigger. The budgets are bigger, there are more people, and there is more hassle. We've got a great team and good people, like Graham Ward, Fred Morton, and Luke Quigley, and we all get on really well. There's never any tension; we'll have a glass of wine at the end of the day, and it feels like a family. Taylor Mackenzie has joined the team as a second rider, and he's fitted right in too. It all works. We all chip in, clean the truck, the toilet, cook food, whatever needs doing, and no one rocks the boat. A happy team is a fast team.

I'll be honest, it was hard to come down to the superstock class. Once you've ridden a full-blooded Superbike, you know it's the best, and everything else just isn't quite the same. However, I'd much rather be competitive on a superstock bike than making up the numbers on a Superbike. Running a Superstock bike is still really expensive but it's far more sustainable. I'm lucky because I have some really good sponsors, so I can afford to run a really competitive team at superstock. Sponsors can turn round any time and stop; I've had it happen to me so many times during my career.

If Batham's pulled out, I would be in trouble, but not just for the money: they do it for the right reasons, and are so easy to get on with. They don't do it to make themselves famous, or even to promote the beer; they do it because they enjoy it. They simply love seeing their beer on the side of my bikes riding round, and they are part of the team, not just sponsors. They really get involved at the workshop and at the races. If you have a sponsor who's on a big ego trip, you've got no chance; it'll be great for a short time and then burn out.

I'm also very lucky to have a girlfriend who is a big motorsport fan. As well as running her own very successful property development business, she is part of a very wealthy family. Her grandfather is called Stanley Ho, and basically he held the monopoly on the Macau gambling industry for seventy-five years. Faye is Macanese, and we first met in 2009, when I was at the Macau Grand Prix, and we always got on well, and kept in touch. Eventually, a couple of years ago, both our circumstances meant that we were finally able to get together, which is something else that I didn't expect.

It takes a lot to surprise me, but Faye managed to in 2018, when she bought me a Honda RC213V, which is a straight copy of the 2015 Honda MotoGP race bike but for the road. Not only is it the most expensive motorcycle that money can buy, but it is the second most expensive product that Honda sells (the most expensive being a jet plane that Honda makes).

It was quite funny how I found out. Just before Macau in 2018 I was calling people about getting a superbike because we didn't have one (well, we do, but it's a TT-specification superbike, so it's a bit heavier and doesn't have the £20,000 engine and other expensive details that all makes it just that little bit better). I knew that Peter Hickman was going to be very difficult to beat, so I was looking to get something exactly the same or better.

Then, just as I was on the phone to someone, about to agree on an arrangement for a superbike to ride at Macau, Alec told me to put the phone down and said that Faye had a surprise for me. She had asked Alec, and a couple of other people in the know, what the best bike in the world was because she wanted to buy me something special. Everyone gave her the same answer (the Honda RC213V), not really expecting anything to come of it, but she went and bought one. It was the road bike, and straight away Alec suggested that I could race it at

Macau, and Faye thought it was a great idea too, so we got straight on with converting it to a race bike.

We could have done with a bit of testing with it before we took it to Macau, because there's so much to learn about any new bike, but in particular the RCV's electronics are very sophisticated and like nothing else we'd come across before. It's an incredible bike, and we really needed something special to beat Peter, and in the end I finished in second place, less than a second behind him.

Looking back, it was 100% the right thing to do; especially from a marketing point of view, it's been massive. The RCV is such a rare motorcycle that everywhere we take it there's so much interest. We've definitely benefitted from a lot of exposure that we otherwise wouldn't have had if Faye hadn't bought the Honda for me. Needless to say, I'd never be able to afford something like it, but luckily I've got a very understanding girlfriend who is also a petrolhead.

I'm coming up to the end of my riding career, but I'm still finding myself having new experiences, and riding something like the RCV is a dream. There's nothing else I've ridden that's as special, and that's why we thought we had to race it at the TT in 2019.

Anyway, back to the team. So we had some good times with Robin, then at the end of 2017 he wanted to take a step back, so we moved to a unit down the road from the Batham's brewery in Dudley, bought my old HM Plant Honda race trailer, which was previously the Castrol Honda WSB race truck when Colin Edwards was riding for them, and Batham's Racing as it is today was formed. In the team, everyone has a say, everyone gets heard. I know that I'm the one that has to make the last decision, but it's right to have everyone say something.

In 2016 I rode the Paton at the TT, and I managed to finish 3rd in the Lightweight race. It was a massive treat for me to be back on the podium with a petrol-powered bike. I don't really think the TT Zero wins or podiums are as valuable as petrol-powered TT wins, but I'll take them anyway. Don't get me wrong, the TT Zero wins aren't easy, but regardless of the purists' debate around electric power versus petrol power, when all is said and done there are simply more people to beat to get onto the podium of a petrol-powered TT race.

The Paton was terrible, mainly because the rear suspension was really old-fashioned and made the bike hard work to ride. However, it was light and fast, which at the TT are probably the two main ingredients for a competitive bike. Paton asked me to go back the following year and said that they had made a lot of changes to it, so I thought I might have a chance, not least because Michael Dunlop didn't have a great bike that year. In contrast, Martin Jessop did have a very good bike that year, which had everything that money could buy thrown at it.

In the race, I thought that if I could catch Martin on the road, I'd be OK, which I managed to do. But he was quite clever: his bike had a bigger fuel tank than mine, so he started the race with more fuel than I did, which meant he needed less fuel putting in at the pit stop. Despite me getting to the pit stop first, Martin put five seconds into me during the stop, so I had to catch him back up again, which was hard going. He rode really well, and during the last few miles he passed me and I passed him back, but it was clear he wasn't going to let me have it. It was a bit like 2000 when I was lapping with Joey, except this time I was the old fella and Martin was the young upstart. I decided to just follow Martin, and I kept the revs down to get my first petrol-powered TT win in nineteen years.

The win felt so much better than it did in 1998. Back then, I never really appreciated it the same way. After my debut win, it was more like, right that's done, let's get on with the next one. I notice that nowadays whenever I get on the podium, I have a really good look around and take it in. I'll stand there and think to myself that it could be the last time. I find myself taking longer to look round and soak up the details like the crowds and photographers, and buildings. The TT is so special, and to win there is the ultimate win anyway, but it means even more now that I know I won't be doing it for many more years. I never thought I'd still be going this long, so it's all a bonus to me. I really did my best to have a proper good look around from the top step of that podium.

In 2018, I was doing OK in the British Superstock championship, then Taylor Mackenzie became available and needed a ride for the last few rounds of the season, so I took a back seat. I raced against his dad back in the late nineties, and against Taylor in 2016 for the title, but to be fair I was always chasing him for it. He actually won the title that year, on a BMW, so it was an easy decision to take him on and for me to take a back seat. He fitted right in with the team and started winning races virtually straight away, so it was easy for everyone to just stick together for 2019 and make Batham's Racing a two-rider team.

I knew taking Taylor on was going to be difficult for me personally, as I'd be both a rider and team manager, but I didn't realise just how difficult it would be. At this level you can't afford anything that takes your mind off racing, and I knew in my heart that I wasn't being very successful at being both a rider and a manager. The best thing to do would be to not ride, or to get a team manager in, but the trouble is that I still really enjoy racing it, and I really want to do it. I still love the buzz of rolling out of pit lane, but for now I've got to do the bare minimum and concentrate on Taylor.

The thing is that I'm still doing new things, I'm still getting results on the roads and, most of all, I still love racing. It's a habit, I've been around it since I was born, it's what I know, and I don't know anything else. I can't stop, although without Batham's I'd have had to stop years ago. The team is brilliant, it's enjoyable, but the day I stop enjoying it, I'll just stop. I've just got to figure out what my exact role is in the team.

Some people make the mistake of making a big song and dance about retiring, and then they look stupid if they come back. To ride just on the roads, I would need to do a bit of short circuit racing too, and for that I need to be bike-fit and mentally sharp, so I can't see myself retiring from just one. Either way, if the last three or four seasons have taught me anything, it's that I really don't know what's around the corner, and that there are new experiences and fresh challenges to be had all the time.

23
After the Flag

At Macau recently I was walking back to the hotel with Gary Johnson when I realised that when I look back on it I have had such a laugh, and there are a lot of riders who I know haven't had half as much fun as I have. I mean, they might enjoy that whole training thing, but most don't. They do it because they feel like they have to. We used to be in the pubs and enjoying the social, and we still managed to have a fantastic experience.

If it finished tomorrow, I could look back on it and go 'wow'. I've done virtually everything I wanted to do, but if I'm honest, I could have been better if I'd had some advice and trained hard. It's not regret; it's what I learned. If I knew then what I know now, I could have been on a factory GP bike, but then I'd have missed out on other stuff. I wouldn't change it for the world.

I've often wondered if I would swap one of my TT wins for a BSB championship, and I must say that I probably would. I dearly would have loved to have won a BSB championship. I finished 2nd and 3rd in BSB a few times, but I have never had the balls to go that last couple of percent to win. Likewise, I'd give my right bollock for a Senior TT or Superbike TT win. Having said that, I do take comfort from the fact that the times when I finished in second or third place in the big-bike

TTs, at least I've been beaten by proper legends, like Joey, DJ, Simmo, or McCallen all at the peak of their careers.

I've enjoyed so many of the championships in so many ways and hated others; they're all so different. I've also raced against so many people over the years, from Steve Hislop, Carl Fogarty, Jeremy McWilliams and Niall Mackenzie, right through to Shane Byrne, Peter Hickman and Josh Brookes, and everyone in between including the likes of Mick Doohan, Kevin Schwantz, Max Biaggi, Kenny Roberts Jnr, Alex Criville – the list goes on. You don't realise how fast those guys are; they just operate on a whole different level.

It does make me feel really old to know that I've been racing that long, that there are people that I've raced against and then, years later, I've also raced against their kids. Robert and Michael Dunlop, Ron and Leon Haslam, Niall and Taylor Mackenzie, Johnny Rea Senior and Junior, and Alan Irwin and Glen Irwin. There are so many people that I've raced against. I just can't remember them all.

Cal Crutchlow and Johnny Rea stood out for me; I could always see what was going to happen with them. They were always going to make it to the very top of the sport as they just had that bit extra that others around them didn't quite have. Cal made it through sheer bloody-minded determination and being really headstrong. He can ride a bike until the wheels fall off, and he is a lot like Michael Dunlop in that way. Johnny is more natural and hardly has to try. Whatever 'it' is that the greats of the sport have that the others don't, Johnny has got it. For me, the biggest surprise is that he never got a proper shot in MotoGP, and Honda let him go to Kawasaki. He would have been brilliant in MotoGP once he'd adapted to the different tyres and brakes.

I honestly didn't think Cal would make it as far as he has; he has done so well to get where he's got to in MotoGP, and I'm super impressed. Racing in MotoGP has made him faster and he worked out early on that he needs to go faster or get dropped. It's that simple. He'll go as fast as he can until he falls off, then he'll go again, and go faster. If you're a bit of a wimp, you won't make it to the top, or even make it as a pro. A lot of people knocked Cal, but I tell you what, to stay in the paddock as long as he has, and run in the top five during the Rossi and Marquez era is amazing, and he deserves all the reward and kudos that comes with it. He's been to my house, and I've played golf with him a few times, and I've had some really good laughs with him.

There has also been some massive characters along the way. Jim Moodie, Iain Duffus and Simon Beck were all just that bit larger than life, or that bit more outspoken, and then there was Sean Emmett – he was the one who shocked me; he was just wrong.

Ability wise, Karl Harris was amazing. He was my teammate at Honda and was such hot property that he was part of the reason Honda let me go at the end of 2005. He won the British Supersport title three times, and he won the European Superstock championship too. You could put the back wheel in the front of the bike and the front wheel in the back, and he'd still be fast.

Karl was so naturally gifted and he earned an awful lot of money in a really short space of time, but he lost it all. I think it all happened too fast for him, and he made some bad choices and lost his way. He really could have done with a manager. The night before he crashed at the TT and died, he came round to my motorhome and it seemed like he was in a good place and he seemed happy again, but I felt so sorry for him because he was so skint.

He didn't even have enough money for a bottle of wine which when you consider how much money he made at the start of his career seems incredible. I think he was at the TT because he enjoyed it and not because he needed money. Karl did used to have a lot of crashes, so I never really thought it was the place for him to go. He was such a lovely person, and he had a heart of gold.

Troy Corser is another one who just defies logic. Watching him at the Goodwood Revival in 2018 was spectacular. If you think you can ride a bike, take it from me that you can't until you've ridden with Troy Corser. His ability is amazing. He was so drunk the night before the race that the bouncers had literally picked him up and thrown him out of the place. The next morning, he got up and raced this BMW that's ninety years old or something, with no suspension, and he slid through the corners on its engine cases, across the tarmac. The tyres were inches clear off the ground – there was daylight between the tyres and tarmac. He was balancing the bike on the engine, then tyres, then engine, then tyres. He thrashed the field. What a rider. Absolutely phenomenal.

Some of racing's biggest characters aren't the racers themselves and are probably people you've never heard of. There was this fella called Tricky, who used to hang around with Nick Morgan and help out his team. He was a lot older than us, but he was the bloke that we would take the piss out of. He was always the butt of the jokes, and he was brilliant. Every team needs someone like him to make it more fun. There's always one in any circle of friends, and the piss-taking isn't nasty, so that person enjoys it as well. I should know, because I get plenty too! You really have to have thick skin for life in the paddock.

John Barton was and still is a really good guy to wind up because he's got a really short fuse. He's a good mate of mine who's been racing at the TT for even longer than me. Years ago, I was at Pembrey and I went out for a few drinks with a few others, but John went to bed in his caravan. When we got back, we wound the legs up on his caravan and pushed it down the paddock into a field. It was going well until he woke up while we were pushing the caravan and went mad at us, which just made it funnier.

I've had races with other people who aren't famous but were fantastic racers, and I've made a lot of friends who don't race any more and who I miss. Steven Thompson rode with us for years, and we helped him out with a bike. He had a massive crash at the North West 200 in 2015 when he was avoiding Dean Harrison, who'd lost control in front of him. He crashed at about 150mph and was in a coma for four days fighting for his life with a broken femur, collapsed lung, bleeding on the brain, damaged nerves – and he lost his left arm.

Steven is still one of my closest friends, and I miss him in the paddock because his character wasn't serious, so being around him made it all feel a little less intense. It gets very serious very quick, so it's good to have people like him and his brother Paul around, who will just sit there and take the piss out of each other and you. When I heard that he'd had a massive crash I was gutted, but considering that it left him barely alive he's done really well. He's got a lot of pain still, including false pains in the arm he doesn't have any more. It would be great to get some of the old boys back together; maybe one day we will be in the same place at the same time again for a reunion.

Basically, your regular social life is gone when you are racing. Everyone is off doing normal stuff and socialising at weekends, and I would miss all that because I'd usually be away racing. As a kid I would always want to go with my dad to his races, so it's been pretty much like that long before I became a racer myself. I had friends but not really many close ones, maybe one or two.

Don't get me wrong, it's brilliant when you're there at the race meeting. I still love the whole paddock life; it's been my home since I was a baby. Neil Tuxworth, who ran Honda Racing up until very recently and was around when Dad was racing, has known me since I was a baby.

In the paddock, we all speak, we all joke, but it's mostly acquaintances rather than mates, but after the racing, on Sunday evening everyone in the paddock goes home to their lives until the next meeting. It's a travelling circus, and if you stop and think about it too much, it makes no sense at all, all these people coming together just for a few people to ride round in circles for forty-five minutes or so.

I love being at the circuits – I know it sounds really corny but I've been going to all of them for as long as I can remember – but I hate the travelling now. I've travelled so many miles over the years, to circuits all over the world, and spent so much of my life living out of a case, that it has been normal for me for as long as I can remember.

It's a lifestyle that comes at a price, but it has been such a fantastic privilege to live it. I've met incredible people, and ridden on some of the greatest racetracks in the world. TT course aside, I'd have to rate Brands Hatch, Oulton Park and Thruxton as my favourite UK circuits, and I consider them every bit as good to race on as Mugello in Italy, Phillip Island in Australia and Suzuka in Japan. I also raced at the Twin Ring at Motegi when the Japanese GP was moved there for the first time in 1999, after Daijiro Kato died at Suzuka the year before. It's mad to think of all the circuits I've been to.

Then there are the bikes that I've been lucky enough to ride. The GP bike in 1999 was a really good bike, but it was so slow compared to everything else out there. In isolation it was mega, but against the bikes it was supposed to compete with it was useless. All the bikes have been good in different ways. The HRC Fireblade in 2004 was especially good – not just the race bike but the whole effort behind it by Honda. It was much more than just a race bike; it meant everything to so many people on the other side of the world.

The McCullough Ducati 888 and 916 were brilliant too, because they were really innovative at the time and moved things forward in terms of performance. The Ducati 998 race bikes in 2002 and 2003, and the 1098s in 2008, were stunning in every possible way, and the 1098s especially moved the game on, just like the 888 did in its day. Like people, there has been so many bikes that I've raced over the years that it's impossible to remember them all, but those ones really stand out for me.

The biggest change in the paddock that I've seen is that years ago everyone used to go to the bar for a drink at the end of the day. We seemed a lot closer then as a group of people, and then it started to get a little bit more serious and we weren't allowed to be seen drinking, so we'd just drink in someone's motorhome. Then it went to the next stage, and people would gossip about people drinking in the motor-home. Now it seems that all the fun has gone from it for the younger riders coming through. I don't really see them taking time to actually enjoy the paddock and the variety of people in it; I only ever see them running or cycling, and taking the paddock life just as seriously as the racing. It's a shame, because it's not necessary, but I suppose it's worth it to them.

I met Barry McGuigan, the ex-professional boxer, once at an airport, when I was being flown into Northern Ireland for an awards thing. He was in the same VIP room as me, and we got talking. He was a really interesting bloke and inevitably we got talking about training, and how hard boxers train. He said that my frame and build is so lean that if I trained then I'd get really fit really easily and really quickly. I still didn't bother training.

I can't really knock the current culture because I guess it's a generation thing. The lads racing these days feel that every single aspect of racing has to be taken seriously and has to be super competitive. Don't get me wrong: when I'm on the bike, I'm not messing about. Everyone makes much more effort, most of it put into social media, to put across an image to please sponsors, and in my view the racers today just don't know when to stop competing and actually take some time to enjoy the incredible privilege and lifestyle that they've got, because, sure as hell, the moment they don't do the lap times, they'll get the flick.

I know the value of a good sponsor and how important it is to keep them happy. When I started racing, if I fell off my bike then I'd be worried about how I was going to repair it, so I really appreciated it when I started getting sponsors with a few quid, reliable vans and, later on, professional mechanics and creature comforts like motor-homes. It's ironic that nowadays, because racing is so expensive for young riders they actually have a surprisingly carefree attitude, because to race, they have to have big sponsors to pay the bills. They aren't really learning how to repair stuff, or the value of parts, or the fact that it costs a fortune just to enter the meeting. A lot of them don't even know how to hold a spanner, let alone put their own money in. When I started, if I didn't do it then it didn't get done, and if I didn't know how to do it then I learned.

There's so much more media coverage on TV, the internet and social media that racers can get instant fans, and the fans can see what they're up to from their living room seven days a week, so the riders have to milk it. I get told off all the time for not holding my helmet up to the camera for post-race interviews, because that's what the sponsors who are on my helmet want.

During the days when I was racing for Renegade and HRC, the only way fans could get close to the races and racers was to come to the tracks and spectate, or read *Motorcycle News*. Massive circuits like Donington Park, Brands Hatch and Thruxton would be absolutely rammed with tens of thousands of spectators at every BSB meeting, so as long as I was doing well on track, and getting on the back page of *Motorcycle News*, everyone was happy. Now it's not enough to win races; the riders have to have personal followers and fans on social media that the sponsors want to get in front of – and the riders do it, otherwise the money will go to the next one with more followers on Twitter.

When I was racing, if I wanted a piece of equipment, like a better shock absorber, I *had* to have it, especially if I thought it would make me quicker. I didn't care who I upset to get it on my bike. I didn't see anything else as being important for the team other than what I wanted. Now that I'm running a race team I sort of get that there are other things that also matter to the team, but I used to cause so much trouble and be a right pain in the arse. I'd have hated me if I'd had to work for me.

I think giving up racing will be one of those days when I suddenly say, 'That's it', and that will be it. Who knows when that will be? My problem is that I still love it, and I've never done anything else. I might not give it all up, maybe just some bits of it, and keep doing the things that I really like the most. The Classic TT is good, the Phillip Island Classic, Goodwood, and the Imatra road race in Finland is really enjoyable too. I could do test riding, but it's such hard work. Jeremy McWilliams does it and he is perfect for it because he is such a grafter, and so fast; plus, despite being old enough to know better, he's still not bothered about crashing. He loves it.

The lifestyle meant never being around at weekends, and always being on the move meant that I was a late starter with girls, but as I've mentioned briefly before now, I did eventually meet someone who put up with me for long enough for us to have two kids. I met Sandrine at Macau in 1996, when I was racing there, and she was working for Serge Rosset's GP team as a hospitality hostess.

We got together after the race, during the holiday in Thailand, and some time after that she moved to England from her home in France, and it went from there. I was over the moon about our two girls, Juliette and Cecilia; the last thing I wanted was boys who I feared would want to race. Having said that, my two girls are so competitive. If we go go-karting, they'll slam into me just to win – they aren't shy. Sandrine is really fiery too, so whenever we did anything together as a family, we all wanted to win. Everything was a competition.

It's hard having a relationship with a racer – not impossible, but really hard. You are always on the go, and the highs are really high, and the lows are really low. It's a constant rollercoaster of good weekends and bad weekends. It was hard for Sandrine; she was French and living in England, away from her family, and we were together through the period of my career as it was the GP season, Renegade Ducati seasons, and HRC seasons, so I was away a lot and under a lot of pressure from the teams I was with to perform. I had to be especially selfish during that period, and we split up after ten years together.

When I had kids, a lot of people said it would slow me up, but I don't think it did. I think if anything it made me a bit quicker – you know, I had to do well. Juliette and Cecilia never really entered my mind when I was racing. Maybe a couple of times at the TT, and other really dangerous circuits I'd think, I've got a lot to lose.

The girls came to the TT when they were first born, and they've been a few times since, plus they've been to loads of other races over the years. I really do like having them around, but it's so hard to look after yourself that to look after someone else at a race is even harder. Now that they're older, if the girls come to a race I'll put them to work and get them to do my pit board, make lunch for all the team, fetch timing sheets and keep the pit garage tidy.

Away from racing, I love having people around, and especially when the girls come to stay; I absolutely love it. It's a shut-down for me, and we'll do whatever they want to, or if there's something I need to do, or a race I need to go to, they'll follow and support me all the way.

It's been thirty years since my nan left me that small bit of inheritance which I used to start racing in 1989. I was just about to pack it in because it was running out fast and I wasn't getting anywhere. I really didn't want to spend it all on racing, mainly because I knew she didn't want me to spend *any* of it on racing. Then I got a break in 1993, and since then I have had the most extraordinary life as a racer … so far.

Career Summary

1989	Suzuki RGV250 VJ21
1990	Suzuki RGV250 VJ22
1991	Suzuki RGV250 VJ22
1992	Honda RS250, Ducati 888 one off rides, Harris Ducati one off rides
1993	Medd Kawasaki ZXR750RR
1994	McCullough Ducati 888
1995	McCullough Ducati 888 & 916
1996	McCullough Ducati 916 & 955
1997	V&M Honda RC45
1998	Honda Britain RC45, Motorcycle City Honda CBR600* & CBR900*
1999	Joe Miller Honda NSR500V, Daily Star Honda CBR600*
2000	Level 3 Yamaha R7, V&M Yamaha R1*
2001	Kawasaki ZX-7RR
2002	Highland Springs Renegade Ducati
2003	Red Bull Renegade Ducati
2004	HRC Honda HM Plant CBR1000RR Fireblade
2005	HRC Honda HM Plant CBR1000RR Fireblade
2006	Paul Bird Motorsport Honda CBR1000RR Fireblade
2007	MSS Kawasaki ZX-10R
2008	Northwest 200 Ducati 1098R
2009	Northwest 200 Yamaha YZF-R1, Crescent Suzuki GSX-R1000, SMT Honda CBR1000RR, MSS Kawasaki ZX-10R, Ducati 1098R, Bathams Suzuki GSX-R1000*
2010	Riders Ducati 1098R, SMT Honda CBR1000RR*, HM Plant Honda CBR1000RR*
2011	Rapid Solicitors Ducati 1098R
2012	MSS Kawasaki ZX-10RR, SMT Honda CBR1000RR Fireblade (Macau only)
2013	Bathams IWR Honda CBR1000RR, Honda Legends**
2014	Bathams BMW S1000RR, Yamaha YZF-R1*
2015	Gearlink Kawasaki ZX-10R, Penz13 BMW S1000RR*
2016	Bathams Racing BMW S1000RR
2017	Bathams Racing BMW S1000RR
2018	Bathams Racing BMW S1000RR, Honda RC213V*
2019	Bathams Racing BMW S1000RR, Honda RC213V*

* Denotes Road Racing only (NW200, TT, Macau)
** Denotes Road Racing & World Endurance

Career Statistics*

British Superbikes
431 Starts (1993-2016)
29 Wins
109 Podiums

British Superstock 1000
44 Starts
1 Win
12 Podiums

MotoGP
16 Starts
0 Wins
0 podiums

World Superbikes
20 Starts
0 Wins
1 Podium

Isle of Man TT
72 Starts
58 Finishes
7 Wins
18 Podiums

Northwest 200
83 Starts
14 Wins
34 Podiums

**Macau Grand Prix **
24 Starts
8 Wins
20 Podiums

Ulster Grand Prix
2 Starts
0 Wins
1 Podium

World Endurance
4 Starts
0 Wins
0 Podiums

Classic TT
18 Starts
2 Wins
5 Podiums

Frohburg Road Race, Germany
6 Starts
3 Wins
5 Podiums

Imatra Road Race, Finland
3 Starts
1 Win
3 Podiums

Stars of Darley
11 Starts
6 Wins
11 Podiums

---

* To end of 2019 season
** To end of 2018 season

www.ingramcontent.com/pod-product-compliance
Lightning Source LLC
Chambersburg PA
CBHW060347100426
42812CB00003B/1163